As one of the author's former students, reading *The Emergence of 'Extremism'* was a journey of self-discovery. As a Muslim who has been subject to the surveillance of 'extremism', it enabled me to take myself out of the pre-criminal space and to see the unfair targeting and criminalisation of Muslim students. This book brings to light the way government policy is all too often used to gaslight Muslims in schools, universities and medical settings. The book shows how the emergence of 'extremism' and 'violence' has positioned British Muslims as antithetical to security and preservation of the state. Muslims often find themselves second guessing their theological beliefs as incompatible with the state – not because they are, but because policy has left no space for these beliefs without suspicion or scrutiny. The book highlights how counter-terrorism measures that target 'extremism' are doomed to fail. I hope this book can be used as a guide to facilitate reformation of both conversations and policies that uphold counter-extremism measures, as the answer to a question that is in of itself misconstrued.

Munadiah Aftab (Academic, Faith Inspired Activist
and former student of the author)

The Emergence of 'Extremism'

The Emergence of 'Extremism'

Exposing the Violent Discourse and Language of 'Radicalization'

ROB FAURE WALKER

BLOOMSBURY ACADEMIC
LONDON • NEW YORK • OXFORD • NEW DELHI • SYDNEY

BLOOMSBURY ACADEMIC
Bloomsbury Publishing Plc
50 Bedford Square, London, WC1B 3DP, UK
1385 Broadway, New York, NY 10018, USA
29 Earlsfort Terrace, Dublin 2, Ireland

BLOOMSBURY, BLOOMSBURY ACADEMIC and the Diana logo are trademarks
of Bloomsbury Publishing Plc

First published in Great Britain 2022

Cover design by Rebecca Heselton
Cover image taken from There Is No Alternative, an exhibition about Prevent
branding by Navine G. Khan-Dossos at The Showroom, London, 2019

A catalogue record for this book is available from the British Library.

A catalog record for this book is available from the Library of Congress.

ISBN: HB: 978-1-3501-9949-1
PB: 978-1-3501-9950-7
ePDF: 978-1-3501-9952-1
eBook: 978-1-3501-9951-4

Typeset by Deanta Global Publishing Services, Chennai, India
Printed and bound in Great Britain

To find out more about our authors and books visit www.bloomsbury.com
and sign up for our newsletters.

CONTENTS

FIGURES

PREFACE

On the morning of Thursday 7 July 2005, I joined millions of other Londoners to take the Underground to work in Central London. Judging by the faces of the other commuters on my train, I wasn't the only one who lacked enthusiasm for the job that I was heading towards. This was my first permanent job after university, and I had already worked out that I was unlikely to ever be enthusiastic about finding jobs for accountants in the recruitment consultancy that I had fallen into to pay the rent. Thankfully, within the next year I would find a job that I was enthusiastic about when I started work as a trainee teacher.

Sitting down at my desk to trawl through CVs, the office filled up around me as my colleagues arrived at work. But, by 9 am when everyone would normally have been at their desks, there were still some empty chairs. Then someone said that there had been a bomb. Twenty-four-hour rolling news soon informed us that there had in fact been three bombs on trains near Aldgate, Edgware Road and Russell Square stations. Shortly afterwards, another bomb would destroy a double-decker bus in Tavistock Square. In less than an hour, Central London had experienced the most devastating bombing campaign since the Blitz.

Like thousands of others across London who had also just arrived at work, I started to phone around to check that my friends and family were safe. Thankfully, everyone who I called that morning did pick up the phone. But, for family and friends of the fifty-two people who had been killed by the bombs, the day would be devastating. Hundreds more had been injured.

As more detailed timelines of the bombers' movements have since been published, I have made the same mental calculation over and over again and even find myself doing so sixteen years later as I read accounts of the day (BBC 2015). If the bombers left Kings Cross Station on an Underground train at 8:38 am and if one of them travelled east on the Circle Line before detonating a bomb and killing seven people between Liverpool Street and Aldgate stations at 8:49 am, and if I also travelled on an eastbound Circle Line train from Kings Cross and got off two stops before Liverpool Street to arrive at work after a short walk just before 9 am, was I on the same train as the bomber? Was I in the same carriage? Was I squeezed up next to him on the crowded train? Were people who I shared my commute with now injured or worse?

I mention this not to propose that I am in any way exceptional, rather to suggest that this was a tragedy that was felt very closely by many people and even by those of us who were fortunate enough to have not lost anyone close to them. With subsequent acts of political violence killing and injuring many more people in the United Kingdom, it is in everyone's interest that we have a robust strategy to prevent future death and destruction. Unfortunately, as will be explored in the following chapters, aspects of the United Kingdom's current counter-terrorism strategy appear to achieve quite the opposite. The Prevent Counter-Terrorism Strategy and government efforts to counter 'extremism' seem to promote rather than prevent violence.

Three hours after the first bomb had been detonated, Prime Minister Tony Blair read out a joint statement from the leaders of the G8 countries who he was hosting at the Gleneagles Hotel in Scotland for the annual G8 Summit. The bombings already overshadowed the previous day's news that accident-prone President George Bush had collided with a police officer and fallen off his bike (Jones 2005). In his statement, Blair insisted that the terrorists would not impose their 'extremism' on us and the analysis that follows indicates that this marks a discursive shift towards the naming of 'extremism' and 'extremists' as causes of political violence that was not seen in the wake of previous bombing campaigns in London or elsewhere.

Counter-extremism initiatives that seek to prevent future acts of violence have flourished since the London '7/7' bombings and Blair's speech at Gleneagles, yet the common-sense presumption that 'extreme' views and opinions can act as a predictor for future acts of violence is based on a fundamental misunderstanding of the democratic process. Rather than being a predictor for violence, our ability to air supposedly 'extreme' views and be heard prevents us from having to resort to violence. Far from being the defenders of democracy, governments, civil servants and a growing field of well-funded counter-extremism professionals have been seduced by the authoritarian logic that the state should police what people think. 'Extremism' has radicalized them against democracy. This book explores what has caused this to happen and suggests that the supposed 'radicalization' of our politics and the apparently growing problem of 'extremism' can only be resolved if we first abandon the counter-extremism industry.

This will be no easy task as counter-extremism is a global industry. Promoted by the Home Office here in the United Kingdom and the Department of Homeland Security in the United States, counter-extremism has also been promoted around the world. Joint conferences between the UK and other governments to promote counter-extremism are now commonplace (Foreign & Commonwealth Office 2018, UAE 2019). This global export of counter-extremism is also supported at a multinational level by UNESCO (UNESCO 2018). Having faced extensive criticism for how it is born out of and also catalyses the oppression of Muslims in the United Kingdom and the United States, this global export should be a concern for us all, not least in consideration of the oppression of Muslims around the world. It is hard to see how Western governments can effectively argue for the protection of persecuted Muslims in China, India, Myanmar and elsewhere without first adopting the moral high ground and abandoning their own misguided efforts to counter 'extremism'. As such, while this book focuses on the emergence of 'extremism' in the United Kingdom, it should also act as a warning over the expansion of counter-extremism around the world.

The emergence of 'extremism' is a tale of both language and politics, and of how they are inseparable from one another. As such, it ranges over political theory, discourse analysis and a critique of reality itself. It is also personal, so begins with my experience of serving as a teacher to a predominantly Muslim community in East London. It was the children who I taught who told me that they had been silenced when the Prevent Counter-Terrorism Strategy tasked their teachers with reporting views or opinions that they perceived to be 'extreme' to the police, and this is explored in Chapter 1. Working as a schoolteacher, I was well aware that children explore the world with their language and that this often involves them saying controversial or 'extreme' things. This is why teenagers can be difficult, but their 'extreme' views are a way of negotiating their expanding social relations. I cannot think of a time when someone said something controversial or even offensive in my classroom that did not ultimately bring the whole class closer together as we resolved our differences and learned from one another. In the wider world, politics can also bring us closer together if we are able to properly discuss our concerns; politics also drives us apart if we cannot discuss our concerns. Efforts to police 'extremism' with counter-extremism strategies prevents these discussions from happening, driving us further apart and making a significant contribution to the emergence of 'extremism'.

Chapter 2 opens with an example of how support for counter-extremism is maintained by relying on a small field of idealogues who help to marginalize critical views that would otherwise inform better policymaking. Critique is fundamental to understanding 'extremism' and this starts with recognizing the importance of language so that we can consider what people are talking about when they refer to both 'extremism' and 'radicalization'. While there have been some efforts to address the Far Right with counter-extremism measures, the original and continuing primary focus of counter-extremism strategies is on Islam. This can be read in the Prevent Strategy documents and in the statistics published by the Home Office that show that Muslims are considerably more likely to be referred than any other group in the United Kingdom.[1] This focus on Muslims has a long-standing historical precedent in the *Orientalism* that was described by Edward Said and which might be seen as a precursor to the more recent academic field of critical race theory (CRT). CRT is the idea that people who are not white have tended to have a raw deal through recent history and thus face certain systemic disadvantages. Histories of colonialism and slavery mean that the historic disadvantage described by CRT is a fact. Thankfully, there are many examples of black CEOs. But, in the same way that gravity not affecting the astronauts on the International Space Station does not disprove gravity,[2] successful Muslims do not disprove CTR. Despite this, campaigns against CRT and the understanding of injustice that it offers have been made by Conservative politicians and right-wing commentators in the pages of the *Spectator* (Fox, Doyle et al. 2020, Nelson 2020).

Such a contested field of inquiry demands that we consider the ideological assumptions and positions adopted in this debate that has seen Conservative politicians and journalists denouncing academic research. Thus, Chapter 2 closes with an exploration of the different forms that ideology might take before settling on discourse as a more useful concept from which to understand the world. This finishes with an exploration of neoliberalism as a fundamental ideology, or discourse, from which to understand the emergence of 'extremism'.

Chapter 3 proposes that careful analysis of language can help us to better understand the world. Initial exploration of the frequency and usage of 'extremism' in government documents, in Parliament and in the media shows that there has been an exponential increase in the usage of 'extremism' since 2005 and that it has also become progressively more associated with violence during this time. Chapters 4 and 5 analyse the use of 'extremism' and 'radicalization' in Parliament over the last century. This shows a clear pattern of 'extremism' being used to denounce independence movements on the fringes of the diminishing British Empire. It then creeps closer to home as 'extremism' in Northern Ireland is referred to before an enemy within is created by targeting British Muslims. This final step enables 'extremism' to be used to police dissent on the British mainland and results in a dramatic shift in the usage of 'extremism' as it ceases to be seen as a product of the failure of government and in demand of political solutions. Tony Blair's New Labour Government's reframing of 'extremism' as a threat in of itself resulted in them developing legal and policing strategies to prevent it. In ceasing to regard 'extremism' as emergent from their policy decisions, Blair's government undermined a vital mechanism that had previously prevented the emergence of 'extremism' and this is referred to as 'parliamentary calculus'.

Chapter 6 explores how the failure of parliamentary calculus under Tony Blair's New Labour Government was enabled by the language that New Labour adopted. This has in turn enabled the maintenance of white supremacy as Muslims have been targeted by counter-extremism strategies that remain unconcerned by Conservative politicians who make proclamations that are as divisive as those of the most violent terrorists (O'Regan and Betzel 2016). The chapter goes on to look at how the counter-extremism industry has been supported by the process of 'murketing', or the funding of faux independent lobby groups, in a process that mirrors the global proliferation of neoliberalism via think tanks with obscure funding arrangements. Chapter 7 proposes that a new understanding of language change over time offers the opportunity to transcend the ongoing and seemingly inevitable vicious cycle of violence that is caused by the targeting of 'extremism'. This leads to a consideration of eight factors that must be overcome if 'extremism' is to be transcended.

Finally, Chapter 8 describes the emergence of 'extremism' as part of a series of associated crises, of our ecology, our ethics, our economy and our very existence. To overcome or transcend these crises, we must take a deep look at the basis of our existence and what we really are. By doing so, it can be seen that we all too often exist in a world of demi-reality that is only a poor reflection of the world. It is this demi-reality that sustains the emergence of 'extremism', and it is only by appealing to the metaReality that is described in this book and by other critics of counter-extremism that 'extremism' might be overcome. As such, the book finishes with an exploration of what is currently sustaining counter-extremism and a consideration of how it might be overcome.

The book is split into three parts, and these reflect its philosophical foundations in critical realism. Critical realism contends that Western philosophical investigations since Plato have tended to be distracted by what we think about the world (epistemology), rather than what the world really is (ontology). To correct this, critical realism defines a split between the actual, the empirical and the real. To reflect this separation of our *actual* observations, that can be defined using *empirical* data, and the *real* generative mechanisms that we might theorize from these observations, the book is divided into three parts. Part I refers to my *actual* experiences as a teacher who was compelled to adopt the Prevent Counter-Terrorism Strategy and to surveil my young students for supposed signs of 'extremism'. Part II uses *empirical* data to describe the emergence of 'extremism'. And, Part III analyses this data to establish what is *really* happening to cause the emergence of 'extremism'. Critical realism describes a laminated ontology where theorized generative mechanisms (the real) are also felt as actual experiences. Thus, Part I also describes real generative mechanisms, such as racism, as these are also felt as actual experiences. The distinction between these theories and those proposed in Part III is that the latter presents theories that are not so well established or that are not described outside of my published work.

While the discussions that follow are necessarily complex at times, it is vital that philosophy is grounded in reality. So, as well as arguing that 'extremism' is a political construct that must be abandoned, each chapter starts with a vignette to show that 'extremism' is connected to: the global economy; dreary meetings in local government offices; political machinations in London; and the needless death of a newborn child in Northern Syria. This paints a diverse array of scenes that will also include frequent reference to my own personal experiences, as counter-extremism and the Prevent Counter-Terrorism Strategy have come to impact on every aspect of our social and political lives.

It is my hope that some who read this will see that the only way to promote a more cohesive and hospitable society is to abandon counter-extremism programmes. As these programmes expand to include evermore types of dissent, from the far right to environmental campaigners, there can be little doubt that doing so will lead to more and not less violence. It is notable that counter-extremism programmes have been in existence for more than a decade and a half and that this is enough time for many to have forged successful careers as counter-extremism experts. That some of these people might have the humility to reconsider their role in relation to democracy and the promotion of violence may seem like a naïve hope. But, critical realism is unashamedly utopian and thus demands that we try and persuade them that the world would be a better place if we stopped trying to police 'extremism'.

ACKNOWLEDGEMENTS

I am eternally grateful for Prof John O'Regan's guidance over very early versions of the text. His advice has been invaluable to both my writing and thinking about the issues that follow. My thanks are also extended to Prof Priscilla Alderson and Gary Hawke for running the Critical Realism Reading Group at UCL. The existence of this group and their guidance has been invaluable. Priscilla's care to go over the basics of critical realism and Gary's efforts to communicate the complexities – most notably in his book, *The Order of Natural Necessity* – have almost certainly helped many others on this journey.

This book emerged from research that was initially guided by Dr Sue Askew. I became a schoolteacher in 2005 in the hope that I might help children have a slightly less dull time in classrooms than I had at school. Ten years later and with Sue as my teacher on a master's course at UCL, I finally enjoyed the thrill of learning for myself and am eternally grateful for this.

I hope that I have helped some of the children who I have taught to enjoy learning in the way that Sue showed me was possible. While I was nominally 'the teacher', I have constantly enjoyed learning from those who I have taught and have been fortunate enough to teach both children in secondary schools and adults on master's courses at university. I have learned as much from the ten-year-olds as from the fifty-year-olds and will be forever thankful for what they have taught me, much of which has informed this book.

Sadly, recognition that learning is a shared experience between teacher and pupil has been winnowed away as recent curriculum reforms have seized ever more control of what and how we learn in schools and universities. All too often, this leads to the brightest, most inquisitive and curious students being labelled as 'naughty'. It has always struck me that schools discouraging students from challenging authority holds a mirror up to the society that has created them. So, I have the utmost respect and gratitude to my former colleagues who still work in a school system that works against humanity by imposing evermore testing, assessment and surveillance onto our children.

There are so many more people to thank that I have had to give up in making a list as it got too long, but Tarek Younis, Shereen Fernandez, James Bridle and Prof Alison Scott-Baumann deserve a special mention. One particular mention must also go to my wife Suja, whose patience and support made this book possible.

Finally, the book would not have happened without the growing community of academics and activists who also bear witness to the emergence of 'extremism'. In the climate of rising Islamophobia that is precipitated by the emergence of 'extremism', the bravery of Muslim academics and activists who speak out against the injustice of the war on terror and counter-extremism is notable. It is a privilege to be guided by their excellent work and to count many as my friends.

PART 1

The Actual

CHAPTER 1

Counter-terrorism in the classroom

'Something has to be done'

On a Friday evening in January 2016, I was in the council's offices with community representatives from across the borough of Tower Hamlets in East London. We had been brought together to review the use of the Prevent Counter-Terrorism Strategy in the borough. It was the end of a long day; the lights were off in the rest of the building as everyone else had gone home. We had all arrived from our various day jobs, yet our commitment to do right by the children who we worked with meant that all eight of us were in heated debate about Prevent – the strand of the British government's counter-terrorism strategy aimed at countering the supposed threat of 'extremism'. Nobody seemed to like this strategy that made informants of teachers, doctors and social workers in our borough and across the rest of the United Kingdom, but every time that someone mentioned the risks of 'radicalization' and 'extremism' the urgency of the conversation increased. Despite our reservations, it did seem that something had to be done to address these apparent threats. However, my pupils told me that government efforts to police 'radicalization' and 'extremism' with Prevent were leaving them fearful of engaging in the political debates that had previously been a vital aspect of their navigation through, and engagement with, the world.

Worrying about being labelled as an 'extremist' following the implementation of the previously ignored Prevent Strategy in 2014, my students had withdrawn from political debate and the school had ceased to be a safe space for them to test and discuss their views. This fear was heightened for the Muslim students as efforts to police 'extremism' were predominantly focused on the supposed threat of 'Islamist terrorism', with 'Al Qa'ida' and 'Islam' referred to 184 times in the Prevent Strategy document issued by the Home Office. In promoting this threat, it has been argued that Prevent and counter-extremism more generally have emboldened the far right in their vilification of Muslims and enabled a downplaying of the violence of white supremacists, a position supported by Nadya Ali, who argues that 'Prevent operates through racialized understandings of radicalization and extremism that "border" Muslim populations as a collective threat to white Britain' (Ali 2020).

This oppressive and often violent focus on Muslims that aligns elite right-wing politicians with hooligans on Europe's streets has been exposed in Hilary Aked, Melissa Jones and David Millar's work *Islamophobia in Europe: How Governments are Enabling the Far-Right 'Counter-Jihad' Movement* (2019). The alignment of policymakers and street protesters and their support for one another, as described by Aked et al., is epitomized by the Quilliam Foundation[1] that has both received in excess of £1.2 million from the Home Office and also offered a platform and financial support to convicted fraudster and nationalist street protest organizer Stephen Yaxley-Lennon, who refers to himself as 'Tommy Robinson' (Damian Green MP in Hansard 2011, Aked, Jones et al. 2019). Aked et al.'s observation that counter-extremism can be traced back to the far right is supported by Liz Fekete, executive director of the Institute of Race Relations (IRR). In her book *Europe's Fault Lines* (Frekete 2018), Frekete cites countless examples of where the security services and growing state-supported counter-extremism apparatus across Europe has provided employment for members of far right organization such as Greece's neo-Nazi and recently declared criminal organization Golden Dawn.

This 'counter-jihad' that has been waged in Westminster and also on the streets in recent years meant that many of my students faced the twin threat of being cast as potential 'extremists' at school and of being vilified online and on the street by the rising tide of Islamophobia in the United Kingdom (Marsh 2018) that was encouraged by the vilification of Muslims in the Press (Baker, Gabrieltos et al. 2011, Centre for Ethnicity and Racism Studies 2012, Centre of Media Monitoring 2019). So, while I felt that something ought to be done about the apparent threats of 'radicalization' and 'extremism', I was also uncomfortable with the idea that Prevent and associated counter-extremism or anti-radicalization initiatives were the answer.

Being involved in the council's review of Prevent led to me spending time with Prevent workers from across the country and to being briefed on the need for Prevent by senior police officers and advocates for Prevent from the Home Office over the course of the next year. Far from convincing me of the need for the strategy, as the authors of these briefings intended, my discomfort grew to such an extent that I decided to carry out research at UCL institute of Education to understand why this strategy continued to be promoted by the British government. It explains that the emergence of 'extremism' can be understood through the careful analysis of language and that government efforts to predict which innocent people might go on to become violent criminals in the future are not only doomed to fail but, in making suspects of us all, are more likely to promote than to prevent violence. It became apparent through this research that those who were pushing for initiatives to counter 'extremism' did not have faith in the democratic state to deliver a harmonious society. Turning the language back onto the bureaucrats who promote Prevent, they had become 'radicalized' against democracy and were carrying out a national and coordinated grooming campaign to recruit people to their dangerous cause. 'Grooming' may seem polemic, but it was recently reported that the Royal United Services Institute (RUSI), a defence think tank, had found that 'Teaching youngsters to make anti-extremism videos [is] "effective" in tackling radicalisation' (Harley 2020).

I first encountered Prevent when it became part of my professional duties as a schoolteacher in 2014. I became concerned that Prevent was having a negative impact on the school experience of children who I worked with on the day that allegations that British schools were being infiltrated by so-called 'Islamic extremists' were debated in Parliament (Hansard 2014); this became known as the 'Trojan Horse' 'hoax' (Abbas 2017). It was on 9 June 2014, and the Muslim students in my class, many of whom had previously been active participants, withdrew from our ongoing discussions and debates. While it may seem strange to be able to pinpoint this date so precisely, the newspaper headlines from the day indicate why some of my students were suddenly unwilling to engage in our daily discussions. From 'Spot Checks for Trojan horse Plots' on the front of *The Telegraph* to 'OfSTED [the schools' inspectorate] to Raid Trojan Horse Schools' on the *Sun*, and a variation of the same theme across the front covers of other national newspapers, the media and the parliamentary debate that they reported on that day made it quite clear to Muslims that they were now suspicious in the eyes of the state.

As is explored later in this chapter, in the section on the Trojan Horse 'hoax', this vilification and suspicion of Muslim communities and the schools that served them led to the introduction of Prevent. This inferred various duties on schools and teachers and the aspect of the strategy that appeared to be of greatest concern to my pupils was 'support for vulnerable people through *identification, referral* and *intervention*' (HM Government 2011 emphasis added). The discussions about and the implementation of Prevent were prompted by OfSTED recommending that schools should follow the Prevent Strategy. No doubt because of the predominantly Muslim community who lived there, a particular focus was placed on the local authority (Tower Hamlets) where I worked by Michael Wilshaw, the chief inspector of schools in England and head of OfSTED (Wilshaw 2014). This was a year before the Counter-Terrorism and Security Act (HM Government 2015) and the Prevent Duty Guidance (HM Government 2015) imposed a legal duty for schools to follow Prevent.[2]

As a result of my concerns for the negative impact that Prevent was having on my relationships with my students, I spoke out against the strategy in school meetings. As a result, students learnt of my concerns and felt empowered to speak out in my classes again. Having found their voices, these students frequently expressed their concern that they were being targeted by Prevent, a strategy that they told me they thought was a racist and overzealous state surveillance operation. They told me that they did not express these views to other adults as they feared that doing so would result in their referral to the police. Similar concerns to those expressed by my students have previously been explored by Kundnani in his 2009 report for the Institute of Race Relations, *Spooked: how not to prevent violent extremism*

(Kundnani 2009). A previous home secretary, Amber Rudd, more recently confirmed my student's suspicions when she told a BBC Question Time audience that,

> [Policing] is not where we get the intelligence from. We get the intelligence much more from the Prevent strategy. (Rudd 2017)

As a result of the conversations I had had with my students, I contributed to reports for legal and human rights lobbying organizations that challenged Prevent on the grounds that it violated the human rights of British citizens (Open Society 2016, Rights Watch (UK) 2016). Involvement in these reports resulted in the impacts of Prevent that I had witnessed being reported in the national press (Bowcott and Adams 2016) and led to many more students coming to talk to me, placing me in a privileged position where I learnt of concerns that these students told me they did not share with other adults and teachers. I was told by many more students that they feared that Prevent could result in them being reported to the police. The following three examples that I learnt from my students illustrate how they were altering their behaviour because of these fears.

What does Prevent do?

Children's fear of seeking the support of adults

A student told me that Prevent had prevented him from seeking the support of adults when he became concerned for the safety of one of his peers. He became worried about a fifteen-year-old friend of his who he said was spending too much time playing Call of Duty.[3] He feared his friend was being drawn into supporting Islamic State by exposure to online propaganda that borrowed the branding and aesthetic of Call of Duty to glamorize the self-proclaimed caliphate. To provide support, my student told me that he and a group of his peers had arranged to spend more time with their vulnerable friend, devising a rota to ensure that someone was spending time with him every day of the week after school. By the time my student discussed the situation with me, he reported that the friend was less socially isolated and that he was no longer worried by his activity online or that he might be supporting potentially dangerous views and opinions.

During this child-led intervention, despite his concerns for his friend's continued isolation and safety, my fifteen-year-old student did not seek help from any adults. He told me that he did not seek help as he feared that Prevent made it their duty to report the situation to the school, who would escalate the referral to the police, and he felt that the intervention of government counter-terrorism workers in this sensitive situation would undermine his own successful efforts to help his friend. Since then and as part of my professional duties as a teacher, I have undergone training in what type of situations should be reported as a result of Prevent. Having received this training, I am confident that my student was correct in his concerns that the school and any of his teachers would have been obliged to escalate his referral to the police, and it is reasonable to suppose that their involvement would have undermined his successful efforts to help his friend.

Fear of resisting calls for a caliphate

Another student who would frequently engage me in compelling theological conversations explained how Prevent was preventing him from challenging the views of people who he perceived to be 'extreme' and potentially dangerous. He explained that on a number of occasions outside a local mosque, he had been approached by people who were calling for the support of a caliphate and who he felt were misrepresenting the teachings of Islam by their lack of respect and pragmatism with regards to the laws of their home country. However, on every occasion that he was approached by these people, rather than challenging them with his pragmatic views on Islam, he had turned his back and refused to talk to them. He refused to engage due to his fear that association with these people was likely to result in a referral under Prevent and that this would result in the police intervening in his life and the potential stigma of becoming known as an 'extremist'. As a result of this, he did not engage his extensive theological knowledge to challenge views that he perceived to be 'extreme' and dangerous.

Silencing of classroom debate

In 2013, I was a form tutor to a particularly lively class. In our allotted form time every morning and afternoon, we would discuss the news of the day. In one particularly heated encounter, a group of students cited the Koran to argue that gay people should be denied equal rights. The argument was by no means split along religious lines; other Muslim students proclaimed support for equal marriage and students of different faiths, and none, joined in on different sides of the debate. The ensuing argument that engaged the whole class became heated and lasted for more than a few days as everyone's views were challenged. A few months later in July 2013, when the Equal Marriage Act was being debated in Parliament, I prepared myself for the next onslaught as the students who had opposed gay marriage raised the topic again. This time, they argued that it was surely right and kind to call a union between any people 'a marriage', no matter what their sexuality. This was a view that they had heard from me in the earlier classroom debate. I had also learnt from them that they were not trying to be difficult, 'extreme' or radical in their earlier assertions, and they were responding in a non-critical manner to what they understood to be received wisdom. The heated debate and the children's willingness to change their views showed that even the most dogmatic positions can change in response to discussion and debate. A year later, a local Prevent Counter-Terrorism Strategy had been implemented in the school, and these same students were among those who informed me that they no longer engage in political debates because they feared being reported under Prevent. As one of them had quoted the Koran to justify harming gay men in our earlier discussion, it is likely that they would have been reported if they were to repeat our earlier debate.

These three examples show how Prevent: had prevented a concerned student seeking support for a friend who he believed was being drawn into supporting the Islamic State; was preventing a student from challenging the views of other Muslims that he perceived to be 'extreme', undermining a mechanism by which apparently 'extreme' views might have been moderated; and, was preventing and silencing classroom debates and disrupting a mechanism by which political views were being moderated.

These conversations on equal marriage indicate that it is possible for debate to dramatically change one's position on a political issue. The Royal Assent of the Equal Marriage Act on 13 March 2014 indicates that such changes can be brought about in the highest political institutions. In the same way that Parliament recognized the importance of 'marriage' in 2014, we must believe that they will one day recognize the importance of *not* policing and criminalizing 'extremism' and 'radicalization'. The current failure to do so means that Prevent is not only undermining our democracy by labelling some people 'extremists', but is also silencing them and, in so doing, denying them the opportunity to participate in debate that is vital to the moderation of all of our views and opinions.

The idea that Prevent shuts down debate has often been challenged by supporters of the strategy who say that the intention of Prevent is to *promote* classroom debate. This has happened in the media (Fenton-Smith 2017) and in my own direct contact with local Prevent workers and more senior civil servants. This must be countered with the real-life experience of students and the obvious point that the intentions of Prevent may be different to its outcomes at a local level. There is some truth to the claim that Prevent promotes classroom debate, and I have spoken to teachers and observed lessons where the discussion of news that students have travelled to ISIS-held territory is promoted. However, having an abstract discussion about a story in the news, as I witnessed in these classes, is different to having a more authentic and dialogic exchange where opposing views are aired and challenged (Alexander 2008). Such an authentic exchange was demonstrated in the aforementioned example from my classroom and resulted in students altering their common-sense beliefs on marriage. My students' experiences indicate that these authentic exchanges where we have the confidence to reveal views that others may perceive to be extreme are being suppressed by Prevent. By claiming that Prevent promotes classroom debate, Prevent workers are conflating the abstract discussion of a news story with a more authentic, dialogic, exchange of views. This might result in Prevent workers masking their silencing of authentic exchanges by fooling themselves that they are promoting a more valuable from of debate.

It was as a result of my developing expertise on Prevent and the rapidly growing counter-extremism industry that I found myself in those council offices on a Friday evening in 2016. I had been approached by the London Borough of Tower Hamlets, which co-opted me as a member of the Tower Hamlets Overview and Scrutiny Committee into Prevent. The committee was convened in 2015 to investigate how Prevent, which was by now a controversial strategy, could be better implemented in Tower Hamlets. The committee was convened for six months and met every three weeks, including a day spent meeting the Prevent team in Birmingham and being briefed by representatives of the police and Home Office's Office for Security and Counter-Terrorism (OSCT). Alongside me on the committee were local government officials and local residents, and I was bought in as an academic and schools' expert. In this capacity, I organized focus groups with school students and local government officials from across Tower Hamlets to enable the officials to hear about the local impact of Prevent. The student participants in these focus groups indicated that they, like the students in my classes, thought that Prevent was changing their behaviour, shutting down debate and undermining the mediation of 'extreme' views. This suggested that my previous concerns about the impact of Prevent, which had been forced into my classroom by the Trojan Horse 'hoax' that is explored in the following paragraphs, were representative of a wider trend.

The Trojan Horse 'hoax' and the Prevent duty

The Trojan Horse 'hoax' that led to the implementation of Prevent in Schools across the United Kingdom can be understood from two main conflicting perspectives. From one perspective, the schools involved were being run by a hugely successful and experienced school leader who was helping to ensure the best life chances for his students. Tahir Alam, chairman of Park View Educational Trust that ran the schools at the centre of the scandal, ensured that his schools were praised by the inspectorate (OfSTED) and that the students exceeded the Department for Education's predictions in their exam results. He did this by valuing 'the cultural background of all the children in the school', ensuring that the children's religious and cultural heritage were supported and, in doing so, helped parents buy into and support their children's education (Abbas 2017). The other perspective is provided by Peter Clarke, the ex-head of the Metropolitan police's counter-terrorism unit, who was appointed by Michael Gove MP to carry out an investigation into the schools. Where others saw a successful Muslim community being vilified by unfounded allegations, Clarke (2014) described an 'Islamist' plot to take over the schools, in his report published in July 2014.

There was little evidence of an Islamist plot but by the time the cases Clarke had constructed against the Muslim teachers were thrown out by the High Court (Adams 2016), the hysteria whipped up by the British press had ensured that 'Trojan Horse' had become a byword for the threat of Islamism that right-wing politicians and the increasingly Islamophobic British public imagined (Marsh 2018). Professors John Holmwood and Therese O'Toole have written the seminal book on the Trojan Horse affair (Holmwood and O'Toole 2018), and Holmwood latterly compared the Birmingham hoax to the Hillsborough scandal. 'Holmwood said he could think of no other case in which the Government and media had so destructively colluded to create a false narrative of events that vilified an entire community' (Oborne 2018).

To understand how the hoax started, we need to go back to articles in the *Times* newspaper from 2014. In March 2014, the *Times* (Kennedy, Hurst et al. 2014) and the *Sunday Times* (Cavendish 2014) reported on a letter that had been sent anonymously to the leader of the Birmingham City Council which described a 'Trojan Horse' plot by so-called 'Islamic extremists' to take over the management of the schools in Birmingham by infiltrating the governing bodies. The provenance of the letter is not discussed in either article but has since been referred to by Parliament's Education Select Committee, who quote the anonymous note that accompanied the letter:

> The document [the letter] had been sent to the leader of Birmingham City Council in November 2013, with a covering letter (also anonymous) stating that 'This letter was found when I was clearing my bosses [*sic*] files and I think you should be aware that I am shocked at what your officers are doing.' The letter writer adds 'You have 7 days to investigate this matter after which it will be sent to a national newspaper who I am sure will treat it seriously'. (House of Commons Education Select Committee 2015)

Evidently, the letter did find its way to a national newspaper, and this led to a media-orchestrated public outcry which resulted in the extraordinary inspection of twenty-one of the city's schools by the UK schools' inspectorate (OfSTED). The aforementioned Select Committee has since reported that

> No evidence of extremism or radicalisation, apart from a single isolated incident, was found by any of the inquiries and there was no evidence of a sustained plot nor of a similar situation pertaining elsewhere in the country. (House of Commons Education Select Committee 2015)

The notion of a 'Trojan Horse' plot by 'Islamists' to take over schools by stealth has provenance in the then secretary of state for education, Michael Gove MP, who was previously a journalist at the *Times* and who had written a book in the wake of the 7/7 bombings in London. In the book, *Celsius 7/7: How the West's Policy of Appeasement has Provoked Yet More Fundamentalist Terror – and What Has to be Done Now* (Gove 2007), Gove presents the relationship between Islam and the West as inherently problematic. A chapter in the book titled 'The Trojan Horse' describes the existence of Islamic ideology in the United Kingdom as a 'symbolic' 'fight', and Gove questions if the United Kingdom would be 'strong enough to defend the idea of Secular space' (Gove 2007). He suggests that the United Kingdom needs to do more to defend itself in this 'fight', and this might provide some insight into Gove's motives for prompting the intervention in Birmingham. Sources at Birmingham City Council have since told me that they did not think that the 'Trojan Horse' 'scandal' was representative of a problem that needed to be addressed, saying that they saw any efforts to incorporate a religious or cultural ideology into the management of the criticized schools as a well-meaning attempt to make the schools representative of the marginalized Muslim communities that they served, a perspective that is shared by the former chair of the schools trust at the centre of the 'scandal' (Abbas 2017) and the deputy head of one of the schools (Donaghy 2014). This also chimed with my experience as a teacher in a school serving a Muslim community in East London, where respect for the children's cultural heritage was vital to the successful functioning of our school community.

Following the initial revelations of the 'Trojan Horse' letter, allegations of the infiltration of schools by so-called 'Islamic extremists' were made in the UK media and in Parliament throughout 2014: 'Trojan Horse: how we revealed the truth behind the plot' (Gilligan 2014); 'OfSTED's slur on the Muslim community of Park View School' (Donaghy 2014); 'Trojan Horse Debate: We were wrong, all cultures are not equal' (Pearson 2014); '"Trojan Horse 2" in London' (Griffiths and Kerbaj 2014, Griffiths and Kerbaj 2014); 'Extremism & Birmingham Schools' (Hansard 2014). The allegations centred on schools in the boroughs of Tower Hamlets and Birmingham, schools that served predominantly Muslim communities and which were exceeding the Department for Education and OfSTED's expected performance measures in their exams (OfSTED 2005, OfSTED 2012, Tower Hamlets 2013, OfSTED 2014, OfSTED 2014, OfSTED 2014).

In response to the Trojan Horse allegations, the schools' inspectorate (OfSTED) was instructed by Michael Gove MP (in his capacity as the secretary of state for education) to inspect twenty-one schools in Birmingham. The inspectorate downgraded fifteen of the schools from 'good' or 'outstanding' to 'inadequate'. Sir Michael Wilshaw, Her Majesty's chief inspector of schools, claimed that 'Birmingham City Council has failed to support a number of schools in their efforts to keep pupils safe from the potential risks of radicalisation and extremism' (Wilshaw 2014). All of the schools were instructed that they could improve if they implemented the Prevent Strategy (OfSTED 2014, OfSTED 2014, OfSTED 2014). On the day the reports were published, the supposed threat to the United Kingdom from 'violent extremism' and the threat to Birmingham's schools from Islam were debated in the same sitting of Parliament (Hansard 2014). Eleven days after this debate, headteachers in Tower Hamlets received a letter offering their schools the services of the Home Office Prevent Counter-Terrorism Programme in lesson planning (Vickerie 2014). The head teacher of a school in Tower Hamlets, whom I spoke to at the time, expressed their concern that these services were at odds with their school's inclusive agenda but – in reference to the Trojan Horse debate in the media and in Parliament, and the threat of intervention by the schools' inspectorate, OfSTED – told me that 'in the current climate we can't afford to ignore this'.

Soon after this, allegations were made in the press that the infiltration by 'Islamic extremists' was worse in Tower Hamlets than in Birmingham. Griffiths and Kerbaj (2014) quote a 'senior Whitehall source', saying,

> Tower Hamlets is expected to be the next Birmingham, but even worse, because the problems surrounding Muslim fundamentalists imposing their views on education seem to be more embedded. (Griffiths and Kerbaj 2014)

These allegations were rebutted by Tower Hamlets Council in a statement published on their website (Tower Hamlets 2014) but, in light of these accusations, staff at the school in Tower Hamlets where I was teaching were warned on the day after the article was published to expect an inspection and that the school might suffer a similar judgement to the schools in Birmingham. Weeks later, OfSTED did come to Tower Hamlets and visited Sir John Cass School, which is down the road from the school where I worked. Sir John Cass School was criticized by OfSTED for not providing the students with 'sufficient guidance about how to keep themselves safe from extremism' (OfSTED 2014), and the same report downgraded the school from 'outstanding' to 'inadequate'. OfSTED's first instruction for how they could improve was that they should adopt the Prevent Strategy (OfSTED 2014). Soon after the inspection of John Cass School, Prevent Strategies for Tower Hamlets (2014) and for the school where I worked were emailed to all staff. Date stamps on the documents indicate that both the borough and the school strategies were written less than ten days after 3 July 2014 when Sir John Cass School was inspected. Seven years after the Prevent Strategy had been written, the government had finally forced it into schools by co-opting the threat of OfSTED. As I reported earlier in relation to debates in Parliament and newspaper headlines a month earlier on 9 June 2014, the moral panic over 'extremism' had already silenced my Muslim students. Prevent had embedded this same panic into the local government bureaucracy and schools of Tower Hamlets.

Throughout this period, many Muslim students at the school where I taught continued to voluntarily attend the lunchtime prayer room. During Friday prayers (*Jumma*), the students had previously given their own sermons, but soon after the inspection of Sir John Cass School the students giving the sermons were requested to submit scripts to the school for approval. This was no easy task for the students who had previously given oral sermons that were not written down. It was clear from discussions at the time that this change in the running of the prayer room was related to the downgrading of John Cass School by OfSTED and the implementation of the Prevent Strategy. As someone who volunteered to supervise the prayer room, I was engaged in this censoring process by email but expressed my discomfort and was not required to pass judgement on the children's sermons. However, a number of sermons were subsequently censored by other teachers and the students were given preprepared scripts to read from instead. The Prevent Strategy, which had previously been ignored, now appeared to be informing the day-to-day running of the school.

Prevent was reinforced six months later when on 12 February 2015 the Counter-Terrorism and Security Act made it a duty for schools to 'have due regard to the need to prevent people from being drawn into terrorism', stating that the 'The Secretary of State may issue guidance to specified authorities about the exercise of [this] duty' and that they 'must have regard to any such guidance in carrying out that duty' (HM Government 2015). Thus, when the 'Prevent Duty Guidance for England and Wales' was published by the Home Office on 12 March 2015 and instructed schools and other specified authorities such as healthcare providers and universities how to adopt Prevent, they were also dutybound by the law to follow the strategy.

A brief history of Prevent and counter-extremism

The Prevent Strategy was first proposed by the New Labour government's security and intelligence advisor, Sir David Omand, in a presentation to the Cabinet Office on 1 April 2003, two weeks after the start of the Second Gulf War. It was proposed as, and continues to be, a part of Contest: a five-year strategy for countering international terrorism. Yet, much like the aftereffects of the Gulf War, Prevent is still with us after nearly two decades. In his presentation to Tony Blair's Cabinet, Omand proposed that by 'reducing the threat' and 'reducing the vulnerability' to terrorism, Prevent might 'reduce the risk'. Yet, far from 'reducing the risk', Prevent might better be described as *promoting* the perceived risk of terrorism. Tom Pettinger (2020) describes how Prevent does this by 'normaliz[ing] the suspicion of banal and everyday behaviours . . . through worst-case imaginations'.

Since Omand's initial proposal, there have been two versions of Prevent. Published first in 2008 by the New Labour government of Tony Blair PM, Prevent was then reviewed and republished in 2011 by the Conservative-led coalition government of David Cameron PM. The language adopted in these two different documents has been described by MacDonald et al. (2013) as representative of the progression of post-9/11 government discourses that first promoted multiculturalism, then Citizenship and Community Cohesion (CCC) in 2008 and then Preventing Violent Extremism (PVE) in the later strategy (MacDonald, Hunter et al. 2013, Thomas 2014). The government have subsequently rebranded their efforts to a more overt focus on counter-extremism (HM Government 2013, HM Government 2015, HM Government 2015), and the most recent shift has been towards Challenging Hateful Extremism (Commission for Countering Extremism 2019).

In my interactions with civil servants at the Home Office, this rebranding of Prevent and counter-extremism has been used to avoid critique: on questioning aspects of counter-extremism I've been told that Prevent is part of the counter-*terrorism* strategy; critique of a specific 'community' project to counter 'extremism' and a typical response might be 'that's part of the Building a Stronger Britain Together programme and not Prevent'; every line of critique is denounced by referring to one of the many rebrandings of the same work that is carried out by the Home Office. To avoid critique in the manner described earlier, civil servants have referred me to the work of the Office for Security and Counter-Terrorism (OSCT), the Research, Information and Communications Unit (RICU), the Counter-Extremism Unit (CEU) and the Building a Stronger Britain Together Programme (BSBT). There may be other parts of the Home Office and of government more generally that are working on similar work, and, should efforts to counter 'extremism' continue, it is reasonable to suspect that others will appear as this policy area grows. The growth of counter-extremism seems likely to continue for the foreseeable future, and Michael Jones (2020) of the Royal United Services Institute (RUSI) has described 'Communications-Based Activities to Prevent and Counter Violent Extremism' as 'a flourishing industry'.

Despite the denials of supporters, counter-extremism and Prevent are contingent on the same idea, which is that there is a knowable process of 'radicalization' or that observable characteristics of 'extremism' are valuable predictors of future acts of violence. Dr Katy Sian has convincingly shown how, rather than developing a new field of valuable knowledge, Prevent reinforces 'earlier iterations of positivist criminology and race-thinking' (Sian 2017). The lack of scientific basis for the Home Office's proposals to counter 'extremism' leaves civil servants with no reasonable defence of this work, so the constant rebranding that was referred to earlier has become their only option in response to the onslaught of critique from academic researchers, civil liberties organizations and politicians.

The latest iteration has been to promote the supposed threat of Hateful Extremism (Commission for Countering Extremism 2019). This has come after supporters of Prevent have apparently tied themselves in knots with their own 'logic' and been unable to answer, 'if counter-extremism isn't to counter terrorism, and if we live in a democracy, why are you trying to police "extremism"?' Having posed this question to a number of civil servants, the most curious answer that I have been given was, 'Nick Timothy told us to target extremism before he left the Home Office'. Nick Timothy was Theresa May's special advisor when she was home secretary, and given the lack of research to justify the costs, disruption and controversy of continuing to target 'extremism', the continuation of this policy area as a result of the whimsical diktat of an unelected advisor is as reasonable an explanation as any other that I've been offered.

As the counter-extremism industry has 'flourished', related propaganda campaigns have been developed and are referred to as 'Strategic communications . . . to effect behavioural and attitudinal change' by the Home Office's Research Information and Communications Unit (RICU). RICU have had a hand in campaigns from the Armed Forces Muslim Association to Facebook pages that are apparently targeted at non-white and teenage British citizens – the inference being that those identified as the racialized 'other' are to be defined as a security risk (Hayes and Qureshi 2016, Cobain and Osman 2020). Latterly, the Building a Stronger Britain Together (BSBT) programme has seen the Home Office collaborate with advertising agency MC Saatchi to support and promote community initiatives to counter 'extremism'.

BSBT offers 'targeted funding for specific projects with demonstrable outcomes which provide a positive alternative to extremist voices', and the groups supported include sports clubs, community support networks and arts organizations (Building a Stronger Britain Together 2017, Home Office 2018, HM Government 2019). At a time when a decade of austerity has left communities around the United Kingdom desperate for funding, there can be little doubt of the incentive to become a Prevent or counter-extremism entrepreneur, and this process of creating grassroots organizations that might not have formed or continued without the hand of central government has been described as 'astroturfing' (Birt 2019). In Chapters 6 and 7, I will explore how astroturfing inevitably creates a cacophony of voices in support of even the most flawed government agendas, drowning out genuine research and critique. Without first addressing this active promotion of groupthink at the heart of government, there is little hope for the creation of effective and evidence-based policy, in counter-extremism and other policy areas.

The violent discourse of radicalization and extremism

The constant rebranding of government efforts to counter 'extremism' has created a level of confusion that demands analysis that goes beyond the surface of what work is being done in this area by the Home Office and associated Prevent entrepreneurs. Changes to the usage of the words 'radicalization' and 'extremism' that are explored in later chapters indicate that there are discursive mechanisms at play that are creating a 'common sense' support for counter-extremism that is dangerously misguided.

The mechanism that creates this common sense will be referred to here as the violent discourse of 'radicalization' and 'extremism' or RadEx – the use of such a portmanteau is characteristic of critical realism, the philosophy informing this book. Critical realism can sometimes be impenetrable to those unfamiliar with it, and, as such, I will keep overt reference to it to a minimum. However, I hope that readers will see that critical realism is an invaluable tool for those willing to take the plunge and endeavour to see through the epistemic fallacy that has dominated Western philosophy since Plato. I follow Bhaskar in believing that this has left far too many great thinkers trapped in considerations of how we know the world, rather than what the world really is.

The use of abbreviations like RadEx is often necessary in critical realism as its focus is on ontology (what we believe is real) as opposed to epistemology (what we think is reliable evidence about reality), and this can result in the need to describe things that are new and previously unknown. In describing the 'violent discourse of radicalization and extremism', this book will explain the generative mechanism for Prevent and the ever-expanding counter-extremism industry and how 'extremism' and violence inevitably emerge from it. Unlike some other branches of philosophy, critical realism is unashamedly concerned with Utopia, and the later chapters of this book will propose how we might move beyond the emergence of 'extremism' and its institutionalization of racial inequality and violence.

Professor John O'Regan is a prominent exponent of a critical realist approach to discourse analysis, and, along with Dr Ann Betzel, his analysis of discourses of extremism and multiculturalism shows how valuable an approach this can be. They analyse speeches made by Mohammad Siddique Khan (the leader of the 7/7 bombings in London), Michael Adebolajo (murderer of Lee Rigby), Anders Breivik (white supremacist Norwegian mass shooter and bomber) and David Cameron (British prime minister from 2010 to 2016). Referring to the discourses of the former 'Islamists and white supremacists' as 'discourses of extremism', they describe the similarities to those of politicians like Cameron who are promoting multiculturalism:

> the discursive construction of identities in discourses of extremism and multiculturalism, on the part of Islamists and white supremacists on the one hand and UK politicians on the other, and the way in which cultural essentialism and outsiderness may be seen to dominate the lenses of both discourses. (O'Regan and Betzel 2016)

O'Regan and Betzel's work is a useful demonstration of the complexity that can be encountered when attempting to define discourses. Even discourses such as those of multiculturalism and the so-called 'extremism' that might appear to be distinct and even contradictory to one another may in fact share similarities when submitted to closer analysis. In exploring the emergence of 'extremism' in later chapters, I use similar close analysis of texts to reveal that the development of post-9/11 counter-terrorism discourses on 'radicalization' and 'extremism' have been a significant contributory factor in the construction of the supposed threat. In later chapters I will explore how they may even have precipitated the violence that they purport to prevent. But first, the development of post-9/11 counter-terrorism discourses on CCC that subsequently developed into the concerns for 'radicalization' and 'extremism' which led to Prevent will be discussed.

Multiculturalism, community cohesion and 'extremism'

Riots in the north of England in 2001 led the government to commission the chief executive of Nottingham City Council, Ted Cantle, to write a report into community cohesion (Home Office 2001). While the Cantle Report does not refer explicitly to 'multiculturalism', criticism of divisions between different communities can be found throughout:

> Whilst the physical segregation of housing estates and inner city areas came as no surprise, the team was particularly struck by the depth of polarisation of our towns and cities. The extent to which these physical divisions were compounded by so many other aspects of our daily lives, was very evident. Separate educational arrangements, community and voluntary bodies, employment, places of worship, language, social and cultural networks, means that many communities operate on the basis of a series of parallel lives. These lives often do not seem to touch at any point, let alone overlap and promote any meaningful interchanges. (Home Office 2001)

Alongside this criticism, the Cantle Report lauds community cohesion, bemoaning its 'breakdown' (p.21) and insisting on its promotion as a solution to the problems described:

> we believe that a commitment to promote community cohesion through the development of organisations from top to bottom is now required. (Cantle 2001)

Professor Paul Thomas suggests that the shift to community cohesion shown in the Cantle Report marked a return to policies of assimilation – whereby minorities would be expected to resemble the dominant group – and signalled the death of multiculturalism and the promotion of multicultural diversity in government policy (Home Office 2001, Thomas 2014). While, in Thomas' view, the Cantle Report's focus on community cohesion signals that the government is stepping away from multiculturalism, the report is notably different from later PVE and CE discourses in not using the term 'radicalization', and in the nine times that it uses 'extremist' it always ties it to the far right, a focus that distinguishes it from both the 2008 and 2011 versions of Prevent that are predominantly focused on the threat of 'Al-Qaida-influenced' and 'Al-Qaida-inspired' terrorism.

In response to the disaffection of Britain's migrant communities that the Cantle Report expressed and the apparent exposure of these communities to 'organised terrorism oversees', Dr John Mackinlay suggests that British security officials thought 'that the country had become unusually vulnerable [to terrorism]' and needed 'a more unified and convincing national strategy' (Mackinlay 2009). Not only is Mackinlay a formidable scholar, but as an ex-officer in the British Gurkha regiment, defence fellow of Churchill College Cambridge and teaching fellow at the War Studies Department of King's College, it would be hard to imagine a more establishment figure. This may be the reason that he was able to gain access to the architects of Prevent not seen in the work of other academics critiquing post-9/11 British counter-terrorism strategy. In his 2009 book, *The Insurgent Archipelago*, Mackinlay describes the actions of senior civil servant, Sir David Omand, in 2002 that would ultimately lead to the government's focus on 'radicalization' and 'extremism'. Sir David had recently moved from his role of permanent secretary to the Home Office to become security and intelligence coordinator for the Cabinet Office in 2002 when,

> On the 22nd October he [Omand] achieved his first organisational objective by convening a meeting of all the involved departments and agencies. His critical mass included parts of the Cabinet Office, Home Office, Treasury, Foreign Office, Ministry of Defence, the Security Services as well as the Metropolitan Police. There were so many attendees that, rather than use the conference facilities in Whitehall, the meeting had to be held at the Civil Service Sports Club. In his opening brief he established himself as national co-ordinator and called on the participants to engage as a whole in helping to construct a national strategy rather than by simply following their departmental priorities. He urged them to cross departmental boundaries and to think nationally. His plan was to create a national structure to address Britain's vulnerability to attack, improve its ability to respond to an attack and to counter growing disaffection or 'radicalisation' of Muslim communities, in addition to supporting the pursuit of the existing terrorist networks at home and overseas. It was intended as an immediate response, a five-year plan, but not as a long-term operation that could support a widely advocated political narrative. (Mackinlay 2009)

The intended short-term nature of Omand's intervention is confirmed in the recently released confidential Cabinet Office briefing presentation on 'a 5 year UK strategy for countering international terrorism' that was gained via a Freedom of Information request and that is referred to earlier. Mackinlay suggests that Omand had a long-term intention to address the issues laid out in the Cantle Report, to build 'healthier, more integrated migrant communities at home'. However, he describes resistance from the Education, Local Government and Community Cohesion departments in Whitehall as they did not want to be linked to counter-terrorism. Added to this resistance, the growing architecture that was already referred to as 'Prevent' (Omand 2004) was shrouded in secrecy so as to avoid this new domestic branch of the war on terror becoming linked to the politically toxic invasion of Iraq in 2003 (Mackinlay 2009). The Office of Security and Counter Terrorism (OSCT) emerged

at the time to coordinate the growing architecture that Omand
had instigated:

> In Whitehall the Office of Security and Counter Terrorism (OSCT)
> was designed as a hub around which Government departments,
> intelligence and the police coalesced and co-operated. The
> OSCT's achievement was to reconcile the actions of a very
> disparate array of actors and to keep them fixed on the objectives
> of CONTEST. In the Whitehall hierarchy the OSCT was a
> subordinate part of the Home Office, but in the context of the
> operation it was required to reach far beyond its boundaries and
> draw together officials from the allied departments of Transport,
> Education, Local Government, Energy and Rural Affairs. The
> OSCT also had a co-ordinating function for the Foreign and
> Commonwealth Office, Ministry of Defence and the Security
> Services.... Had a campaign of such a scale and complexity been
> organised by the military there would have been an operational
> order. (Mackinlay 2009)

Such an operational order was not issued as it would have
interfered with the 'pre-existing *modus operandi*' of the police and
civil authorities and would, thus, have been seen as 'intrusive and
unconstitutional'. This lack of operational order meant that OSCT
were unable to 'steer their efforts at a local level' (Mackinlay 2009).
There is limited reference to the organizational structure of OSCT
or of its relation to Prevent on government websites but Mackinlay
describes OSCT as taking a leading role in the implementation of
Prevent, through the overarching CONTEST Strategy (Mackinlay
2009). OSCT's connection with Prevent has also been corroborated
by the fact that I have had meetings with civil servants from the
'Prevent Unit' of OSCT.

Though named in Omand's 2004 Contest presentation (p.5),
Prevent was not developed into or written as a separate strategy
until after the bombings in London on 7 July 2005 when it
was rapidly drafted and deployed; Thomas describes this rapid
conception and operationalization as a problem that has dogged
Prevent from the outset (Thomas 2014). He suggests that the dual
purposes of Prevent, securitization and community cohesion, exist
as an unhappy marriage. And, in his paper, 'Divorced but still co-
habiting?', Thomas (2014) shows that these two aspects of the

strategy were led by the OSCT and the Department for Communities and Local Government (DCLG). He explains that the community cohesion agenda of the DCLG was side-lined by OSCT and quotes a senior civil servant as saying that 'Prevent took over cohesion' as a result of OSCT's control of funding (Thomas 2014).

As a co-opted member of a local government scrutiny committee into Prevent in 2016, I saw how the requirement of community cohesion projects to reapply to central government via the Home Office for funding as often as every six months rendered control over this type of work to OSCT. At this time, the only projects that could be commissioned had to be selected from a list prepared by OSCT and listed in the Prevent Catalogue (Home Office 2015). This short-term funding model was a frustration to those providing this work as they were unable to guarantee that projects would be recommissioned, meaning that youth groups and other community projects were frequently forced to abandon the children and adults who they had just started to work with as their funding ran out. This frustration, that Prevent could only offer short-term initiatives rather than developing longer-term and more meaningful projects to support effective cohesion work, was still being aired by civil servants who I spoke to a year later in October 2017.

The control of the Prevent agenda on funding was further demonstrated at a local level in discussions that I have had with youth workers who described resisting requests to hand over the contact details of the young people they worked with to Prevent workers. In one case, I was told by the leader of a youth group that his continued refusal resulted in funding from the Home Office being cut off. The youth workers' observations that funding was tied to intelligence sharing and the lack of interest in effective and longer-term cohesion projects is in line with Amber Rudd MP's comments on BBC Question Time that, 'We get the intelligence much more from the Prevent strategy' (Rudd 2017). This focus on intelligence gathering, both at the heart of government and at a local level, seems to confirm that the focus of these Prevent projects was intelligence gathering rather than the promotion of community cohesion.

Arun Kundnani's report, 'Spooked' (Kundnani 2009), publicized the embedding of police and counter-terrorism units at all levels of Prevent and decision-making in local government. Kundnani's work is described by Thomas as 'crystallizing' the perception that

Prevent was a large-scale surveillance operation on British Muslims (Thomas 2014). Though, my own conversations with youth workers and Amber Rudd's comments in the BBC seem to confirm that this was not just a 'perception' but was a crystallization of the *fact* that Prevent was a large-scale surveillance operation on British Muslims. Either way, this lack of trust in Prevent caused the 2010 House of Commons Communities and Local Government Committee report, Preventing Violent Extremism, to recommend that, 'If the Government wants to improve confidence in the Prevent programme, it should commission an independent investigation into the allegations made' (House of Commons Communities and Local Government Committee 2010).

An investigation into Prevent was carried out by the government in June 2011 (HM Government 2011), in the wake of the 2010 general election and the formation of David Cameron PM's coalition government. In response to this review, the new Prevent Strategy was released in June 2011, moving focus away from New Labour's CCC agenda and on to the PVE agenda of the new coalition government. The new strategy is categorical in its rejection of the previous version, stating, 'The Prevent programme we inherited from the last Government was flawed' (HM Government 2011). The primacy of the OSCT's securitization agenda over the community cohesion agenda of the DCLG was confirmed by this new version of Prevent.

The OSCT-aligned securitization discourse of the new Prevent Strategy was not new and had previously been adopted by the British prime minister, David Cameron, in his speech to the Munich Security Conference in February 2011 when he proposed that there was a battle for values and ideology playing out in the supposed contest between 'Western democracy' and 'Islamic extremism'. Cameron rejected the importance of social factors such as poverty and grievances over foreign policy and described his position as 'muscular liberalism' (Cameron 2011, O'Regan and Betzel 2016). Cameron's 'muscular liberalism' has all the hallmarks of 'authoritarian liberalism' that is described by Professor Mitchel Dean. Dean proposes that this form of liberal policing of 'those who have not, or perhaps cannot, achieve extant versions of liberal notions of self-Government' is a 'fundamental notion of sovereignty' that can be seen in 'China's one child policy and Nazi Germany's notion of racial hygiene', but that is now applied to 'a substantial majority of the world's inhabitants' (Dean 2007).

Cameron would later be more specific in his aspirations for a muscular form of liberalism when he criticized Muslim women for not learning English, warning that it left them more susceptible to 'extremism' (Hughes 2016). Cameron's additional suggestion that this 'limited opportunity' for women who may have chosen to care for their families rather than go out to work illustrates that his version of authoritarian and paternalistic liberalism might promote notions of freedom, but that they are narrowly defined as a freedom to sell one's labour rather than to choose a role such as being a carer to one's children for its inherent value. This perverse undervaluing of vital caring roles such as nurses, carers for the elderly and even supermarket shelf stackers has been highlighted by the coronavirus pandemic that has revealed the 'uncomfortable truth [that] the people we need the most are often the ones we value the least' (O'Connor 2020).

Cameron's notion of a battle for ideology is replicated by his government's report from the Task Force on Tackling Radicalization and Extremism (TREFOR) in December 2013. TREFOR repeatedly employs the terms 'extremist' and 'extremism' without qualification, seventy-nine times over nine pages, reinforcing the notion expressed by Cameron that this is a problem of 'extreme' individuals or ideologies rather than of social conditions (HM Government 2013). This report was published in the wake of the murder of soldier Lee Rigby in Woolwich on 22 May 2013 when one of his murderers was recorded on a mobile phone attempting to justify his actions.

The publication of the TREFOR report indicates that the PVE agenda of the Home Office and OSCT had been incorporated across central government, having already been adopted by the DCLG in their Creating the Conditions for Integration report (Department for Communities and Local Government 2012). Thomas describes the DCLG's report as 'a flimsy and woefully inadequate document' (Thomas 2014). However, we might also see that, far from being 'inadequate', the report indicates a shift in the agenda of the DCLG. The report demonstrates that the community cohesion agenda was losing the DCLG as its main supporter as the department aligned itself with the PVE agenda of Prevent and OSCT.

Though the PVE agenda of OSCT had been adopted across government departments, it continues to be controversial. In the BBC Radio 4 programme, Understanding Prevent (Fenton-Smith 2017) – a programme that I also appear on – Sir David Omand, the original architect of Prevent, reflected on the effectiveness of the strategy that he conceived in 2002, saying,

> I have some doubts as to whether it was the right way but I retired in 2005 so am very much an outside observer. The risk in taking that approach [Prevent] was that it was bringing together two strands of work, one part of counter-terrorism focusing on potential risks of violent crime, the other much more general objective about community cohesion and our values. By bringing those two together the risk was it would be perceived by the Muslim communities in Great Britain as being something that was actually hostile to them. (Omand in Fenton-Smith 2017)

When asked if he thought that Prevent has been effective, he responded, 'If it is not accepted, then it's not going to be successful' (Omand in Fenton-Smith 2017). While my Muslim students had been largely silenced by Prevent, their guarded conversations with me indicated that they were anything but accepting of it. While it may seem obvious why my students did not accept Prevent, it continues to be accepted by some academics and policymakers. What lies behind this schism is explored in the next chapter.

CHAPTER 2

Terrorism studies

Lord Carlile 'may be somewhat biased'

If we abandoned Prevent, then terrorist acts which we have been able to avoid as a result of that policy would happen. I admit I played a part in it, so I may be somewhat biased towards it. (Hansard 2018)

Lord Carlile informing a House of Lords debate in 2018 that he might be 'somewhat biased towards' Prevent is 'somewhat' of an understatement. Seven years earlier he had carried out the review that created the very strategy that he is referring to. He also offered his 'considered and strong support' for Prevent in the foreword that he wrote for the strategy (HM Government 2011), was a member of the secretive Prevent Review Board and has continued to offer his unflinching support to Prevent in the House of Lords. Lord Carlile offered this support in a House of Lords debate on an amendment to the Counter-Terrorism and Border Security Bill that would force the government to review Prevent, something that Carlile tells us in the same debate that he 'regard[s] as unnecessary'.

Despite his self-professed bias, Lord Carlile was appointed as the government's 'Independent' Reviewer of Prevent nine months later in August 2019. I wrote to Carlile in November 2019 to explain that I would not be submitting evidence, explaining that his predisposition to support Prevent did not put him in a position to carry out an informed review that would listen to supporters and critics of Prevent in equal measure. To his credit, he invited me to discuss this in person and we were due to meet in January 2020, but our meeting was cancelled without explanation in late December. Over the next few days, it became apparent that Lord Carlile was to be removed as the reviewer following a legal challenge from human rights advocacy group Rights Watch (UK).

The government had removed Lord Carlile before his appointment was able to be challenged in court, 'testament to the strength of the case against Lord Carlile and the overwhelming evidence of his lack of independence, and the lack of faith from the community in a Review conducted under his leadership' (Rights Watch (UK) 2019). Rights Watch (UK) go on to note that Lord Carlile's 'long-standing objection to any kind of criticism or overhaul of Prevent is no secret and he has a track record of discrediting those who raised concerns about Prevent', explaining that 'this meant the Review lacked buy-in and cooperation from those it most needed to engage'.

At the time of writing, William Shawcross was being touted, and would eventually be appointed, as the new reviewer (Hymas 2020). As the former director of the right-wing Henry Jackson Society, Shawcross had indulged the white nationalist Great Replacement conspiracy (Charlton 2019) that white Europeans are being replaced by ethnic minorities when he was quoted as saying,

Europe and Islam is one of the greatest, most terrifying problems of our future. I think all European countries have vastly, very quickly growing Islamic populations' (Ramesh 2014).

Moving on from the Henry Jackson Society in 2012 to become chairman of the Charity Commission, Shawcross faced criticism for unfairly targeting Muslim charities (Ramesh 2014). While it seems that Shawcross would be more likely to champion than to critique the racialized targeting of Muslims under Prevent, his views do not set him apart from his circle of fellow right-wing thinkers.

Associate editor of the *Spectator* who took over from Shawcross as director of the Henry Jackson Society, Douglas Murray infamously gave a speech titled 'What are we to do about Islam?' in which he stated that 'Conditions for Muslims in Europe must be made harder across the board' (Bridge Initiative 2018, Initiative 2018). Writing in the *Spectator* to defend his speech, it is notable that Murray does not actually quote any of the words that he is defending (Murray 2010). As he had referred to the 'infection' of Europe by Islam, it may be that he was aware that some of what he had said was indefensible. The connections to the Henry Jackson Society come full circle back to Lord Carlile, who spoke for the Henry Jackson Society on '40 Years of Terrorism Legislation Reviews' in 2019 at an event hosted by Suella Braverman MP, who would be appointed attorney general shortly afterwards by Prime Minister Boris Johnson.

Soon after Shawcross was first fingered as a potential reviewer of Prevent, the government announced that 'Lord Walney will take on a new unpaid role as independent adviser on political violence and disruption' (Home Office 2020). Rather than committing to a serious review of Prevent, the government were asking Walney when 'far-right, far-left and other political groups . . . cross into criminality'. Supporters of Prevent have often defended it to me by saying that it does not seek to criminalize people, Lord Walney appears to have been commissioned to do the opposite by seeking to criminalize political views. Curiously, Walney, who is also known as John Woodcock, has previously been associated with Shawcross as both were members of a consortium that bought the *Jewish Chronicle* in April 2020 (Jewish News 2020, Wolfson 2020). This deal faced much criticism from Jewish Chronicle chairman Alan Jacobs:

A bid for the Jewish Chronicle using money from an unidentified source and fronted by a group of individuals who refuse to tell the world anything of their plans looks like a shameful attempt to hijack the world's oldest Jewish newspaper. (Jewish News 2020)

Following the debacle over Carlile's independence, a situation compounded by a 'public appointments process, in line with cabinet manual guidelines' not being followed to recruit him in the first place, the government were forced to follow a 'full and open' recruitment process for Carlile's replacement (Smith 2020). However, Shawcross being touted as 'a frontrunner to review Prevent' in the *Telegraph* three months before his official appointment begs the question of just how open and transparent the process really was (Hymas 2020). This concern has been raised by former chief Crown prosecutor for North-West England and fellow applicant for the role Nazir Afzal:

The fact that it was leaked that Shawcross was the Government's favourite even before I was interviewed by ministers suggests that the Government had already made up its mind about its preferred candidate from the outset, and was simply going through the motions to avoid scrutiny about the appointment. (Afzal in Ahmed 2021)

However partial or impartial Carlile's replacement turns out to be in their new role, the terms of reference for the review are inadequate as they assume that 'extremism' and 'radicalization' are harmful and, in this assumption, prevent the review from addressing the main criticism of Prevent.[1] That is, the flawed hypothesis that 'radical' and 'extreme' views are a useful predictor for future acts of violence. Added to this, the Counter-Terrorism and Sentencing Bill that came into law in 2020 removed the legal requirement that the government respond to the review's findings within six months of them being delivered. The review's findings are now due to be delivered in August 2021, but removing this requirement gives the government the option of kicking them into the long grass by not responding to them if they choose to. Despite raising my concerns about the terms of reference and the Counter-Terrorism and Sentencing Bill with the team behind the review, efforts to mitigate them had not been made at the time of writing.

Soon after his appointment, Shawcross wrote a letter to the *Guardian* that was titled 'I want to hear the case for and against Prevent' (Shawcross 2021). Expanding the quote from which the title was taken, Shawcross tells us, 'I want to hear the case for and against Prevent based on evidence that can be tested'. By insisting that evidence should be able to be tested, Shawcross is revealing an allegiance to a largely debunked mode of testing scientific validity that was promoted by Karl Popper. While Popper suggested that falsifiability was a necessary test of scientific validity, subsequent philosophers of science have suggested that this proposal falls down in the real world where scientific theory exists in open systems (Hartwig 2007). This was explored earlier in the introduction where we saw that the existence of black CEOs is clearly not a reason to debunk structural and historical disadvantages experienced by black people. Thus, it might be suggested that attempts to denounce critical race theory (CRT) and other aspects of the social sciences that are explored throughout this book reveal something of the outdated thinking of the proponents of such culture wars, a position that is further demonstrated by senior Conservative minister Liz Truss MP denouncing Foucault:

> These ideas have their roots in postmodernist philosophy – pioneered by Foucault – that puts societal power structures and labels ahead of individuals and their endeavours. In this school of thought, there is no space for evidence, as there is no objective view – truth and morality are all relative. (Truss in Stone 2020)

Tellingly, this speech that was described as 'utterly bonkers' by Liberal Democrat deputy leader and education spokesperson Daisy Cooper was soon redacted from government websites (Stone 2020).

Carlile's unconditional support for Prevent and the challenge that led to his removal as reviewer are characteristic of the heated debates and entrenched divisions that Prevent and counter-extremism strategy tend to provoke. This chapter attempts to situate these debates in the context of academic fields and the broader political landscape. As such, the areas covered are wide ranging. Attempts are made to explore literature on 'radicalization' and 'extremism', *Orientalism*, CRT, democracy and critical realist understandings of critique, ideology, power and discourse. The final brief exploration of neoliberalism offers some insight into the analysis of the final chapters. An exploration of notions of a *Clash of Civilisations*, in particular the book of the same name (Huntington 1996), is notably absent. While such hawkish interpretations of the West's supposed encounter with Islam are clearly a significant factor in the expansion of the global war on terror that Prevent has emerged from, the main focus of his book is on the self-fulfilling generative mechanism for 'radicalization' and 'extremism' that are found in the language itself. That is not to say that this mechanism is not catalysed by racist screeds and right-wing political agendas such as *The Clash of Civilisations* that vilify Islam. But, while such powerful agendas support government efforts to counter 'radicalization' and 'extremism', they are easily bought to light, and I have often silenced a meeting of civil servants who are intent on challenging 'Islamism' in the United Kingdom by asking why they have a problem with religion informing political opinion as employees of a church state. The generative mechanisms explored here are subtler and require more than a back-handed comment to elaborate.

Disagreement has come to define my interactions with civil servants since I began researching 'extremism', and this is best explained by the division between Orthodox and Critical Terrorism Studies (OTS and CTS) (Jackson 2016). The former addresses problems as they are seen in the world, while the latter questions the social structures that might have contributed to the existence of the problem in the first place. Thus, my efforts to understand the discursive structures that have resulted in the emergence of 'extremism' situate this book in the field of CTS.

Literature on 'radicalization' and 'extremism'

In line with CTS, Mark Sedgwick, professor of Arab and Islamic Studies at Aarhus University in Denmark, explores the different understandings of 'radicalization' in his paper, 'The Concept of Radicalization as a Source of Confusion' (Sedgwick 2010). Referring to dictionary definitions, he suggests that 'radical' should be seen as synonymous with 'extremist' (Sedgwick 2010, p. 481), and this understanding of both terms is adopted in here.

Sedgwick suggests that there are different understandings of 'radicalization' from different agendas and that this may result in 'radicalization' working to undermine the conflicting agendas of integration, security, foreign policy and Islam. This occurs as each one of these agendas co-opts 'radicalization' as a means to their own ends. An example of this is a non-violent organization that is promoting a conservative version of Islam with regards to homosexuality. Such an organization may be seen as supporting a security agenda by diverting potentially violent actors into non-violent political activism, but might also be seen to undermine integration in a society such as that found in the United Kingdom that has more liberal views towards homosexuality (Sedgwick 2010). 'Radicalization', thus, may be applied to undermine such a group by those supporting an integration agenda, yet the existence of the same group might act in the interests of a security agenda for the reasons described earlier, so 'the security and integration agendas not only differ, but actually conflict' (Sedgwick 2010).

This conflict between integration and security agendas was made visible throughout 2019 by the reporting of protests by Muslim parents over the sex and relationships education that their children were offered in primary schools in Birmingham. The disagreement that led to the protests was portrayed in the press as an argument between the schools and the apparently traditionalist parents who were opposed to the 'No Outsiders' programme of lessons that introduced their children to LGBT+ relationships. In characteristically polarized responses, local Labour MP Roger Godsiff told protesters, 'I will continue to fight your corner because you're right' (Vernalls 2019), while his colleague and fellow local labour MP Jess Philips described the parents' actions as 'bigotry' (BBC 2019).

What Philips failed to recognize and what was rarely mentioned in the press was that the initial protests were sparked when the head teacher of Parkfield Community School, Hazel Pulley, suggested that the lessons were being introduced 'in response to Prevent' and to 'reduce radicalization' in the vilified parents' young children. In the same presentation that the head teacher introduced the No Outsiders lessons to the parents, she offered statistics on the number of their children who had been referred to Prevent and then on to the counter-terrorism unit of the local police force. Though the parents were attacked in the press and by at least one of their local MPs, they were offered support for their opposition to their young children being cast as potential terrorists in a letter to the *Independent* newspaper that was signed by community groups, teachers and academics, including globally renowned feminist and queer ethicist Professor Judith Butler.

> We support the inclusion of LGBT+ identities within RSE at both primary- and secondary-school level. However, we reject the ways in which LGBT+ issues are being deployed in the Government's discourse about the requirement to teach 'Fundamental British Values' as part of their 'Prevent' counter-extremism and counterterrorism strategies. (Judith Butler et al. 2019)

This episode that saw Muslim parents vilified as homophobic and 'aggressive' (BBC 2019) for protesting against their children, some as young as four years old, being cast as potential terrorists clearly demonstrates the conflict that Sedgwick described between the security and integration agendas to target the supposed threat of 'radicalization'. An additional and enlightening perspective to understand this conflict is that of homonationalism.

Homonationalism describes the process of celebrating the emancipation of those who were previously regarded as queer and deviant and replacing them with a queer and deviant Muslim other, the same accusations of sexual and moral deviance now placed on Muslims as was previously ascribed to gay or queer people (Perry 2014, Puar 2014). Puar notes that in the United States, legislation granting freedoms to homosexuals has often corresponded with legislation withdrawing freedoms from ethnic minorities (Puar 2014). While scholars such as Mavelli have explored the secular interpretation of Muslims as irrational subjects and how this has removed secularism's responsibility for the societal conditions that might lead to acts of political violence expressed by *them* (Mavelli 2012), the homonationalist representation of Muslims as queer and deviant has justified acts of political violence from the West against Muslims (Perry 2014).

Perry (2014) and Puar's (2014) homonationalist interpretations that Muslims are seen as queer and deviant are supported by Baker, Gabrieltos and McEnery's work, *The Representation of Islam and Muslims in the UK Press*, 1998–2008 (2011).This study analysed 200,000 articles in the UK press and, like Jess Phillips MP's portrayal of the Muslim parents in Birmingham, found that Muslims were represented as 'being quick to anger, oppressive towards women, possessing extremist beliefs and at risk from radicalisation' (2011, p. 2), and most references to Muslims saw them as associated with or participating in conflict (2011, p. 3). Muslims were referred to by generalizing terms such as 'the Muslim world' and 'the Muslim community', and frequently constructed subgroups include Muslim leaders who were characterized as quick to anger, Muslim women who were seen as oppressed victims and young males who were at risk of 'radicalization' (2011, pp. 2–3).

Sedgwick shows how this portrayal of Muslims being at risk of 'radicalization' can be instrumentalized in the example of American Sufi leader Hisham Kabbani reporting to the US State Department in 1999 'that 80% of American mosques had been taken over by extremists' (Sedgwick 2010). Such an allegation supports Kabbani's interpretation of Islam and is correct as a relative description from his stance but Sedgwick argues that 'it was certainly not true that 80% were extremists in any terms other than Kabbani's' (Sedgwick 2010). Sedgwick's solution to the concern that the line on the continuum from 'radical' and 'extreme' to 'moderate' might be drawn at a point to suit any agenda is to 'recognize the inherently relative nature of the term "radical," and cease treating "radicalization" as an absolute concept' (Sedgwick 2010). In line with Sedgwick's solution regarding 'radical' and 'extreme' being synonymous, it is clear that his advice on the relative nature of 'radicalization' should also be heeded with regards 'extremism'.

Concern for 'radicalization' is a recent phenomenon, and Sedgwick uses the appearance of 'radicalization' in Google News searches to show that its usage was rare before 2005. This observation will be supported in the data presented in Chapter 4 that shows the exponential emergence of 'extremism' since 2005. Sedgwick goes some way to explain this recent explosion in the usage of 'radicalization' by referring to Professor Peter Neumann (director of the International Centre for the Study of Radicalisation and Political Violence in London), who has said:,

> Following the attacks against the United States on 11 September 2001, however, it suddenly became very difficult to talk about the 'roots of terrorism', which some commentators claimed was an effort to excuse and justify the killing of innocent civilians. Even so, it seemed obvious (then) that some discussion about the underlying factors that had given rise to this seemingly new phenomenon was urgent and necessary, and so experts and officials started referring to the idea of 'radicalisation' whenever they wanted to talk about 'what goes on before the bomb goes off'. (Neumann 2008)

This way in which 'radicalization' recently came to be used is something that I have previously written about, describing Neumann's labelling of 'radicalization' as a process of 'nominalization' (Faure Walker 2018). Nominalization being the description of disparate processes as a single entity (Fairclough 2003), and there is a risk that this nominalization of 'radicalization' might hide the causes of violence, both mystifying the causes of and denying human agency to the phenomenon described (Faure Walker 2018). In later chapters it will be shown that it was only possible for counter-extremism strategies to emerge once 'radicalization' and 'extremism' had become perceived as entities through this process of nominalization. As strategies to counter 'extremism' will be shown in later chapters to be a significant factor in the emergence of 'extremism', this process of nominalization has also been a significant contributory factor.

This nominalization also goes some way to explain how Neumann is able to exceptionalize 'this seemingly new phenomenon'. It is unclear if he is referring to 9/11 and associated acts of political violence or the 'roots of terrorism'. But, either way, it seems absurd to suggest that political violence or its causes are new. Even the suggestion that the heinous violence of 9/11 is exceptional does not stand up to scrutiny when compared to other campaigns of political violence that have been rendered from the sky against civilians – the Blitz and the bombing of Dresden spring to mind. Added to this, for as long as there has been 'terrorism', it must have had 'roots'. Perhaps, the exception that Neumann refers to is the breaking of the state monopoly on political violence. This being the case, 'radicalization' and the corresponding emergence of 'extremism' represent an effort by the state to reclaim its monopoly on violence. However, even in this singular aim, 'extremism' and 'radicalization' run into contradictions and complications.

Sedgwick not only demonstrates that different agendas might apply 'radicalization' in different ways, but he also shows how approaches to counter-radicalization differ between different governments as they struggle to decide what their threshold for intervention should be. He describes this as a question of what constitutes 'threat-radicalization'. Applying his analysis to different countries, Sedgwick suggests that Britain uses the broadest definition for 'threat-radicalization' by using a circular argument that he summarizes as 'the type of radicalism that is a threat is radicalism that is a threat' (Sedgwick 2010). Such a circular argument, when applied to the targeting of a relative concept like 'radicalization', is likely to do little other than make space for pre-existing biases and oppressive forces such as racism and white supremacy as are discussed in the following text in the context of CRT.

Kundnani explores the oppression of Muslims by the security services in the name of the war on terror in his book, *The Muslims are Coming* (Kundnani 2014). Focusing largely on the domestic war on terror in the United States, Kundnani's book presents example after example of the entrapment of otherwise innocent Muslims. Reading his carefully researched book, there can be little doubt that the efforts of the policing services in the United States have made a significant contribution to the creation of the imagined threat of Islamist terrorism – that is not to say that there have not been terrorist attacks committed by Muslims, there clearly have, and 9/11 is no exception – but to imagine that there is a conspiracy that demands that all Muslims should be regarded as suspect terrorists is as absurd as Neumann's claim that political violence is a 'new phenomenon'.

It is perhaps not surprising that Neumann, as one of the foremost supporters of counter-extremism, would subsequently reveal an allegiance to the right-wing conspiracy theory that all Muslims should be suspected of supporting terrorism in an exchange that saw him investigated by his university for 'bullying' a Muslim academic. Dr Tarek Younis questioned Neumann's assertion on Twitter that 'terrorism was leading to the "gradual implosion of French society"', suggesting 'that the actions of the French state had also contributed to social divisions in the country'. To this, Neumann appeared to question whether Younis supported recent terrorist attacks or not. It was subsequently pointed out by numerous commentators that Neumann appeared to be directing this question to Younis *because* he was Muslim (Ullah 2020).

Neumann had inadvertently demonstrated the divisive rhetoric and oppression that Younis had initially pointed out. Neumann's brazen attack on Younis and the research described in later chapters suggest that the oppression of counter-extremism has become even more pervasive than Kundnani proposed, embedded both in the language that we all use and in 'normal' social relations. Thus, while the focus of this book is on counter-extremism in the United Kingdom, it also sounds a warning for the continued expansion of counter-extremism and Prevent-like policies around the world (Cobain and Ross 2020).

While counter-extremism is now promoted in bilateral conferences at the highest levels of government (Foreign & Commonwealth Office 2018), its initial emergence to target Muslims in the United Kingdom is best described by the normal and hidden processes of white dominance that are elaborated by both *Orientalism* (Said 1978) and CRT (Gillborn 2005, Crawford 2017) and that are now explored.

Orientalism

Later analysis, particularly in Chapters 4 and 5, will draw on Said's seminal exploration of *Orientalism*, a theory first put forward in his book of the same name in 1978. Said proposes that the 'Orient' has been constructed as a 'constellation of ideas' that – much like the Islamist threat described by Kundnani – exists independently of any real Orient (Said 1978). Said suggests that the relationship of the West, or 'Occident', to the Orient is one of power and domination, defining '"us" Europeans against all "those" non-Europeans' (Said 1978). Orientals are 'endowed with a historical subjectivity' that contributes to the Europeans' political, intellectual, cultural and moral superiority (Said 1978). While much of this book looks at the construction of 'radicalization' and 'extremism' in a British context, the analysis of Chapters 4 and 5 indicates that this focus emerged from colonialist discourse as British politicians referred to struggles for emancipation at the fringes of the diminishing British Empire. By casting calls for self-rule as 'extremism', politicians were able to denounce and even dehumanize the reasonable demands for self-government made by the people whose countries they had colonized. The discursive mechanisms that are described later in this book might therefore be regarded as significant in the maintenance of Orientalism, both at the height of the British Empire and today.

Later analysis of parliamentary texts, thus, supports Said's observations from 1978 that *Orientalism* was being applied to the further reaches of the British Empire throughout the early twentieth century. More recently, Said has turned his attention to the war on terror, and, in the introduction to a new edition of *Orientalism*, he suggests that British and American military intervention in the Middle East has been justified by a continued Orientalism that still contributes to an essentialized view of 'them' and that spirits away human suffering and pain (Said 2003). While Said explores how *Orientalism* has enabled the waging of the war on terror in the Middle East, later chapters here explore how 'radicalization' and 'extremism' have in turn emerged from the war on terror and enabled it to be turned back on the domestic populations of the West.

In the final chapters of this book, the government's formation and funding of quasi-independent civil society and non-academic 'research' bodies, such as the Commission for Countering

Extremism, that support the emergence of 'extremism' are explored, and parallels can be drawn between Said's exploration of the construction of knowledge of the Orient that emerges from the work of paid 'scholars'.

> A new dialectic emerges out of this project. What is required of the Oriental expert is no longer simply 'understanding': now the Orient must be made to perform, its power must be enlisted on the side of 'our' values, civilisation, interest, goals. (Said 2003)

Said continues in this passage to discuss how this power results in the 'assertion of control' of 'the White Man' over the Orient. Those familiar with Prevent, and the enforcement of 'Fundamental British Values' (FBV) that is so central to the strategy, will also be familiar with this observation of Said's that this knowledge has been 'enlisted on the side of "our" values, civilisation, interests, goals' (Said 2003). Dr Tarek Younis, who has carried out extensive research into the implementation of Prevent in the National Health Service (NHS), including attending countless Prevent training sessions at different hospitals and NHS trusts, describes how Prevent and counter-terrorism has become a deeply moralizing subject. Both in conversation and in his written work, Younis is keen to emphasize the importance of this moralizing in the Prevent training sessions that he has attended, and he often refers to its importance in reinforcing and embedding Prevent in the NHS (Younis and Jadhav 2019).

Younis tells us that this moralizing reinforcement of Prevent occurs in several ways. First, 'counter-terrorism is a sensitive and moralising subject', and this 'moral dimension of counter-terrorism and the need to fulfil the statutory duty of Prevent made our subject [Prevent] difficult to discuss critically'. Prevent itself promoted a 'moral panic of Muslim (non)integration in British society' that invoked racialized and 'prejudicial thoughts' in health workers towards their Muslim patients (Younis and Jadhav 2019). Younis (Younis and Jadhav 2019) traces the emergence of these prejudicial thoughts and the moralizing nature of Prevent back to the invention of 'terrorism', something that is expertly elaborated by Dr Lisa Stampnitzky in *Disciplining Terror: How Experts Invented 'Terrorism'* (Stampnitzky 2013). In summarizing Stampnitzky's work, Younis explains how this moralizing dimension that is so fundamental to Prevent emerged:

Previously, counter-insurgents were seen as (morally deplorable) rational actors. The introduction of 'terrorism' re-framed political violence as irrational, erasing political agency and framing violence as a moral evil in-and-of-itself. (Younis and Jadhav 2019)

The designation of 'terrorism' might have made sense to the United Nations and in the context of the international consensus of the second half of the twentieth century. However, the far right's recent rise to power in their member states – not least in the United States – has resulted in a reappraisal of the wisdom of the moralizing defence of state violence that counter-terrorism offers as UN experts 'expressed profound concern over a recent statement by the US Attorney-General describing Antifa and other anti-fascist activists as domestic terrorists, saying it undermines the rights to freedom of expression and of peaceful assembly in the country' (United Nations 2020). Despite the United Kingdom being an active member of the UN and having faced direct criticism of Prevent by UN special rapporteurs in the past (HRC 2017, OCHCHR 2018), Prevent and counter-extremism persist. A police document that lists left-wing, anti-racist and anti-fascist symbols as of interest to the counter-terrorism police demonstrates that, despite the UN's intervention over the US targeting of anti-fascist groups, counter-terrorism in the United Kingdom continues to be used to target them (Dodd and Grierson 2020).

Given counter-extremism's occupation of the nexus of the racist interests that have coalesced around the counter-jihad movement that was described in Chapter 1, it is perhaps not surprising that it is used to target left-wing, anti-fascist and anti-racist groups. The routine privileging of white interests that this represents and that has a clear provenance in Said's *Orientalism* has more recently been elaborated by CRT.

Critical race theory and fundamental British values

Critical race theory (CRT) is a perspective focused on an examination of the association between race and racism at the intersection of power; in particular, the approach seeks to identify and resist the routine but devastating racism that saturates the everyday world of 'business-as-usual' in nations such as the United States, the UK, and Australia. (Crawford 2017)

I met the author of the text provided here, Dr Claire Crawford, when we were booked to speak on the same panel at a conference in Birmingham in 2018; her story as a former teacher and now academic who was compelled to write about the racism and injustice of Prevent and its enforcement of 'fundamental British values' was all too familiar to me. She presented the aforementioned definition for CRT while examining Prevent in her paper, 'Promoting "fundamental British values" in schools: a critical race perspective' (Crawford 2017). She suggests that an agenda to teach FBV in British schools is closely related to the implementation of Prevent. This connection is made by demonstrating that the definition of FBV is taken directly from the UK counter-terrorism strategy's definition of 'extremism', a definition that is repeated verbatim in Prevent:

> Extremism is a vocal or active opposition to fundamental British values, including democracy, the rule of law, individual liberty and mutual respect and tolerance of different faiths and beliefs. (HM Government 2011)

Crawford's paper makes an important contribution to the analysis of Prevent, and she explains that it is vital to understand Prevent in the context of CRT and racism more generally. In line with the description of homonationalism provided here, she tells us that Prevent serves to construct and present '"white British" norms and mores' as superior; 'decivilize Muslim lifestyles and identities'; and forces British teachers to 'to take up roles as instruments of surveillance and defenders of the white hegemonic order' (Crawford 2017).

She proposes that analysis from the perspective of CRT might offer a number of insights that can contribute to our understanding of Prevent:

- '"race" and "racism" are a product of social thought and power relations'
- 'the ideology and assumptions of racism are so deeply entrenched in the socio, legal, and political structures of Britain, that it is viewed as "natural" and "ordinary"'

- 'racism is a "permanent" and "pervasive" feature of society'
- 'the importance of the experiential knowledge of minoritized groups [to] challenge . . . the experience of "white" people as normative'

(Crawford 2017)

The agendas behind Prevent that Crawford elaborates are clearly of vital importance to understanding the emergence of 'extremism', and this book describes an additional aspect of state and normative social power that compounds these agendas, the construction and subsequent violent nominalization of those considered to be 'radical' or 'extreme'. 'Normative' for what is 'extreme' or 'radical' other than that which is not 'normal'? 'Violent' for it will be shown in the analysis of later chapters that the words 'extremism' and 'radicalization' became progressively synonymous with violence between 2009 and 2014. Thus, while CRT does not form the basis of the understanding of Prevent explored in this book, it indicates that the likely targets of counter-extremism and Prevent will be non-white minorities, and this helps to demonstrate that the language underpinning recent counter-terrorism efforts are likely to facilitate what Professor of Critical Race Studies David Gillborn describes as

the most dangerous form of 'white supremacy' [which] is not the obvious and extreme fascistic posturing of small neo-nazi groups, but rather the taken-for-granted routine privileging of white interests that goes unremarked in the political mainstream. (Gillborn 2005)

Mac an Ghaill and Haywood (2017) and Miah (2015) critique this routine privileging of whiteness in the classroom. Both books warn that 'teachers' embodied whiteness became a space where class difference could be displaced' (Mac an Ghaill and Haywood 2017). They explore how teachers' middle class becomes a code for whiteness, the Bangladeshi and Pakistani students who Mac an Ghaill and Haywood interview referring to how they share more similarity with their white working-class peers than and in relation to their shared difference to their middle-class white teachers (Mac an Ghaill and Haywood 2017, p. 207). Prevent's targeting of the far right can be seen as operating on the same planes of difference that these children had identified, othering the working-class white children as a threat, by comparison to their middle-class teachers.

Aked, Jones and Miller make an important distinction between how different cohorts of the far-right counter-jihad movement are accommodated by the mainstream, noting that 'some are even members of the UK's political elite', whereas neo-Nazis and 'Islamists' are not (Aked, Jones et al. 2019). While it is welcome that the counter-jihad movement, and, by extension, counter-extremism, is not aligned with neo-Nazism, the targeting of the far right by counter-extremism is no less problematic than the targeting of Muslims. Far from demonstrating that Prevent isn't racist as is often suggested by supporters of Prevent, it is entrenching the racialized class distinctions that Mac an Ghaill and Haywood describe (2017, p. 207 & 213). It is also notable that the silencing of supposedly extreme voices as is described in Chapter 1, the impact of which is theorized in later chapters, will be just as pernicious whoever is targeted and silenced.

Predictably, as I am the embodiment of the middle-class white teacher that Mac an Ghaill and Haywood (2017) and Miah (2015) describe, it was only after I had taught for many years that I recognized the importance of the whiteness of the classrooms in which I taught. This process of recognition was helped along in the first lecture of my teacher training at the Institute of Education in London in 2006. In an auditorium where every one of the 900 seats were taken, a trainee teacher at the back stood up and challenged the lecturer on his proposals for how we might address racism in our classrooms after we had qualified as teachers and were teaching our own classes. She explained that as she had progressed through primary school, secondary school and a university degree, she had not been taught by a single person who resembled her as a black woman, and now she was being lectured on challenging racism by another white man. She was understandably frustrated. A recent report from the Institute of Education shows that there has been little progress and that 'a gap persists between the proportion of students and teachers from minority ethnic groups in England' (Tereshchenko, Mills et al. 2020).

Dr Shamim Miah, whose research on CRT is referred to earlier, made a similar point when he spoke at the conference in Birmingham where I met Claire Crawford. With similar frustrations to my fellow student teacher who years earlier had challenged our lecturer, Miah discussed the need for researchers to appreciate the whiteness of their research and to recognize the racism that might be implicit in failing to recognize the racial hegemony of their research. This held a mirror up to me and my research, which up until then had been fixated on the semiotic aspect of the emergence of 'extremism' and 'radicalization' that is described in later chapters. Miah's presentation left me feeling nervous and exposed as I stood up soon afterwards to deliver my research that did not foreground race; I need not have worried.

As is explored in Chapter 1 in the context of counter-jihadism and in later chapters in the context of semiosis, Prevent and 'extremism' are both emergent from and further catalyse the 'taken-for-granted routine privileging of white interests' that Gillborn (2005) describes. Thus, with the recognition of the importance of CRT that Miah had offered me, my research was immediately situated in the context of this field and in a way that contributed to an understanding of race, racism and the privileging of white interests by Prevent. I hope that this book is able to offer other researchers a similar opportunity to see how CRT will not undermine or challenge their existing research. Rather, it offers a new dimension that will help genuine researchers to understand the most pernicious of social structures through their own research, in a way that can make a positive contribution to their research and to society more generally.

Despite, or perhaps because of, the impressive scholarship that forms the foundation of CRT, it recently came under attack on a website and in a jointly signed letter in the *Spectator* on 30 June 2020. The campaign, Don't Divide Us, claims:

> Those who favour the identity-based politics of grievance and academic critical race theory are redefining racism. The achievements of civil rights movements in the past – that effected positive material impacts on the lives of ethnic minorities and increased equal treatment – are now being denied and undermined by those who claim racism is on the rise.

Don't Divide Us has clearly been formed with the intention of challenging growing movements for social justice and anti-racism like Black Lives Matter as the letter goes on to denounce them. However, the failure to recognize that black lives matter because they have historically mattered less than others is a clear example of the 'taken-for-granted routine privileging of white interests' described by CRT. It is also notable that Don't Divide Us is forced to create a strawman to argue against in their denunciation of 'those who claim racism is on the rise', when anti-racism groups tend to be focused on historic and continuing injustice rather than claiming an increase in racism. Despite the cynical proclamations of Don't Divide Us, we are clearly more united if we recognize historical and continuing injustice as CRT helps us to do.

While the 'taken-for-granted routine privileging of white interests' described by CRT may go 'unremarked in the political mainstream', not least by the signatories of Don't Divide Us who go out of their way to denounce the idea of racism and white privilege, it has very real effects on the functioning of politics at a local and national level. Thus, the following section explores how Prevent and 'extremism' might impact local relations between teachers and students, doctors and their patients, and other people tasked with enacting Prevent and counter-extremism. And, how it might affect the functioning of democracy at a national level.

Democracy and debate: Alexander, Arendt, Buber, Derrida, Mouffe, Przeworski and TINA

A group that is labelled as radical and thus excluded from normal public and political processes may, as a result, be more likely actually to become radical in security terms, since exclusion from normal processes encourages a search for alternative processes. (Sedgwick 2010)

Dialogue is fundamental to any encounter between student and teacher, and Professor Robin Alexander has explored this in his work on dialogic teaching (Alexander 2008). He describes the classroom encounter between teacher and student and suggests that all too often it fails to meet the requirement for true dialogue, students more often repeating known answers to their teachers' questions. A dialogic encounter is one where we do not know the outcome for it is in the encounter, what Buber refers to as the 'true life of dialogue'

(Buber 1947), that knowledge is created. The dialogic encounter according to Alexander is therefore the most fundamental aspect of the teacher–student relationship. I met Alexander in 2015 when he was invited to the school where I was teaching to help develop our capacity for dialogic teaching. His promotion of open discussions with our pupils and encouragement of a move away from the endless exam practice that has come to dominate children's time at school was a breath of fresh air to my teaching colleagues and I. However, while his ideas for what a classroom should look and sound like were exactly what my colleagues and I desired, the reality of the exam dominated system and 'knowledge based curriculum'[2] that we impose on our children didn't allow us to move as far from the rehearsed answers as we would have liked.

Alexander's distinction of dialogic encounter from other forms of classroom interaction might go some way to explaining the appearance of a TINA compromise formation in the application of Prevent. TINA compromise formations are named after British prime minister Margaret Thatcher's slogan, 'There is no alternative', and is intended to highlight the fallaciousness of such an argument in instances where there are clearly alternatives. An ensemble that Professor Roy Bhaskar, the founder of the philosophy of critical realism, tells us is frequently encountered in the social world:

> The greater role of philosophy and methodology [in the social world] means that false philosophical beliefs impinge on the realm of practice and so we get all kinds of mish-mash compromises with reality by virtue of which a false or otherwise inadequate theory/practice ensemble is able to stumble on. The TINA formation is accordingly a cardinal concept for the metacritique of irrealism. (Bhaskar 2016)

The importance of what is also referred to as TINA syndrome was highlighted when a civil servant said to me in defence of counter-extremism measures such as Prevent, 'there is no alternative' – an argument since repeated to me countless times by other supporters of counter-extremism. Hartwig suggests that such a fundamental mistake, for there clearly are any number of alternatives, forces us into 'a series of endless theoretical and / or practical compromises' (Hartwig 2007).

As well as having been told by numerous civil servants and supporters of Prevent that 'there is no alternative' to the strategy, the contradiction between theory and practice described by TINA is also revealed by Prevent workers and other supporters of Prevent frequently telling me that the strategy promotes classroom debate. This assertion has been made in every meeting and panel discussion on Prevent that I have been involved in. Meanwhile, others, myself included, report that Prevent has a chilling effect on classroom debate (Faure Walker 2015, Open Society 2016, Rights Watch (UK) 2016, Busher, Choudhury et al. 2017, Faure Walker 2017, Faure Walker 2017).

Turning back to Alexander, it is possible to see that this disagreement might come from a lack of distinction between the two forms of classroom encounter. In my former professional role as a schoolteacher, I have seen lessons planned and delivered to fulfil the requirements of Prevent and these lessons have often prompted discussions. I have witnessed discussions in which children have criticized their peers who have travelled to Syria to join ISIS and have argued for supposedly 'moderate' interpretations of Islam. In these lessons, issues raised are universally agreed with by those engaging in the debate as students express their opposition to ISIS or to travelling to Syria. The anticipation of expected answers that the students will give in these 'debates' does not give the impression of dialogic encounter in which knowledge might be created. Meanwhile, as is discussed in Chapter 1, my own students revealed that they have withdrawn from debate for fear that Prevent would lead to them being reported to the police. The debates that my students described withdrawing from were dialogic, and one of the great privileges of being a teacher is to be part of that process and to also be changed by it, as students and teacher learn together.

By recognizing the differences in the dialogue that Alexander explores – the rehearsed responses of a Prevent lesson and the dialogic encounter that changes us – we can see that, while Prevent may deliver on its intention to promote debate, it could also be suppressing genuine dialogic encounter. By interrupting these encounters, even though it may also be promoting other types of discussion, Prevent undermines the process by which apparently 'extreme' or 'radical' views could be mediated.

A particularly stark example of this comes from a discussion that I had with a student many years before Prevent was imposed on our classroom. One of my pupils expressed a desire to travel to Afghanistan and to take up arms against the coalition forces who were occupying the country. After a short discussion in which he established that I was also opposed to the occupation of Afghanistan and the war on terror more broadly, I helped him to engage in political action by writing to his MP and exploring other forms of non-violent protest. Anyone working with teenagers in a school or with children of their own will know that the expression of potentially 'extreme' views is not extraordinary. It is how teenagers and children navigate their way through an unfamiliar world, and we help them in our responses to them. With a duty that compels teachers to report these kinds of conversations to the school authorities and potentially on to the police, it is inevitable that these conversations stop, as they did in my classrooms when Prevent was introduced. Far from countering-extremism and political violence, Prevent might in fact be disrupting the process by which 'extreme' and potentially dangerous views would otherwise be moderated and actually prevented from developing into violent acts.

Alexander's concern for the importance of dialogue is shared by a number of other theorists who extend the analysis from the classroom and into the political. Mouffe (2005), Derrida (in Borradori 2004) and Przeworski (1991) all describe the importance of dialogue if violence is to be avoided in a democracy. Belgian political theorist, Chantal Mouffe, has written in her book, *On The Political*, that 'it is undeniable that it [violence] tends to flourish in circumstances in which there are no legitimate political channels for the expression of grievances', and she describes the shutting down of discourse in a democracy as 'letting death in' (Mouffe 2005). The late French philosopher, Jacques Derrida, in his conversations on 9/11 and other work, has described the 'autoimmunity' of liberalism – theorizing that the liberal aspiration to consensual politics can result in a violent backlash (Derrida in Borradori 2004). And, Adam Przeworski (1991) similarly suggests in his book, *Democracy and the Market*, that a failure to be represented by the democratic process might leave violence as the only option for those excluded.

The suggestion that Prevent might actually be promoting violence by suppressing dialogue leads to the supposition that the strategy should be resisted. However, since the Counter-Terrorism and Security Act (HM Government 2015) and Prevent Duty Guidance (HM Government 2015) impose a legal duty on all teachers to employ Prevent, it is possible that resistance might undermine their ability to fulfil their legal duty. Where the call to resist Prevent is at odds with the law, Hannah Arendt might be called on for her efforts to describe the 'not altogether happy marriage of morality and legality, conscience and the law of the land' (Arendt 1969). In Arendt's essay on Civil Disobedience (Arendt 1969), she reflects on the civil rights movement in the United States and how it morphed into the movement that opposed the war in Vietnam. In both instances, she suggests that it is unsatisfactory to suggest that the civil disobedience of, for example, the freedom riders or illegal protestors in Washington is purely justified on moral and legal grounds.

Moral and legal arguments are not always adequate to justify our actions as they would lead to the practice of civil disobedience by single individuals, and Arendt argues that such individuals would have little effect. She goes on to argue that 'significant civil disobedience, therefore, will be practiced by a number of people who have a community of interest' (Arendt 1969). The 'decision to take a stand against the Government's policies even if they have reason to assume that the policies are backed by a majority' thus stems from 'an agreement with each other, and it is this agreement that lends credence and conviction to their opinion, no matter how they may have originally arrived at it' (Arendt 1969). Thus, while Arendt describes the need for a community of interest, she also quotes Puner in saying that civil disobedience is 'a philosophy of subjectivity' that is intensely and exclusively personal' (Arendt 1969).

My own personal reasons for opposing Prevent are multiple, having first felt a sense of unease that I was being asked to spy on my students; experience on the local government committee described in Chapter 1 led me to notice that the language of the policy was affecting my perceptions of the strategy; my research then increased my sense of unease as I started to describe the violent discourse of 'radicalization' and 'extremism' (RadEx); and I realized that the duty to police 'extremism' that I was being asked to engage in may in fact be promoting violence. In addition to these concerns about Prevent, there are likely to be countless other sources of unease that I may not even be aware of. While this combination of concerns might be individual to me, I have often found that I am aligned with others who are opposed to Prevent for other reasons. These include my students, anti-austerity campaigners frustrated by increasing counter-terrorism budgets as funding for social services are cut, legal campaigners concerned that Prevent might act contrary to human rights legislation, critical race theorists and anti-racism campaigners and, frequently, Muslim rights campaigners. Following Arendt, each of these groups or individuals who are opposed to Prevent will, like me, have their own deeply personal subjective reasons for this opposition yet, despite this, we form a single 'community of interest'.

Since the Trojan Horse hoax in 2014, I have been lobbying civil servants and politicians who are responsible for Prevent about the potential harm of 'extremism'. I have done this in person, through the Prevent Digest newsletter and website that I run (Faure Walker 2018), through my contributions to the work of human rights and legal advocacy groups working in this area (Open Society 2016, Rights Watch (UK) 2016) and in articles (Faure Walker 2017, Faure Walker 2017, Faure Walker 2018, Faure Walker 2018, Fernandez, Faure Walker et al. 2018, Faure Walker 2019, Faure Walker 2019) and national radio appearances (Fenton-Smith 2017, Tierney 2019). Despite this, the discourse persists, and this might appear to be contrary to Bhaskar's suggestion that transformative praxis is irreducible to agency and spontaneity in social life (Bhaskar 2016).

However, praxis does not necessarily infer that 'extremism' in its violent connotation will disappear; my earlier research and lobbying on Prevent led to the reporting of my concerns in the media and legal circles (Bowcott and Adams 2016, Open Society 2016, Rights Watch (UK) 2016) and ultimately in my students learning of my opposition to the strategy. This resulted in students feeling empowered to speak to me about their concerns that they were being targeted by an overzealous and racist state surveillance policy, concerns that they told me they did not discuss with other adults for fear that Prevent would result in them being reported to the police. My students who had been silenced by Prevent – a situation that might promote violence according to Mouffe, Derrida and Przeworski – were empowered to speak out again. The real generative mechanisms for violence that emanated from 'extremism' had been, to a certain extent, disrupted by my description of them as the students acted as spontaneous agents in their decision to speak to me in a way that 'extremism', counter-extremism and Prevent had previously prevented.

From a critical realist perspective, the power of the Prevent Strategy and 'extremism' is real and leads to actual responses. My re-evaluation and description of the violent discourse of 'radicalization' and 'extremism' generates reasons to and causes for disrupting the real oppressive aspects of counter-extremism discourse. In doing so, I hope that I may make some contribution to the free flourishing of all, as is the overarching concern of critical realism.

Critical realism as critique

[Critical realism] gives us a solid ontological grounding for all those intuitions that most of us feel we should be able to justify, but are constantly being told by the reigning intellectual authorities we can't: that the world, and other people, are real, that freedom is inherent in the nature of the cosmos, that genuine human flourishing can never be at the expense of others. (Graeber in Bhaskar 2016, back cover)

Critical realism shows us that 'the free flourishing of each human being is a condition of the free flourishing of all' (Hartwig in Bhaskar 2016), and, as such, the current usage of 'extremism' not only limits the freedom of those subjected to its gaze, my former students included, but limits the free flourishing of us all. In Part III of this book, the philosophical errors that have led to the emergence of 'extremism' will be explored. Bhaskar proposes that transformative praxis is inevitable (Bhaskar 2016) if we understand these errors that are fundamental to Western philosophy (Bhaskar 2016). Elaborating an understanding of these errors will help to overcome them and will make some contribution to the free flourishing of us all.

My interactions with civil servants who work in counter-terrorism have indicated that critical realism might be an appropriate paradigm through which to explore Prevent. Firstly, in the conversations that I have had with civil servants from the Office for Security and Counter-Terrorism (OSCT) and associated departments, I have been unable to draw them into discussing the silencing of classroom debate that I have observed as being caused by Prevent. This absenting of debate is of particular interest to critical realism, which takes absence as *prima facie* to presence and recognizes that absence is often ignored or overlooked due to its inadequate theorization in Western philosophy (Collier in Hartwig 2007, Bhaskar 2016). This failure to recognize absence is indicative of the errors that Bhaskar describes as endemic to Western philosophy (Bhaskar 2016), and this fits with Collier's suggestion that 'the absenting of the absence of a concept of absence is shown to resolve most of the traditional PROBLEMS of philosophy' (Collier in Hartwig 2007, capitalization in original).

The second reason for critical realism being an appropriate paradigm from which to explore Prevent is that a number of conversations that I have had with civil servants and Prevent workers have taken a turn that signposted the need for critical realist analysis when they have told me that 'there is no alternative' to the type of pre-criminal interventions that have become the norm for counter-terrorism. As explored earlier, to suggest that 'there is no alternative' in this situation where there are alternatives to current counter-terrorism practice shines a light on the TINA (there is no alternative) compromise formation that forms the foundation of Prevent. TINA compromise formations as described by Bhaskar and his fellow critical realists are a primary target of critique (Hartwig 2007, Bhaskar 2016).

Critical realism also offers 'the intellectual heavy artillery for simple common decency and good sense' (Graeber in Bhaskar 2016, back cover), a sense and decency that has sometimes been lacking from the discussions that I have had with civil servants and professionals working in counter-extremism. In one extreme example, Prevent workers who I had previously met in person tried to discredit me on Twitter by saying that I had not met anyone who worked in Prevent, suggesting that this meant that I did not understand how the strategy worked – at the time I had had extensive contact with the accusers, both in one-to-one meetings with them and in meetings with them and other Prevent teams around the country.

Similar anti-intellectual arguments are used by supporters of Prevent who accuse researchers of being 'academic' when their findings challenge the continuation of Prevent, an accusation that has been levelled at my work by civil servants in public meetings (Khaldun 2018). At a time when online interaction is taking the place of print media, both of these *ad hominem* and anti-intellectual arguments against academic research might reasonably be seen as the rhetorical equivalent of book burning and share an alarming provenance. That they are being used to avoid engaging in critique of the oppressive forces of the far right from which counter-extremism has emerged should serve as a warning from history.

Ideology, power and discourse

Ideology is of prime importance to understanding the emergence of 'extremism'. Any theory of ideology demands that one is critical of fixed dictionary definitions so it is accepted here, in accordance with Fairclough whose approach to discourse analysis is described in the next chapter, that ideology is a contested concept (Fairclough 2015). Both Fairclough and Hartwig agree that definitions of ideology fall broadly into two categories. Firstly, following Marxist tradition, a negative conception of ideology aligns it with notions of false consciousness that are abstracted from material circumstances or real processes of geo-history. Secondly, a more 'positive view' of ideology sees it as political standpoints that are consciously derived from social theory, for example socialism, feminism, liberalism and so on. The brief introduction to these two categories of ideology that follows will go some way to explaining that the legitimacy of either form of ideology does not relate to awareness of the ideology but to the ideologues openness to change their understanding based on the evidence that they are presented with. (Hartwig 2007, Fairclough 2015)

While it would be tempting, from a classical Marxist position, to explain away the second, 'positive' view as false consciousness, this would be inadequate from the perspective of critical realism. Firstly, the impact of either form of ideology on our experience is real; by way of example, when fascists and anti-fascists clashed in Charlottesville, Virginia, the United States, on 12 August 2017, it resulted in damage to property and at least one person, Heather Heyer, being killed (Gunter 2017). This example demonstrates that the second view of ideology, consciously derived political standpoints, describes forces that have real impacts in the world and that, thus, cannot be abstracted and ignored. It is notable that since then, and as is discussed earlier, the US administration of

President Trump tried to designate one side in this conflict, the anti-fascists, as a terrorist organization (United Nations 2020).

The second reason not to explain away the 'positive' view of ideology as false consciousness is because, by self-consciously choosing a critical realist stance, I am adopting a stance that is ideological in this 'positive' conception. Hartwig explains that, from this critical realist perspective, 'ideology is correlative to science' (Hartwig 2007). And, following Bhaskar's idealized scientific method explored in his first book, *A Realist Theory of Science* (Bhaskar 1975), and throughout his career, the possibility of false ideological constructs within the critical realist theory that is adopted is ever present. This is of particular importance if we are following a scientific method as it demands that we constantly test our assertions to try and reveal these constructs. Should such constructs appear, they will be revealed as contradictions in theory or between theory and practice (a TINA compromise formation). Thus, throughout any genuine research process, should any aspect of the research reveal such a contradiction in the theory adopted and developed, retheorization will be necessary.

The openness to theoretical revision described earlier and adopted here means that the critical realist stance is, while ideological, not dogmatic. According to the *Oxford English Dictionary*, to be 'dogmatic' is to be 'inclined to lay down principles as undeniably true'. While 'TINA compromise formation' is a term that is familiar to a critical realist audience, 'dogma' might better communicate this concept to non-critical realists. The aforementioned civil servants who have told me that 'there is no alternative' to the type of pre-criminal interventions that are currently seen in counter-terrorism strategy were expressing a dogmatic position, a position maintained by their denigration of and refusal to engage in 'academic' arguments.

To develop the theory of ideology that is employed here further, it will help to explore power, and, from a critical realist perspective, power can take two forms, P_1 and P_2. P_1 is creative, emancipating power, while P_2 is its shadow side of negative coercive power (Alderson 2015). This distinction is vital to exploring and defining ideology which Hartwig describes as follows:

Produced and reproduced at the intersection of the POWER$_2$ with the discursive / communicative (cognitive) and normative / moral sub-dimensions of the SOCIAL CUBE (the *ideological intersect*), ideology functions in general to secure social cohesion and moral legitimacy in the context of generalised MASTER-SLAVE-type relations, in which class is seen to play a pivotal role. Fundamentally generated by oppressive and exploitative social structures, and reproductive of them, it is in no way intrinsic to power$_1$, or universal or necessary. (Hartwig 2007, italics and capitalization in original)

Bhaskar theorizes that our everyday carelessness results in us tending to live our lives in a 'demi-reality' of master–slave relations (Bhaskar 2016). Hartwig describing this as a complex web of 'ideological ignorance (*avidya*) and illusion (*maya*)' (Hartwig 2007). Unless we make a conscious effort to move beyond demi-reality, we live in a world of *avidya* and *maya* constructed and maintained by oppressive P$_2$ master–slave relations, ideology being the communicative aspect of these relations.

Norman Fairclough is one of the foremost thinkers in CDA, and, though he does not use the terms *avidya* and *maya*, he describes how the ignorance and illusion of ideology can be revealed in texts by identifying 'common sense', and he describes this common sense (which he frequently writes is synonymous with ideology) as being 'in the service of sustaining relations of power', going on to say:

Texts do not typically spout ideology. They so position the interpreter through their cues that she brings ideologies to the interpretation of texts – and reproduces them in the process! (Fairclough 2015)

While critique of ideology is of fundamental importance to this book, it is not carried out directly by either the critical discourse analysis (CDA) or by corpus linguistics that is described in Chapters 4 and 5. Fairclough explains that 'ideology critique is a form of explanatory critique, which is not part of either approach [to discourse analysis]' (Fairclough 2015), and appreciating this distinction is helped by considering the classic critical realist split between

- the *empirical* data from CDA or corpus linguistics,
- the *actual* text, and

- the *real* generative mechanisms that underpin social
  processes (discourse being the communicative aspect of this)
                    (Bhaskar 2016, O'Regan and Gray 2018).

The critical discourse analysis (CDA) and corpus linguistics analysis that are described in later chapters gather *empirical* data through normative critique to describe *actual* aspects of the texts that are analysed. The relations between these aspects of the text and the social must be theorized through explanatory critique to bring us closer to an understanding of the *real* mechanisms, in part ideological, that perpetuate counter-extremism discourses and strategies. The *real* generative mechanisms that emanate from counter-terrorism discourses that focus on 'extremism' and 'radicalization' will also be theorized from the *empirical* data and make up the final chapters of the book.

Due to the contested nature of 'ideology' as explored earlier and the focus of this book on language, I will tend to refer henceforth to 'discourse' in preference to 'ideology'. 'Discourse', like 'ideology', will take one of two meanings: firstly, as language in a general sense to refer to text, spoken word, visual images, body language and so on. 'Discourse' in this sense is dialogically related to other aspects of social life such as events and meaning making; secondly, 'discourse' might refer to particular 'discourses' such as the 'Third Way' of 'New Labour' which has been the focus of much of Fairclough's work (Fairclough 2000, Fairclough 2003). The violent discourse of 'radicalization' and 'extremism' that is the focus of this book is a 'discourse' in this second sense.

The theorization of relations between discourse, society, the interpreter and the text is supported by Bhaskar's Transformational Model of Social Activity (TMSA) (see Figure 2.1; Bhaskar 2016). While Fairclough's recent developments in CDA have seen him following a Bhaskarean ontology, he appears to rely on academic Lord Anthony Giddens's structuration model when describing change (Fairclough 2013). Like Gidden's model, throughout his extensive writing on CDA, Fairclough never offers an account of explanatory critique that includes a time dimension. This is not surprising as Bhaskar himself did not distinguish between his and Gidden's work, initially not recognizing that he had included a time dimension in his own work while time was absent from that of Gidden's. Bhaskar refers to a meeting that he had with Giddens – 'in a very nice restaurant in Greek Street' (Bhaskar 2016) – where they agreed on the similarity of their theories, yet it took his colleague

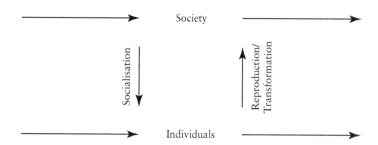

FIGURE 2.1 *Bhaskar's Transformational Model of Social Activity (TMSA) (Bhaskar 2016, Bhaskar 2016).*

Margaret Archer to point out to him that the inclusion of time in Bhaskar's TMSA model was a crucial difference between his TMSA and Giddens's Structuration Theory. The inclusion and distinction of time may appear obvious after the event but Bhaskar tells us that it took Archer 'years' to describe this difference (Bhaskar 2016).

In describing the relationship between society and individuals over time – a relationship that is at least in part discursive – the TMSA helps us to appreciate the relationship between changes to and the reproduction of discourses of counter-terrorism and changes to and reproduction of social structures, both discourses and social structures seen as dependent on each other. The discourses that are embodied in the text that will be later analysed are the communicative aspect of the vertical 'socialization' and 'reproduction/transformation' arrows in Figure 2.1. Thus, this book contributes to our understanding of how society has been transformed and reproduced to engage in countering 'extremism' and how individuals have been socialized to take part. Neoliberalism is one of the – if not the – dominant global discourses and is introduced in the following paragraphs as it will be later shown to have significantly contributed to the emergence of 'extremism'.

Neoliberalism

Governments of different political complexions take it as a mere fact of life (a 'fact' produced by inter-Governmental agreements) that all must bow to the logic of the global economy. (Fairclough 2000)

Neoliberalism is described by Fairclough as a 'new order' or 'a restructured ('global') form of capitalism' (Fairclough 2000). He cites Bourdieu to describe 'a political project for the reconstruction of society in accord with the demands of an unrestrained global capitalism' (Fairclough 2000). This is marked by states and individuals entering into 'intense competition to succeed on terms dictated by the market', resulting inevitably in 'winners' and 'losers' (Fairclough 2000).

The idea that there ought to be winners and losers is sustained by the idea that humans are inherently selfish. This idea has been promoted for centuries, not least by prominent enlightenment philosophers such as Thomas Hobbes (1588–1679) and David Hume (1711–76), and in recent years there has been a slew of books and articles to support this. Yuval Noah Harari (2014), Richard Dawkins (1989), Jared Diamond (2018) and Stephen Pinker (2012) take a historical perspective to argue for our innate selfishness, and, perhaps most infamously by reference to the habits of lobsters, Jordan Peterson (2018) argues that embracing the notion of strong winners and weak losers will lead us out of the chaos that he argues we now live in.

However, as Marcus Paul writes of Harari's selective history of humankind's supposedly brutal emergence:

> The sword is not the only way in which events and epochs have been made. Indeed, to make biology/biochemistry the final irreducible way of perceiving human behaviour, as Harari seems to do, seems tragically short-sighted. (Paul 2018)

Similarly, historian and journalist Rutger Bregman (2020) has recently written a compelling account of how these purveyors of selfishness have been misguided. Using example after example, Bergman demonstrates that we are preconditioned to be kind rather than selfish towards one another. He also follows Marcus Paul in showing how some of the aforementioned authors have based their theories of our selfishness on a flawed interpretation of the data that they cite. Bregman argues that the impact of these books goes beyond just misrepresenting the world and humanity but, in promoting the idea that we are selfish, have encouraged actual selfishness. Even though this is not the world that we have to choose to live in. This selfishness has become a self-fulfilling prophesy or what Bergman describes as a nocebo, the opposite to a placebo. It is notable that the author of *Sapiens*, one of the most lauded books on humanities' selfishness, Yuval Harari writes in a cover note for Bergman's aptly named book that '*Humankind* challenged me and made me see humanity from a fresh perspective' (Harari in Bergman 2020, front cover).

The stories that we tell about ourselves through our discourses and language, such as those critiqued by Bregman and that are told to us by 'extremism', matter and are creative of the world that we live in. Much like our selfishness being emergent from the stories that we tell ourselves and each other, 'extremism' will be shown in later chapters to be emergent from the understanding of the world that is embedded in our meaning and usage of the words 'extremism' and 'radicalization'.

In the world of winners and losers that is created by Harari et al., neoliberal discourse itself is one of the resources deployed by the winners. Mirowski has explored how, even in the face of the global failure of neoliberalism that resulted in the 2008 financial crisis, the neoliberal belief in the primacy of the market led to the protecting of the global elites who had caused the crisis while the losing majority were punished by programmes of austerity (Mirowski 2013). In the same way that the perceived primacy of the market protected elites from their own failure in 2008, it will be shown in Chapters 5 and 6 that 'extremism' was deployed to protect colonial elites from calls for independence and self-rule on the fringes of the crumbling British Empire in the mid-twentieth century.

As well as the inherent selfishness of neoliberalism, Fairclough (2000) and Mirowski (2013) have also explored the new penal logic of neoliberalism, a logic that is intimately explored by Dan Hancox (2018) in his study of the oppression of young black men in *The Story of Grime*. The oppression that Hancox describes started under the leadership of Tony Blair and New Labour (Hancox 2018) and continued 'wounding London's poorest' under the subsequent Coalition and Conservative governments (Hancox 2018). Hancox's description of the oppression of Britain's black community will be shown in later chapters to bear remarkable similarity to the more recent oppression of Muslims under Prevent. This is, perhaps, not surprising as the lineage of both the recent oppression of young black men and the more recent oppression of Muslims is shown in later chapters to have, at least in part, emerged from the neoliberalism promoted by New Labour.

New Labour should not only be seen as an adopter of neoliberalism but also as one of its foremost global promoters:

> New labour has been instrumental in setting up a series of international 'seminars' on the 'Third Way', attended not only by Blair and Clinton but also by leaders from other countries, including Brazil, Sweden, Italy, and more recently Germany. However, in so far as such a new political discourse is emerging, it seems to me to be a centre-left strain within neo-liberalism rather than an alternative or even serious corrective to it. (Fairclough 2000)

The global proliferation of neoliberal discourse inevitably results in changing networks of practices, and these inevitably include changes to the way we interact with one another. The emergence of 'extremism' has played a significant role in this as teachers' and healthcare workers' have adopted new roles as state informants on their students and patients, indicating that the neoliberal state has come to regard all citizens, and particularly Muslims, as potential terrorists.

Fairclough calls for 'co-ordinated action against neoliberalism on the part of critical language researchers' (Fairclough 2000) and sees critical discourse analysis (CDA) as a resource in this struggle:

> CDA can constitute a resource for struggle in so far as it does not isolate language but addresses the shifting network of practices in a way which produces both clearer understanding of how language figures in hegemonic struggles around neo-liberalism, and how struggles against neo-liberalism can be partly pursued in language. It asks: what are the problems facing people, what are they doing in response, how can these resistances be strengthened and coordinated into a plausible alternative, and how specifically does language figure in all this (recognizing the irreducible language factor without exaggerating it)? (Fairclough 2000)

This book aims to make some contribution to this struggle by helping to understand why innocent citizens, including children, have come to be regarded as potential terrorists.

PART 2

The Empirical

CHAPTER 3

The language of counter-extremism

Korzybski's dog biscuits

There is a story that linguists like to tell each other about the founder of general semantics, Alfred Korzybski. One morning Korzybski was delivering a lecture when he pulled a bag containing a packet of biscuits out of his briefcase. Apologizing to his class and explaining that he had missed breakfast that morning, he takes one for himself before offering them to the students in the front row. Waiting until everyone is enjoying their biscuit, he comments on how much he is enjoying his biscuit too, and the students agree that they are indeed nice biscuits. He then removes the packet of biscuits from the white paper bag he is holding, revealing that everyone is in fact eating dog biscuits. Depending on the enthusiasm of the person telling the story, the students now either gag or run out of the lecture theatre to be sick. Korzybski goes on to explain that he has just demonstrated to them that we not only taste our food, but also our words. With his packet of dog biscuits, he had shown that the words can be more important than the food. Or, to bring us back to something that we know Korzybski did say:

> A map is not the territory it represents, but, if correct, it has a similar structure to the territory, which accounts for its usefulness. (Korzybski 1933)

The story or Korzybski's dog biscuits may or may not be true, but it serves to illustrate the importance that language can play in our interactions with and experience of the world. This book stems from my realization that the words 'radicalization' and 'extremism' dramatically alter the way that we experience the world and interact with each other – in turn, altering the structure of society as a whole. The understanding of language that Korzybski offers us indicates that this not only affects the way in which we experience one another, but also affects the functioning of our politics. In this chapter, I will begin to show how the analysis of our use of 'extremism' and 'radicalization' in language can help us to better understand the world.

Korzybski's work on semantics – along with a handful of other great thinkers from the middle of the last century such as Buber, Althusser, Foucault and Wittgenstein – has set the tone for much twentieth-century philosophy. This shift towards the analysis of discourse enables us to question how we construct the world with the language that we use and has laid the foundations for the critical discourse analysis (CDA) that is now used to explore and understand the emergence of 'extremism'.

Critical discourse analysis (CDA)

Fairclough suggests that in carrying out CDA we might also reveal taken-for-granted background knowledge and, in doing so, reveal aspects of the ideology behind the text (Fairclough 2010). The analysis carried out here reveals taken-for-granted knowledge, and theorization of these findings reveals how this 'knowledge' impacts on the semiotic order. A concrete example of such a change in the semiotic order is in the aforementioned recasting of my own professional identity as a teacher to include a duty to surveil my pupils. The analysis of texts that follows goes some way to describe the semiotic changes that led to this change in genre. According to Fairclough, genres are 'the specifically discoursal aspect of ways of acting and interacting in the course of social events' (Fairclough 2003). In the aforementioned example, the role of teacher came to incorporate the new genre to inform – referred to in later chapters as the informant genre.

Alongside my observation of changes made to the usage of 'extremism' and 'radicalization' in the Prevent strategies that is described in the following text, my general reading of media, academic and policy texts around counter-terrorism has indicated that the use of 'radicalization' and 'extremism' to explain acts of political violence has become more prevalent since 9/11. 'Radicalization' and 'extremism' rarely appear in contemporary explanations for the 9/11 attacks on the World Trade Centre and a notable example of this absence is Giovanna Borradori's book, *Philosophy in a Time of Terror* (Borradori 2004). In her book, Borradori interviews Jurgen Habermas and Jacques Derrida about the attacks while they are in New York in the three weeks following the tragedy. The conversations inevitably veer into a broader discussion of terrorism, yet neither Borradori nor Habermas or Derrida use the words 'radicalization' or 'extremism'.

In the years after 9/11, 'radicalization' and 'extremism' start to appear in commentary on terrorism, but as political concepts that have no necessary association with violence. An example of this is the Prevent Strategy from 2008, which creates such a distinction by only using the terms 'radicalization' and 'extremism' alongside references to violence, associating them but drawing a distinction, for if they were synonymous with violence, they would not be used together. However, since then, the Prevent Strategy has been rewritten, and in the glossary of the strategy currently in use, written in 2011, 'radicalization' and 'extremism' are defined by their association with violence. These words that previously described relative political stances have become synonymous with violence. The analysis the second half of this chapter will be used to test and, ultimately, support the following observations:

- That 'radicalization' and 'extremism' are now more readily adopted as explanations for political violence than they were before 7 July 2005.

- That 'radicalization' and 'extremism', when first adopted in political discourse, tended to be collocated with violence or a synonym for violence.

- That the collocation of 'radicalization' and 'extremism' with violence has since become less prevalent.

CDA is used to analyse groups of texts, or corpora, and Mautner suggests that there are two main types of corpus, reference corpora and do-it-yourself corpora (Mautner 2016). The corpus analysis that follows will be carried out on three do-it-yourself corpora and one reference corpus, and these will consist of

- Policy Corpus (2008–17): UK counter-terrorism policy texts;[1]
- Parliamentary Corpus (2006–17): Texts from the UK Parliament that refer to 'radicalization' or 'extremism';
- The News Corpus (2000–17): News articles relating to acts of political violence from 9/11 to the present;
- The Hansard Corpus (1800–2005): An online reference corpus of UK parliamentary debates (Marc Alexander, Jean Anderson et al. 2017).

Both CDA and corpus linguistics are important to the research carried out here as the latter provides an invaluable tool for the communication of the research to policymakers. Corpus linguistics is, however, unable to provide a full account of all of the aspects of the discourse identified through CDA. As corpus linguistics can quantitively describe changes to the usage of 'extremism' that are identified with CDA, changes to the discourse over time can be presented as graphs, and these provide a useful tool for the easy communication of the findings. This ease of communication has been shown in interactions that I have had with civil servants who work in the Counter-Extremism Unit at the Home Office. They have been more willing to engage in discussion of the graphs produced by the corpus linguistics than they had previously been willing to engage in discussion of the more detailed descriptions of texts that CDA offers. Thus, corpus linguistics offers a tool by which policymakers might be encouraged to critically engage with the language that they adopt. As the CDA that I have carried out has previously been dismissed as 'reading too much into the language' by the same civil servants who showed an interest in the graphs, the data created by the corpus study appears to offer a more compelling argument for policy change.

Bringing time into CDA

CDA combines **critique** of discourse and **explanation** of how it figures within and contributes to the existing social reality, as a basis for **action** to change that existing social reality in particular aspects. (Fairclough 2015, emphasis in original)

The various versions of CDA, including Fairclough's, do not offer an account of how changes in language occur over time. That is not to say that Fairclough and others do not describe change; they do. However, the changes described are situated around a specific moment, the marketization of universities or the appearance of New Labour (Fairclough 2010), rather than theorized as part of a progressive change. Reading through much of Fairclough's work, theorization of how changes to language occur over time is absent (Fairclough, Jessop et al. 2007, Fairclough 2010, Fairclough and Fairclough 2013, Fairclough 2013, Fairclough 2015). As is discussed in Chapter 2, Fairclough's reliance on Giddens' Structuration Theory, a theory that does not employ a temporal dimension, limits his critique. By not employing a temporal dimension, Fairclough only offers an account of how the ideology or discourse that he is critiquing *is* or *was* but does not also offer an account of how it *became*.

In later chapters, I address this absence by theorizing how changes to the semiotic order occur over time, the semiotic order being a primary concern throughout Fairclough's work. The Transformational Model of Social Activity (TMSA), which was first discussed in Chapter 2, will help bring a temporal dimension into the explanation phase of the analysis. And, to enable this, data must be collected across different time scales during the critique phase of the research.

While other versions of CDA, most notably Reisigl and Wodak's (2016) Discourse Historical Approach, have explored discourse in its historical context, the development of Fairclough's DRA approach enables the development of a more explicit ontology related to the discourse. Following Fairclough, the initial phase of the analysis carried out here is to recognize that there has been a change in the way that we interact with each other. This is the 'critique' phase and is seen in all of Fairclough's work, and is demonstrated particularly well in his analysis of the marketization of universities and in the emergence of New Labour and the Third Way[2] (Fairclough 2010). However, while Fairclough often critiques texts from different times to highlight different features of the discourses, he does not evaluate how the changes occur over time. To enable this, the dates when texts being analysed were written and published are used in the theorization carried out in the following chapters, and this understanding of discursive change over time proves to be vital to understanding the emergence of 'extremism'.

Choosing texts and developing an approach to CDA

it is not simply a matter of taking a method and applying it to an object of research. The object first has to be theorized. (O'Regan and Betzel 2016)

As a result of my growing concerns about Prevent, I reviewed the strategy to and was struck by the first sentence, 'The Prevent programme we inherited from the last Government was flawed' (HM Government 2011). This indicated that there were likely to be differences between this version of Prevent and the earlier version that it referred to (HM Government 2008, HM Government 2011). Following Fairclough, it is reasonable to suppose that these differences might reveal something of the ideology behind each strategy, the differences shining a light on aspects of common-sense views that might otherwise go unnoticed (Fairclough 2010). This possibility of revealing common-sense knowledge in the texts and, in doing so, revealing something of the ideology behind them led me to critical discourse analysis (CDA) as a possible methodology. CDA is thus a way to systematically analyse texts, with the aim of learning what had caused my students to be targeted by counter-terrorism strategy.

Bringing together recent developments in CDA, most notably Fairclough (2010), O'Regan and Betzel (2016) and Bhaskar (2016), leads to the following approach being adopted.[3] In the preceding chapters (1 and 2), the phenomenon initially observed as the silencing of my students has been theorized and connected to changes in the usage of 'extremism' and 'radicalization' in the Prevent Strategy. These changes are described more clearly in the remainder of this chapter (3) through analysis of the two versions of Prevent and then by analysis of various corpora that show the increasing prevalence of 'extremism' in discourse over the last century. In the following two chapters (4 and 5), 'extremism' and then 'radicalization' are explored by close reading of their occurrence in the parliamentary record, and this enables a detailed understanding of the connection between their usage and the functioning of Parliament and democracy more generally. Following on from this, in Chapter 6, a series of important questions are explored to understand what has caused the emergence of 'extremism' and what barriers there might be to resolving the problem of 'extremism'. These include the following: Whether society needs 'extremism'? Why, if at all, is 'extremism' needed? How is 'extremism' produced and reproduced? Who benefits from 'extremism'? Chapter 7 then explores how the emergence of 'extremism' can be contested and reveals that the emergence of 'extremism' shows us much about the functioning of our politics and how the blight of policy-led evidence has rendered policymakers blind to their actual impacts on society. Finally, in Chapter 8, I reflect on how the emergence of 'extremism' has affected me, and this reveals a concatenated system of global crises that might, however, be overcome by appealing to metaReality. Having established that 'extremism' and associated crises can be overcome, the book ends with an imminent critique of the latest attempts to impose and justify counter-extremism so that we know what must be challenged if 'extremism' is to be transcended.

The emergence of 'Extremism'

Identifying changes to 'extremism'

While trying to understand why I had been compelled by counter-extremism policy to spy on my students, I noticed that there had been a change in the usage of 'extremism'. This change is the phenomenon that is tested in the corpus analysis later in this chapter but is first defined by close reading of different versions of Prevent. New Labour's earlier version of the Prevent Strategy focused on 'violent extremism' (HM Government 2008), while the more recent version from David Cameron's coalition government focused only on 'extremism' (HM Government 2011). The textual analysis below demonstrates that this shift represents the progressive loss of 'violence' from government discourse on 'extremism' between

2007 and 2017. This shows that the British state has become less interested in policing 'extremism' as a supposed precursor to violence and has become more interested in policing 'extremism' itself. This anti-democratic focus on political opinion can be seen in the continued growth of the counter-extremism industry that is demonstrated by the formation of the Building a Stronger Britain Together (BSBT) programme in 2016 and the Commission for Countering Extremism in 2018; both are in addition to Prevent and are explored in the final chapters.

Towards the end of this chapter, the data described shows that sustained focus on any type of 'extremism' is itself a phenomenon that developed after the London bombings of 2005. It is notable that analysis of contemporary news articles about the six bombs that the IRA detonated in London and Birmingham and about a rocket-propelled grenade that they fired at the MI6 building in a campaign from 1 June 2000 to 4 November 2001 does not reveal any use of the words 'extremism' or 'radicalization'. It is also of note that contemporaneous explanations for 9/11 tend not to use 'extremism' or 'radicalization' to explain the attacks on the Twin Towers.

The more recent Prevent Strategy that was written by the UK Coalition Government in 2011 starts its second paragraph by stating 'The Prevent programme we inherited from the last Government was flawed' (HM Government 2011). It was this tension between the different versions of Prevent that indicated that CDA might be an appropriate mode of analysis, the tension offering the possibility of identifying differences between the two and of revealing something of each. Thus, the following analysis of both strategies, from 2008 and from 2011, identifies differences in taken-for-granted knowledge in each. Sections of the text of each strategy are reproduced below along with discussion of the findings and reveal a change in the meaning and usage of both 'radicalization' and of 'extremism'. As discussed in the previous chapter, this change in the discourse can reveal something of the ideologies represented in each strategy.

There is a certain level of irony to exploring the ideological assumptions that underpin Prevent and counter-extremism, as supporters of the strategy such as Will Baldét often argue that Prevent focuses on the ideological causes of violence (Baldét 2017, Baldét 2017, Baldét 2019, Baldét 2020, Baldét 2020). The absence of any serious theorization of this argument seems to presume that those making it are speaking from a position of ideological neutrality. As is explored in Chapter 2, it is not possible for such arguments, or discourse more generally, to exist beyond or outside of ideology. Thus, those making these claims to their own neutrality are either naïve or cynical in presuming their own neutrality. Baldét is a Prevent Coordinator, Fellow of Centre for Analysis of Radical Right and member of the European Union (EU)-funded Radicalisation Awareness Network (RAN), as well as being one of Prevent's most vocal supporters. In response to comments by academic and campaigner Asim Qureshi, Baldét has described himself on Twitter as the 'The Grand Mufti of Counter Terrorism'. Baldét's abrasive approach to critics of counter-extremism has been noted by many, and he recently came under fire for doxing (publishing private information online) a critic of Prevent on Twitter (Hooper 2020).

Baldét inadvertently presages the critique that is made in this book when he writes that Prevent is a 'common sense . . . approach' (Baldét 2020). As is explored in Chapters 2 and 3, 'common sense' understandings of the world have been described by Fairclough as synonymous with ideology and can be revealed by the analysis of texts as is carried out in the following paragraphs (Fairclough 2015). Thus, while Baldét describes it as 'common sense' that counter-extremism and Prevent should focus on the ideological causes of violence, in doing so he is revealing his own position as one of Prevent's most vocal ideologues. The why in which this 'common sense' has come to be expressed in the discourse of 'extremism' and 'radicalization' is now explored by close reading of the two versions of Prevent.

'Extremism' and 'extremist'

'Extremism' and 'extremist' undergo a change in meaning between the two versions of Prevent. In the main text of the earlier strategy, 'extremism/ist' is always collocated with 'violent', written as 'violent extremism/ist', and this indicates that the strategy is targeted at reducing violence rather than at all those perceived to be 'extreme'. The collocation of 'extremism/ist' and 'violent' associates the two terms but draws a distinction, that it is necessary to use them together indicates that they do not share the same meaning.

The latter strategy that was implemented by David Cameron's coalition government, however, offers a specific definition for extremism[4]:

> Extremism is vocal or active opposition to fundamental British values, including democracy, the rule of law, individual liberty and mutual respect and tolerance of different faiths and beliefs. We also include in our definition of extremism calls for death of members of our armed forces, whether in this country or overseas. (HM Government 2011)

The earlier strategy is opposed to and targets violence, yet the more recent strategy targets 'extremism' itself, the aforementioned broad definition of 'extremism' extending to anyone opposing an undefined 'British' value system. These values 'include', but by implication are not exhausted by, 'democracy, the rule of law, individual liberty and mutual respect and tolerance of different faiths and beliefs'. Extremists in this conception are those who do not follow British values; by failing to provide a precise definition of these values, the 'extremist' is defined as the other, that is, as not British, or sufficiently subscribing to Britishness. The labelling of the 'extremist', therefore, offers an opportunity for those compelled by Prevent to report 'extremists' to become or to be more British. The Prevent Strategy is an invitation for public sector workers and others compelled to follow Prevent to prove their Britishness.

'Radicalization'

The changed meaning of 'radicalization' can be seen in the glossary sections of each version of Prevent.

Understanding Radicalisation

We have a growing body of knowledge about the radicalisation process from academic and Government research and from case histories of those who have attempted or perpetrated terrorist attacks. From this data it is clear that there is no single profile of a violent extremist or a single radicalisation pathway. There are, however, factors and vulnerabilities which repeatedly appear in different cases and which can leave a person more susceptible to exploitation by violent extremists.

These factors are set out below. The list is neither exhaustive nor detailed. It is important to emphasise that the presence of these factors presumes neither radicalisation nor engagement in violent activity.

Radicalisers – Radicalisation is often a social process, involving interaction with others. Radicalisers may be propagandists, ideologues or terrorists and may be in face-to-face contact with the subject or in dialogue over the internet.

(HM Government 2008, emphasis in original)

As with 'extremism', throughout the earlier New Labour Prevent Strategy the term 'radicalization' is collocated with references to violence and terrorism, and an example of this can be seen towards the end of the strategy in the section titled 'Understanding Radicalisation' in the aforementioned quote. This shows links being drawn between 'radicalization' and violence as the term 'radicalization' is only used alongside references to violence, for example in phrases such as 'there is no single profile of a <u>violent</u> extremist or a single radicalization pathway' (emphasis added) and 'the presence of these factors presumes neither radicalization nor engagement in <u>violent</u> activity' (emphasis added). While this links 'radicalization' and violence, it also provides a distinction between the two as, were it taken for granted that 'radicalization' meant violence, it would not be required that both phrases be used together. This is further supported towards the end of the quote where it is proposed that 'Radicalisers <u>may</u> be propagandists, ideologues <u>or</u> terrorists' (emphasis added). By including the modal verb, 'may', the text of the earlier strategy suggests that it is possible to go through a process of 'radicalization' without supporting violence or terrorism. That this process might be led by 'ideologues' and 'propagandists', who the text indicates may be other than 'terrorists', suggests that, from the perspective of the earlier strategy, it is possible for 'radicalization' to be a non-violent political process.

The more recent version of Prevent provides a specific definition for 'radicalization':

Radicalisation refers to the process by which a person comes to support terrorism and forms of extremism leading to terrorism.

(HM Government 2011, emphasis in original)

If this latter usage is accepted, 'radicalization' has become explicitly linked to terrorism and acceptance of the glossary definition leads the reader to take it for granted that 'radicalization' will lead to terrorism or the support of terrorism. Thus, the meaning of 'radicalization' has changed to become associated with violence in the second strategy.

Defining the violent discourse of 'radicalization' and 'extremism' (RadEx)

These changed meanings of 'radicalization' and 'extremism', to become more associated with violence and the support for violence, are indicative of what I have come to define as the violent discourse of 'extremism' and 'radicalization', also referred to as 'RadEx'. The wider acceptance of RadEx was demonstrated by senior judge, Mr Justice Hayden, who would later gain infamy for comments about a 'man's right to sex with his wife' (Ames 2019).

In his judgement for the British High Court in the case of London Borough of Tower Hamlets V B, Hayden stated that the definitions of 'radicalization' and of 'extremism' in the most recent Prevent Strategy (2011) 'are so much a part of contemporary life they scarcely need definition' (2016). Despite Hayden's judgement, the British government has been unable to define 'extremism' in a way that will not leave their policing of extremism open to challenge in court; this has been investigated in the press (Hooper 2017) and has been confirmed to me in conversations with civil servants working in the Counter-Extremism Unit of the Home Office.

The research described here indicates that the failure to define 'extremism' in a meaningful way may not only stem from the existential impossibility of defining 'extremism' in a way that is consistent with a functioning democracy, as was explored in Chapter 2, but is also made impossible by the definition apparently changing between different government documents. While these differences between two documents from 2008 and 2011 were described earlier, in the rest of this chapter corpus analysis is used to test whether these changes are part of a wider trend, and this reveals something of the discursive context from which 'radicalization' and 'extremism' have emerged.

Testing the changes to 'extremism' that are seen in Prevent

The Policy Corpus (2008–17)

The Policy Corpus is made up of 974,851 words and 25 documents from various government departments and parliamentary committees. The corpus was collated by searching government archives for 'extremism' and 'radicalization'. The earliest document analysed in the corpus is the New Labour Prevent Strategy from May 2008, the same document that was analysed earlier. The most recent document analysed is from 22nd June 2017 and is a published statement from the Home Secretary, Amber Rudd MP, on the series of terrorist attacks in the United Kingdom in the first half of 2017. As a result of a meeting with a civil servant at the Home Office in October 2017, more recent documents are not included.

The meeting took place after I emailed the address given as a contact on the Home Office's Counter-Terrorism Media Summary. The Home Office's Counter-Terrorism Media Summary appears to be sent to government departments every day to promote awareness of political violence. The editions that I have seen foreground the most shocking acts of violence, no matter where in the world that they have recently been reported, so it seems reasonable to suppose that the intention of the summary is to promote the threat of terrorism to government departments and civil servants. In my email, I asked to be added to the subscribers of this daily news digest but was informed that the summary was only for government departments. However, I was invited to the Home Office for a meeting with someone from the Research Information and Communications Unit (RICU). They showed some interest in my research and explained that their department, RICU, habitually vetted ministerial statements and government documents such as those that make up the Policy Corpus. Showing considerable interest in the trend that is shown in the following graph, they asked for a copy, and I duly provided one.

In his book *Blank Spots on the Map*, Trevor Paglen (2009) explores the geography of the war on terror and famously helped to uncover the global rendition and torture programme that was carried out by the United States and their allies. In this context, Paglan describes 'the observer effect':

> The observer effect in human sciences is quite straightforward: People act differently when they're being observed. The observer effect questions the easy distinction between observer and observed: To observe something is to become part of the thing one is observing. (Paglen 2009)

The person I was sitting opposite to at the Home Office and who had asked for my data had also told me that their unit at the Home Office was involved in writing the same type of documents that I was observing, and they told me that they had an interest in the usage of 'extremism' that I was describing. Thus, it is reasonable to propose that my observation of these documents was likely to impact the production of subsequent documents, particularly as I provided them with details of my findings. I have therefore not added any further documents to the corpus as the pattern described by documents produced after this date would likely say as much about the observer effect as about the emergence of 'extremism'.

The aim of constructing the Policy Corpus was to see if the change that was described earlier, that 'radicalization' and 'extremism' had become conventionally synonymous with violence, was limited to the two versions of the Prevent strategy or was part of a wider trend within government texts. A software package, Wordsmith Tools, was used to investigate the L1 collocation of 'violent' with 'extremism' in each document. 'L1' means that the word ('violent') is located in the word space immediately to the left of 'extremism' ('violent extremism'). For each document analysed, I calculated how frequently 'violent extremism' occurred as a percentage of the total occurrence of 'extremism', and this data was used to create the graph in Figure 3.1 that shows how the usage of 'extremism' has changed over time.

Each point on the graph is a government document and the point at 100 per cent represents the 2009 document, Pursue Prevent Protect Prepare: The United Kingdom's Strategy for Countering International Terrorism. In this document, 'extremism' is only written as 'violent extremism' (100 per cent of the time). Over time, the word 'violent' has been lost so that all of the most recent documents are clustered around 0 per cent. While the close reading of the text

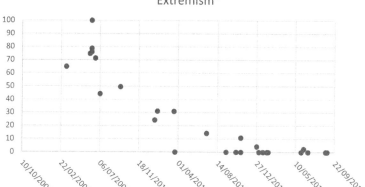

FIGURE 3.1 *Collocation of 'extremism' with 'violent'.*

carried out in Stage 1 showed that the usage of 'extremism' and its association with violence had changed between two documents, the analysis of this corpus has enabled the exploration of many more documents and almost one million words. This shows that the observations that first described the changes in the usage and emergence of 'extremism' in the analysis of aforementioned two documents may be part of a wider trend within government texts, suggesting that the collocation of 'extremism' with 'violent' has been progressively denuded in government documents since 2009.

As well as showing collocations at L1, Wordsmith Tools can be used to search for collocations in different configurations. For example, 'R1' would indicate that the collocated word is found in the word space immediately to the right. The software allows the investigation of collocation between words that are within 25 words to the right (R25) or to the left (L25), and the settings can be altered to test for any L or R collocation between 1 and 25.

It was demonstrated earlier that 'radicalization', like 'extremism', tended to be collocated with reference to violence in the earlier Prevent Strategy but that this collocation had since been dropped. However, it is not possible to demonstrate this so clearly as it is for 'extremism'. Searching for collocations of 'radicalization' with 'violent', 'violence', 'terrorism', 'terrorist' and 'terrorists' from L1 to L25 and from R1 to R25, no pattern was found. Over fifty graphs of the different collocations of 'radicalization' were produced by this method, and, while they failed to show such a pronounced downward trend as the graph for 'extremism' shows, they do show something similar, and two of these graphs (Figure 3.2 and 3.3) are reproduced to demonstrate this. In both the graphs, and

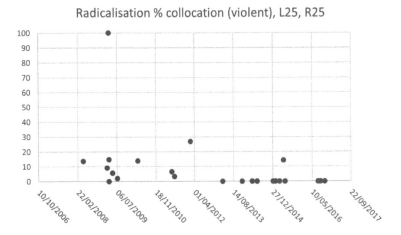

FIGURE 3.2 *Collocation of 'radicalization' with 'violent'.*

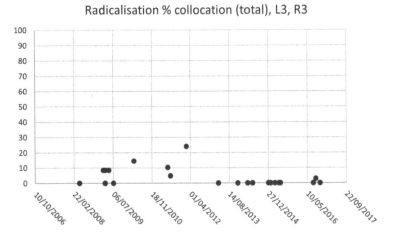

FIGURE 3.3 *Collocation of 'radicalization' with 'violent'.*

in all fifty that were produced, there was a significant clustering of more recent documents of around 0 per cent. Like 'extremism', more recent usage of 'radicalization' tends not to collocate it with 'violence' in government documents

The Parliamentary Corpus (2006–17)

Parliamentary debates are archived back to the 1700s but they are recorded in different databases that relate to different time periods. Despite attempts to generate data from across different databases that would be comparable, the different cataloguing and search functions of each have meant that this has not been possible. Databases from different times catalogue by date, or by minister or by debate topic, and either separate written answers from debates in the chamber or do not. As such, the most appropriate database to use to construct a do-it-yourself corpus of parliamentary debates extends from the present to as far back as 2006. As 'extremism' only entered common parlance in 2005, this represents a significant proportion of the recent emergence of 'extremism'.

By carrying out similar analysis of parliamentary speeches as was done earlier with government documents, a similar trend is described. The loss of 'violence' and other words associated with violence from references to 'radicalization' and 'extremism' over time is seen, along with the characteristic clustering of recent speeches around 0 per cent.

Similar to the Policy Corpus, the Parliamentary Corpus shows that the collocation of 'violence' with 'extremism' has also been progressively lost in parliamentary debate between 2006 and 2017. However, the trend is not as defined as that which is seen in the Policy Corpus. Taking a closer look at the text represented by a single data point on the graph offers some explanation for this. The point at 0 per cent on 20 November 2006 is taken from a debate that includes the following text:

We must recognise, too, that we face stark challenges to our values and our way of life from those who foster extremism and do not hesitate to use violence to further their own ends. (Hansard 2006)

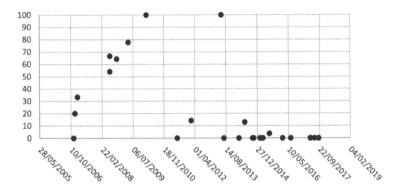

FIGURE 3.4 *Parliamentary Corpus.*

Unlike the corpus analysis that suggests that 'extremism' is not associated with violence in the text, this quote reveals that the two terms are associated in the actual meaning of the text. As this point on the graph is representative of a text that only included the word 'extremism' twice, this misrepresentation of the actual meaning by the corpus analysis has resulted in the point that represents this text being placed at 0 per cent on the graph rather than at 50 per cent. This alters the appearance of the graph as a whole and demonstrates why it is important that any conclusions drawn from the analysis of corpus data should be limited to describing general trends, rather than focusing on the meaning of individual points and specific texts.

The News Corpus (2000–17)

The News Corpus is composed of articles from the *Guardian*, *The Telegraph* and the BBC, and it is hoped that this provides an admittedly limited cross-section of the British media. Leading articles were selected from each news source on the days following the seventeen most recently reported terrorism attacks on the British mainland. Fifty documents that totalled 52,609 words were analysed in this corpus. Despite the relatively large number of documents analysed (twice as many as the Policy Corpus), the

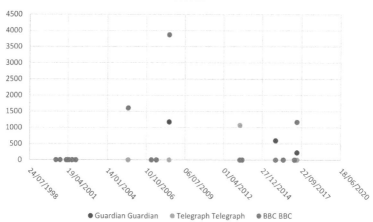

FIGURE 3.5 *News Corpus ('extremism').*

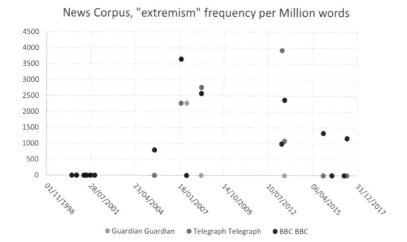

FIGURE 3.6 *News Corpus ('radicalization).*

typical brevity of news articles resulted in there being a limited number of words analysed. For this reason, there was not enough data to investigate the collocation of 'extremism' with 'violent' as was done with the Policy Corpus. However, in the articles analysed, it was found that 'radicalization' and 'extremism' did not appear in any articles relating to terrorist attacks before the 7/7 bombings of 2005. This includes all articles analysed that related to the IRA campaign in 2000 and 2001, and these are represented by the clusters of points at zero on the left-hand side of the following graphs. 'Extremism' and 'radicalization' only started to be used to describe acts of terrorism after the London 7/7 bombings in 2005.

The Hansard Corpus (1803–2005)

The Hansard Corpus differs from the preceding corpora in that it is not a do-it-yourself corpus; it is a reference corpus that was created in 2011 by researchers and academics (Marc Alexander, Jean Anderson et al. 2017) in collaboration with Milbank Systems, which manages records of parliamentary speeches and correspondence. This reference corpus is made up of 7.6 million speeches and 1.6 billion words from parliamentary debates between 1803 and 2005. As such, the Hansard Corpus is used to show changes in language from before the time covered by the Parliamentary Corpus.

'Radicalization' is absent from the record of parliamentary discourse until 1975. It then appears very rarely through the

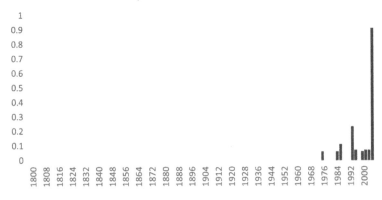

FIGURE 3.7 *Hansard Corpus ('radicalization).*

parliamentary record for the next thirty years, only appearing in 1984, 1986, 1993, 1995, 1999, 2001 and 2003. Of the thirty years of parliamentary discourse recorded between 1975 and 2005, 'radicalization' is absent for twenty-three. There is a sharp increase in the usage of the word in 2005, a 4,154 per cent increase on the average usage since it entered the parliamentary lexicon in 1975. This increase in usage corresponds to 'radicalization' first appearing in the Media corpus, in the same year as the 7/7 bombings in London.

'Extremism' first appears in 1919 but is used infrequently until the 1970s, on average 0.2325 times per million words between its first appearance and 1970 when the usage increases and initially peaks at 2.41 words per million in 1975. The frequency of usage then fluctuates with progressively larger peaks of usage in 1984, 1995, 2001 and 2005.

'Extremist' first appears in 1869 and 1882. However, both instances can be discounted as they represent the term to mean 'the most extreme', as opposed to being used as a noun to describe an extreme person. For example, the first usages are, 'I hope that the Bill will be dealt with the greatest caution and the extremist care' and 'It required Gentlemen of the extremist hardihood to defend the Bill'. This, again, shows a limitation of corpus linguistics. As

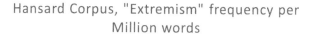

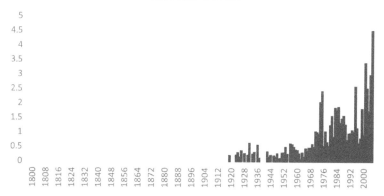

FIGURE 3.8 *Hansard Corpus ('extremism').*

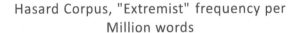

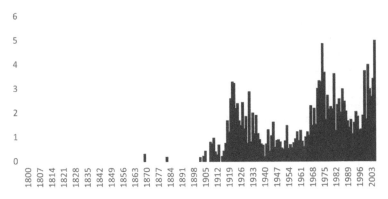

FIGURE 3.9 *Hansard Corpus ('extremist').*

such, and for the purposes of this research, 'extremist' first appears in the record as a noun in 1902 when Sir Lewis McIver describes one of his political opponents as an 'extremist' on account of the 'very strong opinions' that he holds.

Like 'extremism', the frequency with which 'extremist' appears in the parliamentary record then fluctuates, and usage of the term peaks between 1918 and 1933, through the 1970s and, with a particularly prominent peak in 1974, and then again in 2005.

Amalgamated Hansard and Parliamentary Corpus (1803–2017)

This final graph has been created by amalgamating the Hansard Corpus with a corpus of recent parliamentary debate. Thus, while the Hansard Corpus and the current Hansard records are not internally consistent, so should not be used to describe more than a general trend, it is reasonable to infer that there has been a dramatic increase in the usage of 'pre-crime' in recent years.

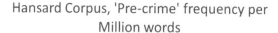

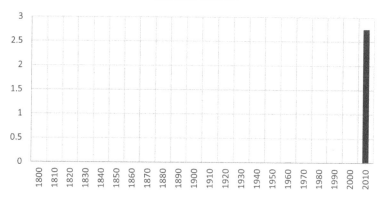

Hansard Corpus, 'Pre-crime' frequency per Million words

FIGURE 3.10 *Hansard Corpus ('pre-crime').*

What the Corpora show

The Policy and Parliamentary Corpora indicate that the change in the usage of 'extremism' first observed in the Prevent Strategy, that the collocation of 'extremism' with 'violent' has been progressively lost since 2009, are part of a wider trend within policy and parliamentary discourse. In the media texts analysed, 'radicalization' and 'extremism' were not used to describe so-called acts of terrorism before 2005 but this has since become more common. So, Prime Minister Tony Blair's insistence that the 7/7 bombers would not impose their 'extremism' on us, that was referred to in the Introduction, did indeed mark a discursive shift. 'Extremism' was not associated with previous bombing campaigns on the British mainland but since Blair's association of 'extremism' with terrorism in 2005 it has become the norm.

Both the Parliamentary and News Corpora suggest that there has been a dramatic increase in the usage of 'radicalization' and 'extremism' since 2005. It is therefore reasonable to suggest that their usage has also significantly increased in parliamentary discourse since 2005, as is also indicated by searching the Hansard database of parliamentary texts from 2005 to the present. This observation is further supported by the analysis of Professor Mark Sedgwick, who showed in Chapter 2 that there has been a dramatic increase in usage of the word 'radicalization' in the 'English-language press' since 2005 (Sedgwick 2010).

In parliamentary discourse, 'radicalization', 'extremism' and 'extremist' are rare or non-existent before the 1970s and have since emerged through progressive and increasing peaks of usage. There has also been a dramatic increase in the usage of 'pre-crime' in Parliament in recent years. This type of corpus analysis should only be used to draw limited conclusions that describe general trends in language use, rather than focusing on the meaning of individual points and specific texts. As such, and in appreciation that corpus analysis does not necessarily describe the actual meanings of the texts analysed, the texts are returned to in the next chapter and submitted to close reading to gain a deeper understanding of their meaning. In later chapters, both the meanings of the texts and the trends over time that were described earlier will contribute to a theorization of the texts, their production and their interdiscursive relationship to other texts and social structures, with a specific focus on how these changes have occurred over time.

This later theorization will show that the sense that 'something must be done' to prevent 'extremism' and 'radicalization' that was felt by me and other committee members at the start of the first chapter was not based in any actual need, but in generative mechanisms that are inherent in the usage of the words that is described in this and the following chapters. While Prevent might seem like 'common sense' to its defenders (Baldét 2020), it is this 'common sense' that is hiding the social and political impact of counter-extremism. Advocates for Prevent accepting the 'common sense' that there should be a strategy to target 'extremism' and 'radicalization' will be shown in later chapters to be hiding their own ideological assumptions. While no doubt well meaning, these assumptions have led to the increasing support for strategies to target 'extremism' and 'radicalization', strategies that the theorization in later chapters indicates do more to promote than to prevent political violence.

CHAPTER 4

The emergence of 'extremism'

'Stop the extremism'

On 9 September 2019, Prime Minister Boris Johnson stood at the Dispatch Box of the House of Commons and announced a debate on an early parliamentary general election, proposing that Parliament would be closed, or prorogued, for over a month to allow for preparation for the election. Johnson had been prime minister for less than two months and had taken the top job after receiving 66 per cent of the vote from Conservative Party members to become leader of their party. The British Electorate is made up of around 45 million people, so the 100,000 votes that he received in support of his claim that he would 'Get Brexit Done' represented a select 0.23 per cent of the British people who would be eligible to vote in a General Election. Johnson's proposed prorogation would see Parliament shut for over a month in advance of the greatest constitutional change for a generation, the United Kingdom's scheduled departure from the European Union (EU) on 31 October 2019. As a result, he faced much criticism for attempting to silence a Parliament that was less enthusiastic about Britain leaving the EU than he was.

The prime minister's apparent move to silence Parliament was met by levels of passion not seen since the infamous debates on the eve of the Invasion of Iraq in 2003 and over potential military intervention in Syria in 2013. The timing of the debate, starting at

10.48 pm, meant that MPs were only given one and a half hours to discuss the proposals before the motion was voted on and passed. Some of the most vociferous interjections during this short debate would come from members of the recently formed political party Change UK.

Made up of former members of the Conservative and Labour parties, Change UK had formed as a pro-Europe and 'centrist' party in response to the referendum vote to leave the EU. They campaigned for a second referendum that they referred to as 'the peoples vote' and that they hoped would overturn the earlier vote by the people of the United Kingdom to leave the EU. If they were not already consigned to obscurity by being founded on such a contradictory position, they were further discredited when Change UK MP Angela Smith referred to ethnic minorities as having 'a funny tinge' in a BBC panel discussion. As one of eight former Labour MPs who claimed they had joined Change UK in response to racism in the Labour Party, Change UK's credibility was irrevocably damaged as it became clear that these Blairite MPs were exploiting since discredited allegations of racism, and specifically anti-Semitism, to undermine their own party leader Jeremy Corbyn.[1]

Towards the end of the debate, Change UK MP Mike Gapes rose to speak from amongst the small band of his fellow anti-Corbyn and pro-Europe MPs. Given the intensity of debate, Speaker John Bercow was forced to shout for 'Order', before going on to say, 'I have never known a situation in which Mr Gapes cannot be heard', before allowing Gapes to continue in his characteristically bombastic manner:

> In this time of national crisis, this country is in a very dangerous place, and it is time that all moderate social democrats, one nation Conservatives and Liberals came together to stop the extremism, which is going to damage our country for decades to come.

Gapes' argument that it is 'extremism' to disagree with his cadre of rebel MPs, presumably he includes the 52 per cent of the electorate who voted for Britain to leave the EU three years earlier, is one of the clearest examples of 'extremism' being used as a relative term. Gapes' use of it to attack his political opponents is so absurd that it would not be out of place as a denunciation by Senator McCarthy in the United States' anti-communist hearings of the 1950s. The analysis that follows will show how Gapes' 'centrist' logic has emerged in parliamentary discourse over the last half century and how it has the potential to irrevocably silence debate that is vital to the functioning of democracy.

Selected references to 'extremism' from the parliamentary record are used in the rest of this chapter to show various aspects of its emergence. In the following chapter, a similar analysis of 'radicalization' is carried out and 'radicalization' is so rarely used in Parliament before 2005 that every instance is cited. This mapping of the emergence of 'extremism' is literally geographical in one aspect as the mechanism by which 'extremism' moved from initially being applied to calls for self-determination at the furthest reaches of the British Empire before creeping closer to home and even into Parliament with Gapes' above reference to the 'extremism' of his fellow parliamentarians. By looking at 'radicalization' and 'extremism' separately, while recognizing them as part of the same discourse, there is a certain level of triangulation in the data as both words show similar patterns of usage over time and the application of the discourse progressively closer to home is enabled by a number of other factors. The move to apply 'extremism' to the home population is enabled by the creation of a domestic other by the war on terror, hence the proliferation of its application to British Muslims. A situation helped along by over a century of British Orientalist imaginings of the Middle East.

The analysis in the following paragraphs shows that, while 'extremism' was predominantly applied to foreign calls for self-determination in the first half of the twentieth century, it has been occasionally applied to the Left. Though these instances are rare, as is the use of 'extremism' in the early decades of the corpus, they reveal something significant about the functioning of parliamentary discourse and debate. They reveal a discourse on the Left that prides itself in and seeks change through being in opposition, even being prepared to celebrate the loss of power as an indication that some level of social justice has been achieved and that the Left are therefore not in demand from the electorate. This genre of the Left is shown in the following chapters to have been abandoned and replaced by Tony Blair's aspiration for New Labour to be in power. As New Labour have been global leaders in the proliferation of a neoliberal style of government, their embrace of the denunciation of 'extremism' also fits with the emergence of 'extremism' alongside the emergence of neoliberalism and the heated politics that this precipitated in the 1970s.

'Extremism' and the British Empire

'Extremism' is initially most frequently used in reference to the break-up of the British Empire, and the quotes that follow have been selected as they are indicative of the usage of 'extremism' in reference to the loss of British colonies in India, the Middle East, throughout Africa during the earlier parts of the twentieth century and, finally, closer to home in reference to the Troubles in Northern Ireland during the 1960s and 1970s. While there is some reference to the 'extremism' of the Left in Britain during this time, it is rare and only comes into common usage in the 1970s. The application of 'extremism' from far-off territories and towards the United Kingdom shows how the word may have enabled an Orientalist view to slowly creep from the fringes of the British Empire and back to the population at home.

India

On Friday 12 December 1919, Knight Commander of the Order of St Michael and St George, Knight Grand Commander of the Order of the Indian Empire, Knight Grand Commander of the Order of the Star of India, former liberal MP for Midlothian, former governor of Victoria, Madras and Bengal, president of the Asiatic Society, former Lord Lieutenant of Peebles-shire, founder of the Scottish Beekeepers Association and, perhaps not surprisingly, a leading Freemason who had been the Grand Master of the Grand Lodge of Scotland and Grand Master of the Grand Lodge of Victoria, Thomas Gibson Carmichael sat in the House of Lords as the 1st Baron Carmichael of Skirling. Opening a debate on the Government of India Bill, Carmichael offers a lengthy account of his sympathies for 'moderate' Indians and makes one of the earliest references to 'extremism' that can be found in the parliamentary record:

I am in sympathy more, perhaps, than most who have been in India – with views which are looked upon as somewhat extreme: I am going further to admit that possibly in the definition of what views were extreme and what were moderate: I would go further in the direction of extremism than a great many of my friends would in saying that certain views were moderate: We have all been younger than we now are: Some of us have modified our views – I know I have – on many points; and as we grow older I think we learn a certain amount of sense: One thing which, perhaps, people in this country forget is that in India those who take an interest in politics are on the whole younger than the men who take an interest in politics here

Carmichael attempts to understand and explain 'extremism', and it is a position that he proclaims sympathy for. 'Extremism' is relative and is a position that he appreciates others might view him as having adopted, a view that some might even see as 'moderate'. 'Extremism' is a position that many, including Carmichael himself, will have adopted in their youth. In this sense, he suggests, that the emergence of 'extremism' in India under colonial rule is understandable. However, in his final assertion that those interested in politics in India are 'younger than the men who take an interest in politics here', he undermines his preceding proclamation of understanding. His arguments that he understands and appreciates 'extremism', that he has even moderated his previously 'extreme' views, serve to present him in a reasonable and informed position from which he is then able to cast the politics of Indians as youthful exuberance. In doing so, Carmichael undermines his proposed understanding, and thus the possibility that he might respond to the real concerns that have led to the emergence of the 'extremism' that he refers to.

Sudan

Four years later in a House of Lords debate about the Foreign Office on 10 July 1924, Viscount Turnour, like Carmichael mentioned earlier, is recorded as attempting to describe the causes of 'extremism'. His contribution is of note because it is the first example of 'Islamic extremism' in the parliamentary record, a phrase that does not reappear until seventy years later in 1995. Turnour, like Carmichael, recognizes the supposed causes of 'extremism' but also uses the word to cast an Orientalist lens onto Muslims, who Turnour refers to as 'Mohammedan',

> It was undoubtedly the fact that the Englishmen who worked under the Turko-Egyptian Government in the Sudan at that time did all that they could to improve conditions, but unfortunately they met with very little success: Finally came the appalling catastrophe of the Mahdist revolt: I do not think there is any question as to what were the main reasons for that revolt: It was not merely a fanatical outburst of Islamic extremism, because governors and governed were Mohammedan people: It was; here there will be no difference of opinion – a Sudan national rising against the gross misgovernment of the Sudan by Egypt, and the latter's exploitation of the slave trade.

While Turnour recognizes 'the gross misgovernment of the Sudan by Egypt, and the latter's exploitation of the slave trade' as a real cause of the 'extremism' of 'the Mahdist revolt', he takes care to note that Englishmen 'did all that they could to improve conditions'. Without making any judgement of the veracity of this claim that the 'Englishmen' were implicitly better for Sudan than the stated 'misgovernment' of the region by 'the Turko-Egyptian Government', this claim sets the 'Englishmen' as superior to 'the Turko-Egyptian Government'. A claim that is aligned with Hochschild's suggestion that an awareness of the 'Arab' slave trade in East Africa was promoted at the time to deflect public scrutiny from colonialist expansion in West and Central Africa (Hochschild 1998).

By describing this generative mechanism for the emergence of 'extremism' while specifically absenting the emergence of a mechanism from the actions of his countrymen, Turnour uses 'extremism' to argue for the superiority of 'Englishmen' and the inferiority of the 'Turko-Egyptian Government' of the area. Thus, though Turnour does explore the causes of 'extremism' he also uses it to promote the superiority of 'Englishmen' over 'Mohammedan people'. This perspective is supported by the statement that 'the Mahdist revolt' is 'not merely a fanatical outburst of Islamic extremism' which works to simultaneously promote and diffuse an Orientalist perspective. Turnour is indicating that he recognizes such a thing as 'Islamic extremism' and that it might act as a generative mechanism or cause of other 'revolts'. However, that it is '*not merely* a fanatical outburst of Islamic extremism' (emphasis added) indicates that, at least in the instance that he describes here, the 'Mahdist revolt' of the 'Mohammedan people' is grounded in an ontology other than the phenomenon of 'fanatical . . . Islamic extremism'. The recognition of both 'Islamic extremism' and other causes of 'the Mahdist revolt' reveals that Turnour is using 'extremism' to cast Orientalist aspersions *and* to explore other causes of 'the Mahdist revolt'.

Both the words 'Mohammedan[ism] and 'Mahdist' are explored by Said (1978) for their capacity to situate the Western scholar outside of and superior to Islam (Said 1978). Thus, even though Turnour tries to understand an ontology for extremism, his contribution to the parliamentary record mentioned earlier is Orientalist and provides some lineage for the situating of 'extremism' in opposition to 'British values' as will re-emerge more than eighty years later with the redrafting of the Prevent Strategy in 2010.

Palestine

Reference to 'extremism' in India is found throughout the parliamentary record and increases through the 1930s when it is also accompanied by the citing of 'extremism' in reference to the 1936–9 conflict in Palestine, reference to which continues into the 1940s. The following contribution from Lieutenant Colonel Sir Arnold Wilson, Conservative MP for Hitchin, from the middle of this period, on 21 July 1937, is made notable by the extent to which he attempts to explore the ontology of extremism:

> The Government are being urged by Members opposite and by the Royal Commission to resume what we may call strong Government in Palestine – further measures against the Press and against anybody who attempts to disturb the public peace. I see from the 'Times' that the Mufti of Jerusalem is in trouble again, and there seems a likelihood that it may be decided to arrest him. I am far from wishing to interfere with the discretion of the Government and its representatives on the spot, but I suggest

that there is still time for a brief respite, a *locus penitentiae*, before we make what is already a very difficult situation perhaps almost incurable by arresting a leader of one side. I say this with reluctance, but I have had the responsibility myself in such a case. I have had a revolution on my hands and have been compelled to arrest and deport ring-leaders who through their extremism had made any moderate expression of opinion dangerous, if not impossible; but I did not find those measures to be, in general, successful. Discontent that is based on sentiment and race is hydra-headed, and little as we have reason to admire the statesmanship or moderation shown by the Mufti of Jerusalem in the past, he is a recognised leader, and I hope His Majesty's Government will go all the way possible to find some via media short of his arrest and removal.

In this contribution, Wilson is recognizing that 'extremism' might emerge from repressive actions of the state, and this leads him to argue for restraint from the British colonial administration. This analysis is closely aligned with that made here, that excessive imposition of state power via counter-extremism measures may result in the promotion of the violence that these measures intend to address. It is also of note that the aforementioned quote is coming from a military figure, someone who might be expected to propose more draconian measures rather than calling for restraint.

As Mackinlay explored in his book, *The Insurgent Archipelago*, also referred to in Chapter 1, the emergence of the Prevent Strategy and counter-extremism more generally occurred as responsibility for counter-terrorism moved from the military and into the civil service (Mackinlay 2009). The transfer of this responsibility has resulted in Mackinley suggesting that the experience of the military in counter-terrorism from before 9/11 had been lost, with the result that OSCT 'did not have the experience to understand that a campaign, which narrowly focusses on the terrorist, tends to obstruct the engagement of the population' (Mackinlay 2009).

This is a particularly important factor in UK counter-terrorism strategy as it means that the extensive knowledge that was generated from decades of military activity, and mistakes, in Northern Ireland during the Troubles was lost. As was the organizational memory of the British Army's time in Palestine referred to earlier. In my own research and advocacy, I have spoken to military officials who served in Northern Ireland during the Troubles, and they have universally shown an appreciation of the argument that repressive counter-extremism measures might be counter-productive, an understanding that has been lacking in my interactions with civil servants working in this area. Wilson's contribution to the parliamentary record, thus, highlights the importance that policy is informed by past successes and failures.

Africa

The first reference to 'extremism' from the 1950s appears in a debate on colonial affairs from 12 July 1950 when Mr Selwyn Lloyd, Conservative MP for Wirral, presages twenty years of repeated parliamentary reference to 'extremism' throughout Africa when he says:

> There were doubts whether they were ready for Western democracy in its fullest form. It was said of one side that either we ought to stay and govern firmly or else it would be better to go.

> Another comment was, 'Why do you let this small group of extremists dominate the situation?' There was a feeling that we had lost interest; that we were defeatists about retaining our connection with West Africa, and that we were about to make a quick departure in the same way as we had gone from India or Burma. I think it is vital that we should disprove that attitude of mind. We must not allow a small group of extremists to poison the relations between Britain and the Nigerian peoples. I say 'peoples' advisedly, because the Right hon. Gentleman knows there is no such thing as a Nigerian people. It is a concatenation of a considerable number of different peoples.

> How are we to deal with this disquiet? I suggest that the first matter to be dealt with is the apparent success of extremism. There is a great feeling that if the extremists shout loud enough they get something. If a time-time [*sic*] has been fixed for constitutional advance and if the extremists agitate enough, they will get the Government to go back on the time-table laid down. I think it is very important that any time schedule for constitutional development should be adhered to.

By asking if 'they were ready for Western democracy' without questioning the appropriateness of the UK imposing a system of government on another region, that by Lloyd's admission is 'a concatenation of a considerable number of different peoples', Lloyd removes agency from those governed and assumes the right of the British to impose a system of government. This non-critical engagement in colonial rule sets the tone of debate on 'extremism' in Africa for the next twenty years of parliamentary debate. The notion of imposing 'Western democracy' on a foreign region also reveals an earlier expression of a political genre that will become a repeated justification for the post-9/11 war on terror sixty years later when US president George Bush Jr infamously promotes the export of democracy to Iraq and elsewhere around the world (Bush 2003).

The tautological analysis of the causes of extremism that Lloyd offers continues through the parliamentary record from the 1950s and 1960s and is further demonstrated by two records from 1960. On 28 March 1960, the Earl of Home, later to be prime minister, Alec Douglas-Home, is recorded in a House of Lords debate on Kenya:

> My Lords, how does one outlaw extremism, whether it be the extremism of the European in the South or that of the African Congress in the North – by decree, by law? Surely the best way is to enlist the moderate, sensible, constructive Africans and Europeans who both recognise that each in Africa is indispensable to the successful and prosperous future of the other.

Like many of his fellow peers and politicians cited earlier, Earl Home is recognizing the need for restraint in government to avoid the inadvertent promotion of 'extremism' by attempts to control it. However, rather than going on to propose that the root causes of anti-colonialist movements – by definition, colonialism itself – be addressed, he proposes the co-opting of 'moderate, sensible, constructive Africans and Europeans'. By proposing this solution, Earl Home is suggesting that ideology, in its second (positive) connotation – described in Chapter 2 as political standpoints that are consciously derived from social theory – is both the cause of and the solution to 'extremism' in Africa. Thus, while he recognizes that 'extremism' might emerge from attempts to outlaw it, he does not attempt to seek out and address its root causes and makes the implicit claim that extremism is emergent from itself.

Earl Home's partial recognition of the causes of extremism is repeated later in the same year on 4 July 1960 when Viscount Hinchingbrooke, Conservative MP for South Dorset, says in a debate on the Commonwealth Prime Ministers' Conference,

> This great concourse of nations, the British Commonwealth, has no future at all in a turbulent world unless it is based upon compassion, tolerance and compromise. In the last few months I have been very shocked to listen to speeches from hon. Members opposite and to read articles in the Press pleading the merits and cause of black Africa, come what may, and showing a great passion for extremism and for a fierce pace of change. I have wondered whether the results of all these things would not be directed in the end towards tearing the British Commonwealth apart.

In calling for 'compassion, tolerance and compromise', Hinchingbrooke is aligned with the calls for restraint from Earl Home and from Lieutenant Colonel Sir Arnold Wilson that were explored earlier. However, he discounts the 'merits and cause of black Africa' as 'a great passion for extremism'. Not only is he using 'extremism' to demean the cause for African self-government, he is also labelling it as a 'passion' and reveals that his initially called for 'compassion, tolerance and compromise' is not extended to 'black Africa'. Hinchingbrooke is dismissing the 'cause of black Africa' as secondary to the British Commonwealth. In doing so, he is casting African calls for self-government as irrational, and this enables him to dismiss them.

All the preceding quotes that refer to opposition to British colonial rule in Africa as 'extremism' make the same implicit claim, that British rule in Africa should persist. While this position may seem unacceptable by current standards, this 'taken-for-granted routine privileging of white interests that goes unremarked in the political mainstream' (Gillborn 2005) is – according to critical race theory – to be expected. Thus, this outdated and racist conception of 'extremism' may hold a mirror up to the current and taken-for-granted usage of 'extremism' and the recent denunciation of critical race theory (Fox, Doyle et al. 2020, Nelson 2020).

Northern Ireland

By the late 1960s, three decades of violent conflict that would become known as 'the Troubles' had begun in Northern Ireland. Correspondingly, references to 'extremism' in Northern Ireland dramatically increase and become more common than those attributed elsewhere. One reason for this seems to be that 'extremism' is repeatedly used in its relative sense and by all sides to denounce one another, such as in the following quote from a debate on the Ulster Defence Regiment on 19 November 1969 when Roy Hattersley, Labour MP for Birmingham Sparkbrook, is recorded as saying:

> My hon: Friends who seems [sic] to criticise the very principle of agreement should not do so on the basis that by co-operating with the Government of Stormont we are co-operating with some sort of Ulster extremism: Nothing could be further from the truth: The genuine voice of Ulster extremism was heard in the House this afternoon when the hon: and learned Member for Antrim, South (Sir Knox Cunningham) described the Defence Regiment as a potential hotbed for I:R:A: infiltration: That was the genuine voice of extremism in Ulster:

In this contribution, Hattersley is reappropriating the language of his opponents. Responding to calls that he is engaging in 'extremism', he turns the word on his opponents and recasts them as the 'extremists'. This might be considered an unwise tactic from the perspective of cognitive linguist George Lakoff, who advises against appropriating the language of our political opponents (Lakoff 1990, Lakoff 2011, Lakoff 2016). However, it could be argued that Hattersley's approach is effective in reframing his opponents as 'extremists'. Yet, the arguments explored in the next chapter and earlier in reference to democracy and debate might suggest that 'extremism', even in this usage, makes an unhelpful contribution to any political debate. While Hattersley may be scoring cheap points by labelling his opponents 'extremists', how he could also be causing more significant problems to the functioning of democracy, as is discussed in the next chapter.

One month later, the formation of the establishment of an Ulster Defence Regiment is again discussed in Parliament when, on

15 December 1969, Lord Winterbottom, Labour peer, is recorded as saying the following during a debate in the House of Lords:

> For it is not by this Bill alone, my Lords, that life and meaning will be given to the Ulster Defence Regiment: Parliament may provide the authority, the Government establish the framework; but it is the people of Northern Ireland themselves who must bring this Regiment to life: They alone can make it, as I am confident every one of your Lordships desires, truly part of the British Army: a symbol of resistance to extremism of communal harmony in Northern Ireland, and of the wider unity of the United Kingdom

This contribution is notable as, unlike those explored earlier, military force is proposed as a response to 'extremism', an approach that earlier contributions suggested had failed elsewhere and had, thus, argued against.

In the preceding sections, the proliferation of the word 'extremism' to Orientalize political machinations in response to the break-up of the British Empire reveals a progressive application of the term ever closer to home, from the further reaches of the Empire to Northern Ireland. It might be suggested that this progression home has since continued with the recent application of 'extremism' being used to describe British Muslims. This recent Orientalization of sections of the British population has been enabled by referring to 'extremism' amongst British Muslims via the emergence of a discourse on 'Islamic extremism' in the 1990s. This is discussed in the following chapters and can be seen as a significant step in the emergence of 'extremism' as it is used today.

Islamic extremism

On 23 February 1995, Lady Olga Maitland makes the first reference to 'Islamic extremism' in the parliamentary record since 1920 when she is recorded as saying the following during a House of Lords debate on the army:

> Paul Beaver, who is well known for his work with Jane's Defence Weekly, in a presentation in the House some weeks ago, identified

44 flash points in areas of British concern for this year. He pointed to the new fighting in regional and ethnic conflicts, the continued regional and ethnic conflicts in former colonies, the proliferation of weapons of mass destruction, the rise in Islamic extremism and the threats to our trade routes.

The nominalization of 'extremism' (in this instance, 'Islamic extremism'), like many of the preceding examples, hides real mechanisms that are generating the concerns that the speakers are purporting to address. But, while bringing Islam into the discourse separates Maitland's quote from most of those discussed earlier, by implying an underlying cause for 'extremism', it is similar in nominalizing 'Islamic extremism'. In doing so, Maitland names a single cause for 'extremism', Islam.

Later in the same year, on 7 November 1995, in a House of Lords debate on Sudanese Human Rights, the Lord Bishop of Southwark says:

My Lords, do Her Majesty's Government recognise that the continuing extreme poverty of a great many Sudanese people – poverty recently seen by the Archbishop of Canterbury when he visited the area – can create a fertile seedbed for Islamic extremism? Can the Minister say whether the Government will allow non-Governmental organisations to engage in development rather than just supplying emergency aid?

The Lord Bishop recognizes 'Islamic extremism' as a product rooted in causes beyond religion. Perhaps not surprising, coming from a religious figure who might be expected to defend against accusations that religion promotes violence. Depending on one's perspective on religion, this could be seen as a *naïve* defence of unjustified religiosity or an understanding of the 'true' nature of the faith in question. The possibility of these two perspectives shows that it is possible that those who refer to 'Islamic extremism' could either be casting themselves as defenders or critics of religion.

A further cause of 'Islamic extremism' is recognized by Mr Raymond Jolliffe, cross bench hereditary peer, on 18 November 1999, when says in response to the Queen's speech:

If international humanitarian law is violated, all of us are affected: Even from a purely Russian perspective, the present course appears self-defeating: I say that because decimating the Chechens is sure to fan the flames of Islamic extremism: Already there are reports of fighters arriving from such countries as Afghanistan and Pakistan to help the Chechens

In recognizing a cause of 'Islamic extremism', Jolliffe's words are similar to those of the Lord Bishop cited earlier. All three aforementioned references are similar in referring to 'Islamic extremism' abroad. Though both the Bishop and Jolliffe endeavour to understand the causes of 'Islamic extremism', the parliamentary record as a whole reveals a somewhat Orientalist perspective in the application of 'extremism' to religion tending to be reserved for Islam. By searching the parliamentary record, one can see that there are very few references to the 'extremism' of other religions; there is no reference to 'Christian extremism' or 'Hindu extremism', and there is one reference to 'Jewish extremism', from Richard Crossman MP on 31 July 1946. There is also a notable absence of 'secular extremism' in the record. This absence of other religious and secular 'extremisms' casts Islam as more liable to 'extremism' than other belief systems and thus contributes to the creation of an Orientalist lens through which to view the British Muslim population.

On 24 September 2002, Nicholas Soames, Conservative MP for Mid-Sussex, further elaborates the potential causes for 'Islamic extremism' during a debate on 'Iraq and Weapons of Mass Destruction':

What the Arab world needs particularly – and if there is indeed as a result of these actions to be regime change in Iraq – is a model that works: a progressive Arab regime that by its very existence would create pressure and inspiration for a gradual democratisation and modernisation around the whole region. That would provide an engine to deal with the widespread poverty, ignorance, repression and humiliation that form the lethal cocktail driving Islamic extremism, especially among the young, and whose consequences remain such a terrible danger to us all.

We are living at a time when we cannot predict, as we did in the cold war, how the enemy will react or behave. We face a number of undetectable threats for which we will have no warning. Given what we know of the Iraqi regime and its weapons, and given the necessity to uphold the authority of the United Nations, we must press on and deal with this issue by acting and operating, as Britain always has, within the full authority of international law. This is no time for us to avoid the hard choices that have always placed Britain alongside her allies in doing what is right and necessary.

In this contribution, Soames describes 'Islamic extremism' as a product of 'poverty, ignorance, repression and humiliation' and, in doing so, recognizes causes for the phenomenon he describes. And, while these causes reveal an understanding of what might cause 'Islamic extremism', going some way to undermine the Orientalist lens, Soames use of 'ignorance' and associated terms such as 'modernity' asserts his superiority over those who he describes.

Having explored the possible causes of 'Islamic extremism', Soames goes on to say at the start of the next paragraph that, 'We cannot predict . . . how the enemy will react', and this is of interest from a critical realist perspective as it presents a TINA (there is no alternative) compromise formation. A TINA compromise formation, as is discussed in earlier chapters, is seen where someone's 'truth in practice [is] combined or held in tension with a falsity in theory' (Hartwig 2007, Bhaskar 2008). This is the case in what Soames is recorded as saying, as he first theorizes the causes of 'Islamic extremism' before saying that we cannot predict how the same 'enemy' will react. In initially offering suggestions as to the causes of 'Islamic extremism', he has already proposed that how the 'enemy' might react *can* be predicted. Thus, his 'truth in practice' reveals a falsity in the theory that he goes on to present. As is explored in earlier chapters, the appearance of this TINA compromise formation reveals something of the fallacious foundations of both Prevent and of counter-extremism more generally.

'Extremism', describing leftism and nominalizing opposition

Returning to earlier references to 'extremism' in the corpus, 'Extremism' first appears in the parliamentary record on 2 August 1919 when Mr Henry Croft, Conservative MP for Christchurch, says:

And yet we have a member of the Cabinet who went to South Wales and settled the miners' dispute in the manner I have indicated, with the result that immediately the extremists in the railway world and in the transport world said, 'Oh, but the leaders in South Wales, by exercising pressure, have managed to get out of the Government all, or very nearly all, they desire, and you, our leaders, on account of the War, have let the opportunity go by'. That was putting a premium on extremism. I hope the Government will not interfere in disputes in the first place again, that we shall not have the Prime Minister going from his task in the Cabinet as a strike conciliator, and that he will not be called in to settle all these disputes over the head of industry.

In this first record of 'extremism' from the parliamentary record, it is being used to describe the ideology of those who are demanding workers' rights for miners and railway and transport workers. Ideology in this sense is employed in its second, positive, conception, to describe consciously chosen political standpoints. 'Extremism' is, thus, described by Croft as akin to socialism or conservatism, though an important distinction should be drawn between these words and 'extremism'. 'Extremism' is also 'extreme' and is, as such, when viewed from a normative position, a pejorative term.

'Extremism' is described by Oxford dictionaries as 'The holding of extreme political or religious views; fanaticism'. And, the dictionary's example of 'extremism' used in a sentence is given as 'the dangers of religious extremism'. To avoid the conflation of the call for workers' rights with other political and religious 'extremism', Croft could have used any number of terms such as 'leftism' or 'trade unionism' to describe this political stance. However, to do so would have recognized this as a consciously chosen political position and, in doing so, Croft would have offered more validation than he does of 'extremism's' position on the spectrum of normal politics. To refer to 'extremism' as Croft does essentializes this relative political stance, and, as is discussed earlier and in the next chapter, has a potentially negative impact on the functioning of democracy more generally.

By casting the political position of advocates for workers' rights as 'extremism', Croft is employing the word as a rhetorical tool to argue against political change. He goes further in his argument by suggesting that negotiating with 'the leaders in South Wales' will encourage others. This is an argument familiar to an audience 100 years later in the government's oft-repeated assertion that they 'do not negotiate with terrorists' for similar reasons (Comments 2004, Telegraph 2004, Watts 2015). Croft's 'leaders' are, presumably, union leaders, and it is notable that they are not named as such, for to do so would situate them within as legitimate struggle for workers' rights and undermine the argument that they are to be ignored as simply being 'extremists'. Croft's suggestion that the government agreeing to the demands of 'extremists' will encourage others shows that he recognizes an ontology for 'extremism'. However, like many of the aforementioned examples, this ontology is tautological in 'extremism' being derived from 'extremism', and Croft thus fails to explore its underlying causes.

Five years later, on 24 April 1924, John (Walton) Newbold, Communist MP for Motherwell, is similar to Croft in using 'extremism' to describe revolutionary left-wing politics. However, while Crofts fails to explore the causes of 'extremism', Newbold is explicit in his description of these causes when he says:

> architecturally, and from the sanitary position, Motherwell is a blight upon the landscape, which has produced the condition of affairs that presented me to this House: I am clearly aware that that is the explanation of the extremism which is manifested in the County of Lanark: . . . the proportion of people living more than two to a room was 70:1 per cent; more than three to a room.

This presents a deeper exploration of the causes of 'extremism' than Croft presents as he is describing 'extremism' as a product of, or a revolt against, poor social conditions. In doing so, Newbold shows an attempt to understand the deeper causes of 'extremism' than Croft.

Two years later, 'extremism' is again used to describe left-wing politics, this time by Conservative prime minister, Mr Stanley Baldwin, when he says on 8 December 1926:

> The great difficulty the Labour party is faced with is that they are on the horns of a perpetual dilemma – an obvious dilemma and a difficult one from which to extricate themselves: They can either throw in their lot with extremism and stir up industrial unrest, or they can cut loose from it.

Though a Conservative politician, Baldwin is describing a debate that would emerge within the Labour Party with the rise of New Labour almost a century later. The New Labour position has been described by Fairclough as using spin, polling data and management strategy to be in power rather than to argue for change by being effective in opposition (Fairclough 2000, Fairclough 2010). Political theorists such as Laclau and Mouffe (1985) have described the other position of effective opposition proposed by Baldwin in their earlier suggestion that it is the very essence of a socialist movement to be in opposition, a position that some have said the Labour Party has recently returned to (Guardian 2016). The internal party debates over the role of the Labour Party and their aspiration to be in power or to be effective opposition have tended not to use the word 'extremism', perhaps because it would cast negative aspirations within their own ranks. There is one notable exception to this usage by Labour MPs, and this is in the maiden speech of Tony Blair MP that is discussed on the following pages. However, Baldwin, as a Conservative politician, uses it not only as a descriptor of this conflict within the Labour Party that would be ongoing eighty years later but as a means of denigrating political standpoints that are in opposition to his Conservative agenda.

Another word used to denigrate political standpoints, in this instance for those related to a single city, is 'Birminghamism'. 'Birminghamism' only appears in a single debate in the parliamentary record but is of note as it is described as being 'always distinguished for its extremism' by Mr Frank Owen, Liberal MP for Hereford, in a debate on 4 November 1930:

> Birminghamism was always distinguished for its extremism and Birmingham and Birminghamism have been true to type in this case. Smethwick and Aston have been true to type; and Birminghamism, more rampant and more virulent than ever, has been let loose upon this country.

This quote is of particular interest as 'Birminghamism', like 'extremism', is being used as a rhetorical tool to nominalize social and political processes and, in doing so, to obfuscate agency and responsibility. In this instance, presenting 'Birminghamism' as a phenomenon disconnected from any cause – only connected, by name, to the city from which it emerges – the agency and responsibility of the people of Birmingham is being removed from the conditions in which they live. In this sense, 'Birminghamism' presents an Orientalist view of the people of Birmingham who are seen as disconnected from the social conditions from which they and their politics emerges. Added to this, 'Birminghamism' is described as 'virulent', a medicalized term that is used to indicate that this apparently disconnected ideology might spread like a virus through the population. Sian (2017) has recently cited Young in her discussions on Prevent to suggest that 'Such a lens limits us to seeing crime, deviance, and political violence as merely a pathology to be eradicated'. She suggests that such 'Orientalist knowledge constructions' limit the capacity for the political responses that would be required to reduce political violence (Sian 2017). This Orientalist view of Birmingham proposes a foreignness to the city that it might be argued was catalysed by a focus on the city's Muslim population ninety years later to produce the 'Trojan Horse' 'scandal' that was discussed in Chapter 1.

The conflict over the role of the Labour Party, to aspire to be in power or to be effective opposition as was discussed earlier, reappears on 16 September 1948 when Mr Douglas Jay, Labour MP for Battersea North, is recorded as saying:

> Nor, finally, can there be any doubt that it is just because we have achieved and maintained this measure of social justice in this country, and because the wage earners have confidence in the fair distribution of our national income, that extremism and Communism make no headway in this country. That is the real lesson of the past two years; and it seems to me something of which all British subjects, and indeed all democrats, might be proud. The hon. Member for South Edinburgh (Sir W. Darling) last night, speaking rather tragi-comically if I may say so, deplored the disappearance of various red patches from the map. He found this humiliating, and apparently took no pride in the achievements which I have tried to recall tonight. Quite frankly, I can feel only pity for anybody whose love of his country is so weak as not to feel pride in these solid achievements of the British people.

Jay is specific in describing 'extremism' as emerging from a lack of social justice. He ties it to communism, and, in doing so, he is describing 'extremism' as a version of leftism as in the preceding quotes. This quote is distinct from those mentioned earlier and is of interest because Jay overtly rejects the notion that the Labour Party should aspire to power and appears to celebrate the loss of support for the Labour Party that he is a member of. Jay's celebration is a particularly powerful example of the genre that, like Laclau and Mouffe (1985), presents the Labour Party as part of a socialist movement that ought to embrace being in opposition and prioritize change towards more social justice over an aspiration to be in power. The increasing social justice that Jay is celebrating is likely to be tied to the expansion of the welfare state after the Second World War by the Labour Government of Clement Attlee. This genre within the Labour Party could be described as aiming to write itself out of politics. Taken to its logical conclusion, Jay's aim is to achieve a utopia in which the resistance that is the foundation of the labour movement has no more injustice to resist, no more social justice to demand.

This need to aspire to a utopia is aligned with critical realisms aspirations for a concrete utopia (Bhaskar 2016, Bhaskar 2016 and chapters 7 & 8). However, Laclau and Mouffe (1985) and Mouffe (2005) warn that the condition for the resistance of hegemony is the maintenance of antagonistic discourse in the political domain, and this will be drawn on in the following chapters to interrogate the wisdom of Bhaskar's call. This indicates that agonistic political relationships might be a necessary condition for utopia.

The explosion of 'extremism' in the mid-1970s

The preceding chapter showed that the frequency that 'extremism' appears in the parliamentary record dramatically increased in the mid-1970s. Looking at the history of the period helps to understand what might have caused this dramatic increase, and Dominic Sandbrook's seminal history of 1974 to 1979, *Seasons in the Sun,* provides valuable context from which to understand the emergence of 'extremism' during this period that he describes as

a pivotal moment in our recent history. It opens on 4 March 1974, when the unprecedented economic and political crisis created by the OPEC oil shock, the three-day week and the collapse of the Heath Government brought Labour's Harold Wilson back to Downing Street as the head of a minority Government. And it ends on May 1979, when, after an extraordinary series of strikes had ripped the heart out of Jim Callaghan's administration, Margaret Thatcher walked into Number 10 as Britain's first woman Prime Minister.

By any standard these were extraordinarily turbulent and colourful years: the years of the Social Contract and the IMF crisis, the Birmingham Bombings and the Balcombe Street siege, the Grunwick strike and the Lib-Lab Pact, the Bay City Rollers, the Sex Pistols and Ally's Tartan Army. They culminated in the industrial unrest known as the Winter of Discontent, which, rightly or wrongly, became the most enduring symbol of the national experience of the 1970s. . . . More than a quarter of a century later, Francis Wheen, who was 20 in 1977, wrote that the 'defining characteristics of the Seventies were economic disaster, terrorist threats, corruption in high places, prophecies of global economic doom and fear of the surveillance state's suffocating embrace'. (Sandbrook 2013)

Sandbrook explores how the Conservative Party and right-wing media have since promoted a 'caricature' of the time through 'haunting images of rubbish piling up in Leicester Square, railway station boards showing a list of cancellations and pickets gathering outside cancer wards', images that 'never went away' (Sandbrook 2013). This is a caricature that Sandbrook goes on to suggest does not fit with people's 'rather better memories of the decade', nor does it fit with more official measures of the United Kingdom's success:

Jobless figures were generally better than during the Blair and Brown years, let alone the Conservative Governments of the 1980s and 1990s . . . there were fewer strikes per year in Britain than in Canada, Australia or even the United States . . . most people were better off in 1979 than they had been in 1970. (Sandbrook 2013)

While Sandbrook presents a conflicted picture of what was happing in Britain in the 1970s, there is one certainty painted by him. The conflicting narratives that Sandbrook presents and which endure to this day reveal that the 1970s were a time of deep ideological division for Britain. A time that, Sandbrook tells us, 'saw the last gasp of an old collective working-class culture and the emergence of individualism as the dominant force in our political, economic and social life. Afterwards, nothing would be the same again' (Sandbrook 2013).

Thus, the increase in discussion of 'extremism', and of 'radicalization', in the parliamentary record of the time might be attributed to many factors that stemmed from both ideological division within Parliament itself, to the very real 'Troubles' in Northern Ireland, and nationwide industrial unrest. Multiple examples of each of these factors being referred to in Parliament and alongside 'radicalization' and 'extremism' can be found throughout the 1970s.

Written in 1975 and published by the Trilateral Commission, *The Crisis of Democracy* (Crozier, Huntington et al. 1975) is a book that offers chilling insight into the neoliberal project that began to emerge in the 1970s. The Trilateral Commission and *The Crisis of Democracy* are very much from the era of the Cold War and in opposition to the global proliferation of communism at the time. In their book, Crozier et al. bemoan the loss of 'traditional means of social control' as a result the increased engagement in the democratic process of citizens of the United States, Japan and Western Europe (Crozier, Huntington et al. 1975). The book is described by Chomsky as giving us some insight into the 'thinking that may well lie behind domestic policies' of the time in Western Europe, the United States and Japan (Chomsky 1981). The 'crisis' was that too many people were demanding change by engaging in democracy; from the perspective of the Trilateral Commission and of neoliberalism more generally, there was too much democracy!

Depending on one's political perspective, the industrial unrest that Sandbrook refers to could be seen as a triumph of the British worker against state and corporate power or, as in *The Crisis of Democracy* (Crozier, Huntington et al. 1975), as a failure of the state and corporate power to 'impose discipline and sacrifice' on the population (Crozier, Huntington et al. 1975). Or, combining these two perspectives, we might see this as a momentary triumph of the British worker before 'discipline and sacrifice' was imposed. Not surprisingly, the history that is often written of this time – a history which has been written from the perspective of the neoliberal ideology that underpins *The Crisis of Democracy* (Crozier, Huntington et al. 1975, Lydon 2017) – paints the last defeat of neoliberalism as a rather more gloomy time than Sandbrook suggests many remember.

The Trilateral Commission continues to this day as a collective of global business leaders and politicians, including the current leader of the Labour party Sir Kier Starmer. The Commission's pro-market position does not appear to have altered as they proclaim support for the 'free enterprise that underpin[s] human progress' on their website. Far from reflecting that the 2008 financial crisis might be the cause to reconsider the pr-market neoliberal project that they promote, the Commission insists that it means that 'the leadership tasks of the original Trilateral countries need to be carried out with others to an increasing extent'. Neoliberalism will, as Mirowski (2013) tells us in his book of the same name, *Never Let a Serious Crisis Go to Waste*.

The hypernormalization of 'extremism'

After the frequency of 'extremism' in the parliamentary record peaks in 1974 and 1975, there is a lull in usage until eighteen days after the election of Margaret Thatcher as prime minister. In a House of Commons debate on the Economy, Pay and Prices, on 22 May 1979, Denis Healey, former secretary of state for defence, chancellor of the exchequer, MP for Leeds East and soon to be deputy leader of the Labour Party , critiques Thatcher's claiming of the 'extreme centre':

> We are today concluding a debate which, by general consent, marks the biggest reversal of policy that any Government have undertaken for 50 years. The Right hon. Lady opened it last week by laying claim to a position on what she called the extreme centre. Her extremism is clear enough, but where is her centre? Her claim to represent the middle way is almost as bizarre as her choice of a quotation from St. Francis – the humble apostle of poverty and equality – to sanctify a doctrine that glories in the conviction that the only valid motive force for social and economic endeavour is naked materialism and selfish greed.

Healey's critique of 'naked materialism and selfish greed' is aligned with Sandbrook's observation that this was a time when individualism emerged as a dominant force. Sandbrook also tells us that the Conservative Party that was now in power 'took a decisive step to the right' (Sandbrook 2013). By casting herself in the contradictory position of the 'extreme centre', as Healey describes, Thatcher is presenting both a fallacious argument and a shrewd piece of political rhetoric. Her argument is fallacious because it is not logically consistent, one cannot be both extreme and hold the political centre ground, even though the very notion of the 'centre' is itself metaphorical (Lakoff 2011, Lakoff 2016). Thatcher's rhetoric is 'shrewd' as it recasts her views, that might otherwise be seen as 'extreme', as in the centre, and, in doing so, might be seen as moving the centre ground of British politics.

The process of moving the 'political centre', as may be the aim of Thatcher's rhetoric has recently been elaborated by a very different politician in the address that Jeremy Corbyn MP, Leader of the Labour Party, made to the party's national conference thirty-eight years later in 2017,

> Conference, it is often said that elections can only be won from the centre ground. And in a way that's not wrong – so long as it's clear that the political centre of gravity isn't fixed or unmovable, nor is it where the establishment pundits like to think it is. It shifts as people's expectations and experiences change and political space is opened up. Today's centre ground is certainly not where it was twenty or thirty years ago.

As well as a tactic to move the centre ground, the fallacious nature of Thatcher's argument might also be seen as part of a tactic that Adam Curtis describes in his 2016 BBC documentary of the same name, *Hypernormalization*.

'Hypernormalization' is described by Curtis as the deliberate promotion of confusion as a political tactic. He argues that hypernormailzation is a tactic that was been used to ultimate effect by Donald Trump in his rise to become president of the United States (Curtis 2016, Laybats and Tredinnick 2016). Laybats and Tredinnick (2016) explore the aspect of hypernormalization that results in emotional responses taking on more meaning than traditional evidence, citing Michael Gove MP's claim that 'people in this country have had enough of experts' as a prime example of this phenomenon (Curtis 2016, Laybats and Tredinnick 2016, Sky News 2016). It is, perhaps, not coincidental that Michael Gove MP was the politician at the centre of the 'Trojan Horse' 'scandal' that was explored in Chapter 1, the confusion created by the since discredited allegations having enabled the intervention of the security services into schools via the implementation of Prevent. The confusion having played as much of a role in the affair as the reality of the allegations.

In his aforementioned quote, Healey is attempting to attack Thatcher's notion that she can be both 'extreme' and at the 'centre' of politics. In doing so, he not only repeats her notion of the 'extreme centre' but also rephrases it in saying, 'Her extremism is clear enough, but where is her centre?' By saying this, Healey is employing the same style of argument as his fellow Labour MP Roy Hattersley that was referred to earlier and that, Lakoff tells us, is likely to fail. As Lakoff writes in his book, *'Don't think of an Elephant'*, this phrase is sure to be ineffective if one is attempting to stop people from thinking of an elephant (Lakoff 1990). By repeating and paraphrasing Thatcher, Healey is reiterating and, thus, promoting her assertion that her 'extreme' position that would later become known as 'Thatcherism' was, in fact, not 'extreme' at all.

This appropriation and (hyper)normalization of 'extremism' is the harbinger of the emergence of new usages of 'extremism' such as the 'extremism' of the right. Less than a year after Thatcher first presented her notion of the 'extreme centre' to Parliament, 'extremism' is used to describe a phenomenon that could be seen as the opposite of previous leftist connotations of the word when Mr John Lee, Liberal Democrat MP for Nelson and Colne, is recorded as saying in a debate on the Northern Region on 21 January 1980:

> Rising unemployment in the regions, particularly where there is a significant minority community, provides fertile ground for extremism, whether of the Left or the Right: In Nelson and Colne within the past week we have for the first time been subjected to a considerable leafletting campaign by the National Front, which is a most unpleasant start to the 1980s.

Like many previous contributions to parliamentary debates, Lee refers to the emergence of left-wing politics from unemployment and a lack of social cohesion, but he also refers to the emergence of 'extremism' of the right from the same societal conditions. By referring to 'extremism' of both the Left *and* the right, we might see the metaphorical centre ground as remaining in the same place, but this would be wrong. It would be wrong because the absence of reference to the phenomenon of emerging right-wing 'extremism' from earlier parliamentary discourse means that its emergence on the apparently 'extreme' right of the metaphorical spectrum of British politics shifts the whole spectrum to the right. This moves Thatcher's position – that may have previously been 'extreme' – towards the centre.

Political division in Parliament seems to have continued through the 1980s as Thatcher's government entrenched the 'naked materialism and selfish greed' that Healey described. This presents two mechanisms that may have caused the increase in frequency of usage of 'extremism' through the 1980s. Firstly, the ideological division that emerged in Parliament at this time and that resulted in MPs accusing each other of 'extremism', the divisions running so deep that even Labour MPs appear to speak out against 'extremism' in its leftist connotation. This is exemplified by Tony Blair, Labour MP for Sedgefield and future prime minister, in the following contribution to a House of Commons debate on the Finance Bill from 6 July 1983, which is also his maiden speech to Parliament:

> The constituency of Sedgefield is made up of such communities: The local Labour party grows out of, and is part of, local life: That is its strength: That is why my constituents are singularly unimpressed when told that the Labour party is extreme: They see extremism more as an import from outside that is destroying their livelihoods than as a characteristic of the party that is defending those livelihoods.

In one aspect, this contribution from Blair is similar to the quotes cited earlier. It is similar in aligning 'extremism' with leftism. It is different and unique in the parliamentary record up this point by being a Labour MP describing 'extremism' as a threat to the Labour Party. It is also notable that Blair nominalizes 'Extremism'; by doing so, it is denied human agency as it could be said that it is seen as a problem to be addressed rather than an indication of an underlying failure of government. This alters the genre of Labour politicians, promoting a legislative genre that dramatically impacts the calculus of the UK Parliament. The term 'calculus' is used here to describe a theory of ongoing and dynamic change in parliamentary discourse, the way in which this has been undermined by changes in the usage of 'extremism' is also explored in the next chapter.

Whether described by Conservative or Labour politicians, 'extremism' reveals a schism in understanding how the UK political system works. On one side, politics is seen as being fought in the metaphorical centre ground, with calls for reform of workers' rights seen as representative of dangerous 'extremism'. On the other side, 'extremism' is seen as a necessary threat against the erosion of equality and social justice. This second conception is best explicated earlier by Mr Douglas Jay, Labour MP for Battersea North, on 16 September 1948, when he describes the loss of Labour votes because of actual political change to support social justice, 'the disappearance of various red patches from the map', as a desirable outcome. Leftist Labour MPs, thus, present themselves as the ultimate pragmatists in arguing against their own potential to be in power to protect workers' rights; a position that is abandoned by Tony Blair.

The crisis of the Labour Party's identity, whether they should follow Blair's aspirations to be in power, or the 'hegemonic struggle' of Laclau and Mouffe (2001, p. xix) that Jeremy Corbyn embraced as leader has continued under the subsequent leadership of Kier Starmer. Starmer, who faced much criticism in the press over his lack of transparency about who financed his successful campaign to lead the Labour Party in 2020, is also a member of global promoters of neoliberalism the Trilateral Commission. Acting as Jeremy Corbyn's sidekick in the Shadow Cabinet, since taking over as leader of the Labour Party, he has since shown his position in relation to Laclau and Mouffe's socialist strategy. Starmer's presiding over his former ally Corbyn and other socialist MPs' suspensions from the party over the aforementioned anti-Semitism allegations shows that his sights are firmly set on being in power rather than forcing social change through being in effective opposition.

The shifting position of the Labour Party and the complexity this shows demands that political change that is enacted in the UK Parliament is understood not through an analysis of individual arguments but through a theory of ongoing change – this will be henceforth referred to as 'parliamentary calculus'. As critical realism is a philosophy that is interested in the exploration of an irregular ontology of real generative mechanisms, it lends itself to the theorization of this complex area; this is elaborated in later chapters. But, first, a similar analysis to that carried out earlier is carried out for 'radicalization'. The occurrence of 'radicalization' in the parliamentary record before 2005 is so rare that every time that it is used in Parliament before then is reproduced in the next chapter, its usage follows a similar pattern to 'extremism' and therefore supports the observations that have been described earlier.

CHAPTER 5

The emergence of 'radicalization'

Fallout from the Six Day War

On 5 June 1975, the American guided-missile cruiser USS *Little Rock* was the first ship in nearly a decade to travel through the Suez Canal. A military ship led the way as the waters were feared to be littered with mines left eight years earlier by the optimistically named 'Six Day War'. The Six Day War resulted from Israeli retaliation against Egypt closing the Straits of Tiran to their shipping. In response, Israel attacked its neighbouring countries, killing over 20,000 Palestinian, Egyptian, Jordanian and Syrian troops. While the newsreels reported on jubilant celebrations in Israel following the war, returning Israeli soldiers recorded their horror at what they had done in creating millions of Palestinian refugees and being part of a campaign that included the murder of civilians. Israeli filmmaker Mor Loushy (2016) documents the horror that the returning soldiers felt at what they had done and reports their accurate predictions and fears for the subsequent violence and apartheid that their actions during the brief war had consigned Israel to. The soldiers, many of whom had survived the Holocaust in their youth make painful comparisons with their actions at displacing Palestinians, 'I could see myself in those kids who were carried in their parents' arms, when my father carried me, perhaps that's the tragedy, that I identified with the other side. With our enemies.'

While Israel's military action would unsettle the entire region for decades, it was also felt abroad when the Yom Kippur War of 1973 saw coordinated military action by Egypt and Syria to retake the territories they had lost. Having challenged the previously unopposed military superiority of Israel, Egypt and Syria placed themselves in a position to negotiate the Israeli withdrawal from much of the territory they had occupied. Acting in defence of the Arab coalition, members of the Organization of Arab Petroleum Exporting Countries (OAPEC) proclaimed an oil embargo on counties perceived to be supporting Israel. While those directly targeted were Canada, Japan, the Netherlands, the United Kingdom and the United States, global oil prices soured and economies around the world would be blighted by highest rates of inflation seen in half a century.

Neoliberalism, the Left and New Labour

While extraordinarily high rates of inflation in the United Kingdom during the 1970s corresponded with those around the world that were also rising in response to the oil crisis, Conservative politicians were quick to blame them on the domestic policies of Prime Minister Harold Wilson's Labour government. This gave cause for Mr Julian Critchley, Conservative MP for Aldershot, to be the first politician recorded as referring to 'radicalization' in Parliament, in a House of Commons debate on the Army on 17 June 1975:

> There was a time when the objective of British foreign policy, like the objective of any country's foreign policy, was the maintenance of security. In the 1960s that objective changed and became the maintenance of prosperity. In the 1970s we are experiencing the radicalisation of politics, and defence has now to compete for attention with the problems of inflation, unemployment and energy. The Labour Party is the inflation party.

It is notable that 'radicalization' was first used to in Parliament to refer to the left when Wilson's Labour government was in power, and not earlier in the twentieth century when the left also included Communist MPs. That Critchley would use 'radicalization' to chastise the relatively moderate government of Harold Wilson seems to corroborate Sedgwick's assertion, discussed in Chapter 2, that 'radicalization' is a relative term. Critchley's comments thus seem to say more about his intentions than about the government that he is referring to.

In referring to the 'radicalization of politics', Critchley is aligning his concerns with those laid out in the same year in *The Crisis of Democracy* (Crozier, Huntington et al. 1975) suggesting that the politicization of citizens be addressed by the state imposing 'discipline and sacrifice' on the population (Crozier, Huntington et al. 1975). Critchley, however, does not propose that the causes of these concerns be addressed so directly; rather, he states that 'The Labour Party is the inflation party'. In saying this, Critchley is appealing to the British electorate to support his Conservative Party, arguing that 'the radicalization of politics' might lead to people voting for the Labour Party and that this will imperil the UK economy, as he seems to claim is demonstrated by rising inflation rates – a claim that is patently absurd in light of the ongoing oil crisis of the time driving up inflation rates around the world.

The concerns laid out by Crozier et al. have more recently been described by Chomsky as fundamental to the political project that has since become known as 'neoliberalism' (Chomsky in Lydon 2017). The similarity of the ideas espoused in *The Crisis of Democracy* to Critchley's argument around the supposed 'radicalization of politics', both from the same year, leads to the supposition that there may be a relationship between Critchley's use of 'radicalization' and neoliberalism. Analysis of 'extremism' carried out in the previous chapter supports this and leads to the theorization of an interdiscursive relationship between the emergence of 'extremism' and neoliberalism in the chapters that follow.

While 'radicalization' has been a frequent topic of parliamentary debate since 2005, it only appears in the parliamentary record fourteen times after its first appearance and before 2005, when it comes into common parlance. As such, every incidence of 'radicalization' in the parliamentary record from before 2005 is referred in this chapter. The infrequency of the word's usage indicates that any real mechanisms that emanate from 'radicalization' during this period are likely to have been limited. However, the usage that can be seen contributes to the later theorization of the real mechanisms that have resulted in the word's current usage and in the exponential increase in its use since 2005.

It is over a decade later until 'radicalization' reappears in Parliament when on 10 December 1986 Mr Dave Nellist, Labour MP for Coventry South East, co-opts the 'radicalization' of the left as a warning or threat to a Conservative government in a debate on the 'Termination of Existing Arrangements [for trades union activity and for the remuneration of teachers]'. Nellist's warning is that the erosion of workers' rights by the Conservative government will lead to the 'radicalization' of voters who will, by Nellist's logic, then vote for a Labour government at the next opportunity.

> The Right of free collective bargaining, like the Right to strike, the Right to vote and every other Right in what is supposed to be a democracy – in so far as it can be a democracy under a Tory Government in the late 1980s – has been won by the struggle of generations of trade unionists, stretching back at least over a century. For a Tory Government to abrogate one of those Rights is an attack on a central feature of democracy. . . . It is escalating the *radicalisation* of the rank and file in ordinary teachers associations throughout the country. . . . It is worth making one small point about the *radicalisation* and the effect of such a draconian measure on the entire profession and on the youths and students in education. . . . The Bill, particularly clause 1, removes the basic democratic Right to free collective bargaining. . . . ..Instead, it substitutes direct control by the Secretary of State. In that sense clause 1 is an undemocratic and reactionary clause in an undemocratic and reactionary Bill . . . its only success will be in *radicalising* and politicising more teachers, taking them away from any support that they, as individuals, may have given to the Tory party and its candidates at election time. In that sense, if what the Secretary of State intends by clause 1 is a solution to the teachers' dispute, it will be counterproductive. (Emphasis added)

Nellist is arguing that failure to allow workers to be represented will result in their 'radicalization'. Both Nellist and Critchley employ the same meaning for 'radicalization', the increased support for the left in response to oppressive policies of the right. This is an undesirable outcome as earlier described by Critchley, a Conservative, as he suggests that it will lead to an increase in inflation. It might be seen as implicit from Nellist's leftist position that 'radicalization' of the teachers is desirable, as it will lead to teachers supporting his party. However, he also makes it clear that the 'radicalization' of the teachers will result in a loss of 'support that they, as individuals, may have given to the Tory party and its candidates at election time'. 'Radicalization' is thus being used as a threat against the imposition of the policies of the ruling Conservative government.

The next occurrence of 'radicalization' in the parliamentary record comes from a House of Commons Intergovernmental Conference on 5 July 1995 when Hon Douglas Hurd, Conservative MP for Whitney, is recorded as commenting on the development of the European Union:

> What is taking shape . . . is not a huge further radicalisation of the European Union or a huge new concept that will pull up everything by the roots and start something entirely afresh. . . . We have to look ahead to the expansion eastwards, and to some extent southwards – to Cyprus and Malta – of the European Union. One aspect that we have to consider to that end is the changes that will be needed in the common agricultural policy and in the structural funds. No one in their right mind would suppose that we could expand eastwards, which is certainly necessary, while conserving the CAP in its present form as the whole thing would go bust.

Hurd, like the preceding politicians, is using 'radicalization' to refer to political change and, like his fellow Conservative Critchley, presents it as implicitly undesirable. He refers to 'changes that will be needed in the common agricultural policy and in the structural funds' but does not regard these as a 'radicalization' of the European Union. Reasoned political change as described by Hurd is, thus, not 'radicalization', and, as such, 'radicalization' is a pejorative term for ill-considered or unreasonable change. It is also notable that Hurd's reference to a 'concept that will pull up everything by the roots' shows an understanding of the etymology of 'radicalization' in *'radix'*, the Latin for 'root', perhaps not surprising from a former scholar to both Eton and Trinity College Cambridge.

Both Conservative politicians Critchley and Hurd are, in line with their party name, taking on a position whereby drastic political change is seen as undesirable. Critchley takes a position from which all change is perceived as undesirable. Hurd takes a more pragmatic position where change is 'certainly necessary' but as a result of an apparently reasonable economic argument. Nellist, a Labour politician, is presenting 'radicalization' as a reasoned response to a Tory 'attack on a central feature of democracy'. By using the threat of 'radicalization' as an argument against the imposition of Conservative policies, Nellist is positioning himself as part of a socialist movement that is necessarily in opposition. That this position is aligned with the theorization of socialist strategy as laid out by Laclau and Mouffe (1985), who regard opposition as the necessary and inevitable socialist position, is explored in later chapters.

In using 'radicalization' in this way, Nellist is employing dissent as an argumentation strategy, a position that is at odds to the Third Way that is later adopted by New Labour and was seen in Tony Blair's usage of 'extremism' in the last chapter. Fairclough describes intolerance of dissent as a genre of government that is characteristic of New Labour (Fairclough 2010). Thus, Nellist's genre, to co-opt the threat of dissent as a political tactic, differs for that which his party will later adopt under Tony Blair.

'Radicalization' of citizens of the Middle East in response to Western military intervention

As well as being used to describe leftist political change and as a pejorative term for unreasonable change at home, 'radicalization' is recorded in the parliamentary record as referring to the catalysing of political change in the Middle East by Western military intervention.

> Will the Right hon. Gentleman try to comprehend the urgency of the need for a debate on what is happening throughout the middle east. We have a unique opportunity in Britain to try to restrain our American allies from their ill-considered interventions in that part of the world. Does he not understand that the more the Americans intervene in any area of the middle east, the more

they increase the inevitability of radicalisation of that area, not only in religious but in political terms as well?

It may surprise contemporary readers that this quote does not refer to the heated parliamentary debates that occurred in the run up to the invasion of Iraq in 2003. It is from nineteen years earlier on 8 March 1984 when Mr Andrew F. Faulds, Labour MP for Warley East, refers to US military interventions in the Middle East in a parliamentary debate on the Iran–Iraq War. Faulds' parliamentary colleague, Sir David Price, Conservative MP for Eastleigh, follows on by saying, 'Many of us believe that Islamic fundamentalism is probably the greatest threat to peace at present'. This is the first time that 'radicalization' and Islam appear together in the same parliamentary debate. Though preceded by Faulds' argument that military intervention causes 'radicalization', Price's brief statement fails to repeat this connection or make it implicit that 'Islamic fundamentalism' occurs as a response to Western military intervention. In presenting 'Islamic fundamentalism' in this way, it is proposed as a threat that is emergent from conditions that are singularly 'Islamic'. This Orientalist view, discussed in Chapter 2, essentializes Muslims and disconnects their actions from the material circumstances from which all of our actions emerge (Said 2003). This disconnecting of 'Islamic fundamentalism' from political responses is a portent to prime minster, David Cameron's, speech to the Munich Security Conference twenty-seven years later in 2011. Cameron is more overt than Price by insisting that the roots of modern terrorism lie in Islamic ideology (Cameron 2011).

On 13 January 1993, Mr George Galloway, Labour MP for Glasgow Hillhead, is recorded as arguing, during a debate on 'The Arab Israel Dispute', that

the failure of the secular nationalist leadership of the Palestinian people to obtain any significant concession has led to that radicalisation and Islamicisation of the whole national consciousness in Palestine?

Going on to state that

The radicalisation and Islamicisation that is occurring across the Arab area and the broader Muslim world will be greatly intensified by what will be regarded as western double standards, whereby the west is ready, at a moment's notice, to pulverise Iraq, but unable, over decades, to do anything about Israel's rejecting and ignoring international law and international standards, or to do anything to save the lives of the tens of thousands of Bosnian Muslims who have died in the current campaign in former Yugoslavia.

A week later, on 21 January 1993, he refers to the US and UK coalition's bombing of Baghdad, equating the bombing campaign to a terrorist attack and saying:

> The attack was a blunder because it has contributed seriously to a wave that will continue for years of further instability, radicalisation and sweeping fundamentalism across the middle east and the broader Islamic arena. I do not know where some of the authorities obtain their information. On Arab streets, in the slums of Algiers, in Aden, in the slums of Cairo and in the mosques of Saudi Arabia, the attack has led to the beatification – if Muslims can be beatified – of that blood-soaked tyrant, Saddam Hussein. His stock has never been higher.

> Believe me, that wave of radicalisation and fundamentalism has been under way in the Arab area for a considerable period. Anyone who is aware of the Palestinian question and who has watched the steady march of the fundamentalist movement, Hamas, gaining ground at the expense of the secular, moderate, nationalist leadership of the Palestine Liberation Organisation, knows exactly the despair and humiliation felt by the Arabs that is leading to the festering problem of fundamentalism.

Like Faulds' reference to US interventions in the Iran–Iraq War, Galloway is exploring the genesis of 'radicalization', which he links to 'Islamicization' and 'fundamentalism'. In his first contribution from 13 January, he claims that 'radicalization' has emerged from a failure of 'secular nationalist leadership' in Palestine, from 'western double standards' in bombing Iraq while failing to hold Israel to account over breaches of international law and for failing to prevent genocide of Muslims in Bosnia.

Again, on 21 January, he refers to 'radicalization' as a response to the bombing of Iraq, going on to suggest that this is leading to 'the steady march of the fundamentalist movement . . . at the expense of the secular, nationalist, leadership of the Palestinian Liberation Organisation'. The 'fundamentalism' that Galloway refers to is implicitly religious due to its stated emergence from the failure of 'secular nationalist leadership'. This is partly Orientalist as Galloway presents the secular perspective as the acceptable norm and dismisses the 'instability, radicalization and sweeping fundamentalism' that emerges from the failure of the secular. However, it diverges from the purely Orientalist positions stated by Price and Cameron as mentioned earlier as Galloway's 'radicalization' is described as emerging from Western military intervention and the 'double standards' of the West towards Israel and the Middle East. Like Nellist, his fellow Labour MP who is quoted earlier, Galloway is using 'radicalization' as a threat to argue against a course of action proposed by the government. 'Radicalization' in this conception is describing an undesirable outcome but is being co-opted as a threat.

Like Galloway, Robert Graham Marshall-Andrews QC, Labour MP for Medway, also links 'radicalization' to Western intervention in the Bosnian War when, on 18 May 1999, he is recorded as saying:

The radicalisation of support for Slobodan Milosevic in Belgrade has occurred because, although he tells his people many lies, he can tell them with complete candour and truth that the action taken against them by NATO is illegal

Unlike Galloway, who describes 'radicalization' as stemming from the failure to 'do anything to save the lives of the tens of thousands of Bosnian Muslims', Marshall-Andrews sees the military action that the West *did* undertake in the Yugoslav conflict as being the cause. Specifically, Marshall-Andrews describes the illegality of the actions of NATO as being the cause of 'radicalization'. That Marshal-Andrews and Galloway could be referring to the threat of 'radicalization' for, respectively, both the *lack* of military intervention in Bosnia and *because of* military intervention in Bosnia indicate that it can be used as an argumentation tactic that does not necessarily have a fixed scenario to which it refers to. Once again, this supports Sedgwick's argument for the importance that 'radicalization' be seen as a relative term and which was discussed earlier and in Chapter 2 (Sedgwick 2010). This contradiction raises serious questions about the intentions of supporters of initiatives to police 'radicalization'.

On 26 February 2003, the impending invasion of Iraq by the US and UK coalition was debated in Parliament. This invasion of Iraq is an issue that many, including the former head of MI5 (Manningham-Buller 2010), have subsequently described as catalysing the 'radicalization' of Muslims, but it is only the Lord Bishop of Guildford who pre-empts this connection in Parliament at the time:

> I return to the anger over what is perceived to be – no matter what we may think about it – American and western imperialism. Will it threaten our social cohesion? Some of my colleagues who live with delicate multi-cultural communities are very worried about the impact of this conflict on social cohesion. We need to think about these matters.

> In my sleepless nights over this issue[1] I have a nightmare that Osama bin Laden is smiling about the prospect of this war in the Middle East. Al'Qaeda works outside the structures of international order and law. Is it possible that a war prosecuted in this way will fulfil its desire to create increasing chaos and disorder; increasing Islamic fundamentalism and radicalisation in the Middle East; and that we will find in this post-Cold War world that we have not yet found a way of living together in peace in the international community? Is there anything this debate can do to exorcise that nightmare, which I suspect is not only in my mind?

The Bishop, like many of the preceding parliamentarians referred to, uses 'radicalization' as a warning as to what might happen if the war proceeds. As the only reference to 'radicalization' in the parliamentary debates leading up to the invasion of Iraq in 2003, an event that would later be regularly linked to 'radicalization', the Bishop is remarkably prescient.

'Radicalization' of Muslims in the United Kingdom

Two years before the aforementioned contribution from the Lord Bishop of Guildford, the Lord Bishop of Birmingham commented on the connection between the 'radicalization of Muslim youth in UK cities' and military intervention in Afghanistan, intervention by the same military coalition that would later invade Iraq, stating on 18 October 2001:

> I hope that we shall not see yet another demonstration of the impotence of power in the face of a weakness that has little or nothing to lose. . . . I conclude by returning to Birmingham and my conversation with my adviser this morning. He is quite clear that, the longer this conflict [Afghanistan] goes on in its present form, the greater the fear for the radicalisation of Muslim youth in our cities and the more difficult for the voice of moderate Muslim leaders to be heard. I have also heard reports from church-run play groups about the fears expressed by Muslim women – fears for their families and for themselves. One might say that, if the young men are carrying the anger, the women are carrying the fear.

This is the first time in the parliamentary record that 'radicalization' of Muslims in the United Kingdom is connected to military intervention abroad. The Lord Bishop of Birmingham is presenting himself, like the politicians in the preceding section, as an insightful actor, someone who knows what is happening at a local level. Like Nellist, the Bishop is using the threat of the 'radicalization' of others as a means of arguing against a certain political tactic. Nellist's concern was for the imposition of new employment conditions on teachers while the Bishop is concerned by the continuing war in Afghanistan.

There are twenty-five seats for Bishops of the Church of England in the House of Lords, known as the Lords Spiritual. While this arrangement has faced criticism in the past (Humanists UK 2018), the numerous references to Lord Bishops in this chapter show them to have an apparently more informed and better understanding of the issues referred to here than is demonstrated by their secular peers.

The emergence of laws to prevent 'radicalization'

It is not until two years later on 1 March 2005 that government interventions to target 'radicalization' are first recorded as being discussed in Parliament when Baroness Anelay of St Johns, a Conservative peer, says in reference to the Prevention of Terrorism Bill (2005):

> My Lords, we do not underestimate the difficulty of the problem facing the Home Secretary. There is indeed no difference between us on the determination to protect our public from terrorism. We know that there are no easy answers but, as I made clear last week, we believe that the Home Secretary has settled on the wrong answers, which may sacrifice essential and long-standing British principles of liberty and justice in a way that is unlikely materially to enhance the security of our people. The Government have quite properly, and laudably, put into effect measures to prevent the radicalisation of groups in our society; these laws, and the sense of injustice that they may create, could completely negate those efforts.

The Baroness' argument that counter-terrorism measures, while perhaps well-meaning, may in fact increase the threat of terrorism are notable as it shows that the concerns that I express in this book are as old as the strategies that they critique. Since the time of the Baroness' critique, the type of strategies that concern her have become ever more oppressive, with the imposition of the latest Prevent Strategy (HM Government 2011) being the current high watermark for this oppression. The argument against these types of strategy, that they may increase the risk of terrorism, becomes ever more urgent as the counter-extremism industry continues to expand.

This urgency is further highlighted by the final record of 'radicalization' to be found in the Hansard Corpus, on 9 March 2005 when David Triesman, a Labour member of the House of Lords, is recorded as saying in a debate on the United Kingdom's forthcoming presidency of the European Union (EU):

> The justice and home affairs agenda will be carried forward in the EU's counter-terrorism action plan and the Hague justice and home affairs work programme, particularly to meet the negotiating deadlines on key measures such as the European evidence warrant and data retention. We want to see the completion of the strategy on radicalisation and recruitment

by terrorist organisations, and progress towards increasing the security of EU travel documents.

Triesman is indicating that the United Kingdom intends to use its presidency to impose its rapidly developing counter-terrorism agenda on the EU. According to Kundnani (2009), this agenda was going through a rapid phase of development at the time. The agenda will go on to be promoted throughout Europe in the following decade by the Radicalisation Awareness Network (RAN) (Fitzgerald 2016, Ragazzi 2018) and globally by UNESCO (UNESCO 2018).

Baroness Anelay has, like the preceding politicians, used 'radicalization' as a warning against proposed government policy. In this instance, the strategy that the Baroness employs 'radicalization' to argue against is the strategy to tackle 'radicalization' itself. Triesman's use of 'radicalization' demonstrates a different genre to his fellow politicians as he does not use 'radicalization' to warn of the consequence of certain political actions. Rather, he calls for the foreign expansion of strategy to tackle 'radicalization'. It might be argued that each of the preceding references have nominalized 'radicalization' and, in doing so, have obfuscated the agency and responsibility behind the process (Fairclough 2003). Triesman's proposal for 'a strategy on radicalization', rather than a strategy to address the underlying causes of political violence, is only made possible by this process of nominalization, a process that Fairclough describes as characteristic of the new language of New Labour, the faction of the Labour Party that Triesman was a leading light in and served as general secretary from 2001 to 2003.

The common cause of 'radicalization'

Every record of 'radicalization' in UK parliamentary debates from before March 2005 has been reproduced and discussed earlier. This is made possible by the infrequency that this now-common word was used in the thirty years since it first appeared in Parliament in 1975. During these first thirty years, 'radicalization' was recorded on average less than once every two years. The texts that are explored show a shift in the usage of 'radicalization' over this time. Initially, 'radicalization' is connected to the left-wing of British politics, either employed as a warning by Conservative politicians who represent it as an implicit threat or by Labour politicians who use the threat of 'radicalization' as an argument against Conservative, counter-terrorism or military policies, even at the risk of losing votes for their own party.

As a harbinger to debates on the Iraq War that will become ever more heated two decades later, 'radicalization' is used in reference to American intervention in the Iran–Iraq War in 1984, and this is also the first time that it is connected to a threat of 'Islamic fundamentalism'. It is only after 9/11 that 'radicalization' is recorded as being used to refer to a phenomenon or process that might affect Muslims who live in Britain and, within two years of this, strategies to prevent 'radicalization' are recorded as being discussed in Parliament.

The following causes of 'radicalization' described at first do not appear to be connected:

- Responses to the erosion of workers' rights

- Inability of an expanding EU to maintain payments via the common agricultural policy

- American intervention in the Iran–Iraq War

- 'The failure of the secular nationalist leadership of the Palestinian people'

- Failure to protect Muslims from genocide during the Yugoslavian War

- Illegal intervention of NATO in Bosnia

- The impeding invasion of Iraq in 2003

However, while these factors may appear disconnected, there is a common theme that joins them all, 'radicalization' is described in each example as a response to the failure of government. As was discussed in Chapter 2, this has been explored by political scientist Adam Przeworski in his book, *Democracy and the Market* (Przeworski 1991). He proposes that revolutionary sentiment in a democracy will only be avoided if 'losing under democracy [is] more attractive than a future under non-democratic alternatives' (Przeworski 1991). Each of the scenarios described earlier as likely to result in 'radicalization' is a scenario where it is explicitly or implicitly argued that continuing under a pre-existing system of government will become less desirable as a result of some described circumstance. Thus, the politicians are presenting themselves as knowing actors who are able to advise on what political decisions should be taken to avoid 'radicalization'.

While limited in terms of the amount of parliamentary debate that is covered by looking at texts containing such an infrequently used word as 'radicalization', we can infer something of the different genres that politicians represent themselves in. In the earliest texts, 'radicalization' is universally described as the call for political change that is to be expected in the face of undesired political strategy, either changes to employment rights at home or military intervention abroad. In all cases, politicians present themselves as knowing actors whose local sources or innate predictive powers enable them to foresee the negative repercussions of policy. By the final quote, the political genre has changed, Triesman does not present himself as a knowing actor. Rather, he presents 'radicalization' as an unquestioned threat that should be tackled by the expansion of policy. In asserting this, it could be argued that Triesman is presenting the much-critiqued genre of New Labour, a managerial genre that by using spin and assertion rather than substance 'discourages dialogue and debate' (Fairclough 2010). For its discouragement of debate, and its embrace of a newly nominalized word, Triesman's contribution is a textbook example of the New Labour genre that Fairclough describes in his book, *New Labour, New Language?* (Fairclough 2000).

Critiquing the usage of 'radicalization' in this book is not based on an assumption that the phenomenon that it describes is illusory. Rather, I follow the penultimate quote from Baroness Anelay in 2005 when she warns that laws attempting to prevent 'radicalization' will result in a sense of injustice that 'could completely negate' the well-intentioned efforts behind their creation.

Absence

An important focus of critical realism is absence, seen as particularly important as it is *a priori* to presence (Bhaskar 2008). The absence of any reference to 'radicalization' or 'extremism' from two debates in Parliament is notable. On 14 September 2001, Parliament was recalled from summer recess to debate the 'International Terrorism and Attacks in the USA', attacks that were yet to be called '9/11'. Four years later, an emergency parliamentary debate on the 'Incidents in London' was convened on the same day as the bombings that would later take on similar symbolism and be referred to as 7/7. In both debates it is notable that the words 'radicalization' and 'extremism' (or any other derivation such as 'extremist') are absent. Perhaps suggesting that the words had not yet become linked to acts of terrorism, an observation that is supported by the analysis of the News Corpus in Chapter 4.

Another notable absence is the absence of discussion of the Prevent Strategy in Parliament before 7 June 2011, when the strategy is discussed in a debate of the same name. This is the debate in which the revised version of Prevent is presented to Parliament by the Coalition government that had replaced New Labour in 2010. The prior absence of any debate or reference to Prevent in Parliament indicates that the implementation of the earlier strategy, first discussed by the Cabinet Office of the New Labour Government in 2004 (Omand 2004) and subsequently published in 2008, was not ever debated in Parliament. This is another example of the genre of New Labour that Fairclough describes as 'discourag[ing] dialogue and debate' (Fairclough 2010). As explored in the quotes throughout this and the previous chapters, there has been a consistent parliamentary discourse on the self-defeating nature of strategies to police dissent. It might therefore be supposed that Prevent would have faced opposition in Parliament and even been prevented from being implemented had New Labour allowed it to be debated.

Analysing parliamentary texts containing both 'radicalization' and 'extremism' in the last two chapters shows that a number of different genres have led to the words' current manifestations and the emergence of strategies to counter them. This heritage can be traced back to the ideological battlegrounds of the 1970s from which neoliberalism emerged, a time when both fears for global instability and ideological differences led to the explosion in usage of the words as was seen in the corpus analysis of Chapter 4. By reading all occurrences of 'radicalization' and 'extremism' from before 2005, it can be seen that these words are originally applied to political opposition to colonialism during the break-up of the British Empire in the early twentieth century, initially attributed to independence movements across Africa, then through the Middle East, before there are extensive discussions of 'radicalization' and 'extremism' in Northern Ireland during the Troubles of the 1970s. As the language crept closer to home, the next place for it to be applied was on the British mainland, and this is enabled by Parliament next discussing the 'radicalization' of British Muslims, rhetoric that might be seen to have contributed to the emergence of strategies such as Prevent. The subsequent expansion of these strategies to target many other forms of political opposition, including environmental protesters (NETPOL 2018), will be discussed in the next chapter. Finally, absence of 'radicalization' and 'extremism' from parliamentary discourse in the immediate aftermaths of 9/11 and 7/7 indicates that their current discursive connection to acts of terrorism is a new phenomenon. It should not be seen as coincidental that strategy to target 'radicalization' and 'extremism' emerged under the New Labour Government of Tony Blair; nominalization is described by Fairclough as a defining characteristic of the 'new language' of 'New Labour' (Fairclough 2000). By enabling 'radicalization' and 'extremism' to be legislated against, their nominalization may have contributed to the increasing usage of both 'radicalization' and 'extremism'.

Throughout the twentieth century, 'radicalization' was described as resulting from failure of government but nominalization has ultimately led to 'radicalization' and 'extremism' now being described as *causes* of violence, resulting in policy that is targeted at them failing to address a deeper ontology for political violence. While the foolishness of attempts to counter 'extremism' are made clear by the brief analysis of this chapter and by earlier reference to political theory, the question of the generative mechanisms that lie behind these changes is yet to be theorized. Thus, the next chapter asks what caused the emergence of 'extremism'?

PART 3

The Real

CHAPTER 6

What caused the emergence of 'extremism'

The death of Jerah

In February 2015, the same month that the Counter-Terrorism and Security Act 2015 came into law, fifteen-year-olds Amira Abase, Shamima Begum and Kadiza Sultana didn't turn up to school in Bethnal Green in East London. Grainy images of them passing through customs at Gatwick Airport revealed the start of their journeys to the ISIS-held city of Raqqa. Over the following years, conflicting stories of their marriages, the death of their husbands in battle, the deaths of their children in infancy and their own deaths in air strikes would slowly emerge through the fog of war that only allowed partial and sensational news out of the region occupied by ISIS.

In February 2019, a journalist from the *Times*, Anthony Loyd, found and interviewed the only survivor of the three girls. Shamima Begum was now nineteen years old, nine months pregnant and living in a refugee camp in Syria. She would soon give birth to her third child. Both of her first children having died in infancy, she named her newborn after her late son Jerah, the name derived from the Hebrew to live, wander or travel. Begum's next appearance to the world was on *Sky News* a few days later when she cradled the tiny bundle of her newborn baby and appealed to be allowed back to the United Kingdom so that she could raise him in safety. With journalists and politicians now travelling freely to and from the camp where Begum and Jerah were living, there would have been no practical difficulty in bringing them home. But, over the next few days, Home Secretary Sajid Javid would take a firm line in insisting that she must not return, going so far as to breach countless norms of international law by revoking her citizenship and leaving her and Jerah stateless. Less than three weeks after he was born, Jerah died in the squalid conditions of the refugee camp and became the third of Begum's children to die in infancy.

A month earlier in January 2019, Javid had announced his intention to become leader of the Conservative Party. His campaign video focused on his Pakistani roots and the importance of providing everyone with the opportunities that had helped him to earn his fortune in the City and then to rapidly rise to the most senior positions in government after moving into politics. Javid was not willing to extend these opportunities to Jerah and claimed to be revoking Begum's citizenship as she posed a security threat to the United Kingdom and, thus, should not be allowed back into the country. Begum had expressed her support for the Islamic State in her media interviews, and supporting this proscribed group was a crime that she could have been tried and potentially imprisoned for if she were allowed back to face the British Justice System. There does not appear to have been evidence that she had committed or was threatening to commit any other crimes

That Javid was willing to deny Begum and baby Jerah the opportunities that he proclaimed to be so important in his leadership video reveals two possible positions. The first is that he did not believe the idea that people could be 'deradicalized'. As 'deradicalization' is the foundation of Prevent and government efforts to counter the supposed threat of 'extremism', this sets him at odds with the security agenda that he as Home Secretary was an active and vocal supporter of. The other possibility is that revoking Begum's citizenship was a tactical decision by Javid to look tough and to appeal to the 100,000 members of the Conservative Party who would shortly vote on the next leader of the party and whose votes he was courting to claim the title of Prime Minister. That he lost out to Boris Johnson when his posturing gamble did not pay off was unfortunate for him. That he might have been prepared to disregard the life of a newborn to make this gamble is surely one of the lowest positions that one can imagine a politician taking. I remain curious as to which position best describes Javid at the time, a mistrust in the value of the counter-extremism strategies that he proclaimed to support or the murderous disregard for a baby who he could have saved.

Writing of citizenship deprivation, Barrister Colin Yeo has described how 'after decades of the power being essentially taboo, associated as it was with Nazi Germany and Soviet Russia, it was resurrected with a vengeance after 2010' (Yeo 2020). Javed oversaw a 600 per cent increase in the use of the power during his short term as home secretary (Dearden 2019). Javid's inhuman response to Begum and her newborn child became the most publicized of the hundreds of British citizens who were abandoned, rather than being brought home to face justice and be monitored in the United Kingdom. This tragic episode illustrates how discourse can solicit dramatic changes in the way that we react to and interact with one another. As was discussed in Chapter 3, this may be represented as a change in the speaker's genre and style. The discourse of the war on terror creates genres of heroes and villains or good and evil, characterized by President George Bush Jr's post-9/11 mantra of 'either you are with us or you are with the terrorists' (Jackson 2005), enabling Javid to present himself as a strong leader as he oversaw a policy that was previously taboo.

Without Javid's actions being underpinned by the discourse of the war on terror, it seems likely that Begum and Jerah would have been regarded as victims and hastily repatriated for their safety. Whether Begum was regarded as a teenage victim of 'grooming' for being persuaded, aged fifteen, to travel to Syria to marry an ISIS fighter, or as an adult terrorist supporter may also have been effected by any number of other discourses around security, race and the perception of gender and age. Jerah would probably have survived if his mother had been regarded as a teenage victim by the home secretary.

The war on terror that has been waged since 2001 shows how discourse can fundamentally alter the way we perceive the world. Mervyn Hartwig has written the following about discourse:

if we get our account . . . fundamentally wrong and do not correct our mistake, we are consequently forced into a series of endless theoretical and/or practical compromises. The upshot is a cumulative, emergent meshwork of figures and concepts that is incoherent and mystifying yet indispensable to our way of being. (Hartwig 2007)

The death of Jerah is perhaps the most profound of these 'compromises', and, despite the war on terror's promotion of previously taboo actions such as citizenship depravation and the well-documented rendition and torture programmes of the United States and its allies, it has become indispensable to the functioning of many countries. The dramatic changes in the way that we interact with one another that are solicited by the emergence of 'extremism' show how the war on terror has turned inwards on our home populations. These changes in human relations make the expansion of the war on terror inevitable and make suspects of us all. By exploring these changes in this chapter, we will see how they make the continued expansion of apparently 'extreme' political positions and violence evermore likely.

The promotion of violence becomes almost inevitable with the nominalization of 'radicalization' and 'extremism'. Before they were nominalized, 'radicalization' and 'extremism' were addressed by resolving the failures of government that were perceived to have resulted in them. Having been nominalized to describe deagentified threats, 'radicalization' and 'extremism' became entities that the government was and is able to legislate against. A call for such legislation was seen in the quote from Mr David Triesman in the preceding chapter when he called for the government to complete 'the strategy on radicalization' on 9 March 2005.

Once the government targets 'radicalization' and 'extremism', with the threat of the intervention of the security services, as is seen both in Prevent (HM Government 2008, HM Government 2011) and in counter-terrorism strategy more generally (HM Government 2015), it becomes inevitable that those perceived to be 'radical' or 'extreme' will withdraw from engaging in debate that risks them being labelled in the new violent connotation of the words. As was explored in Chapter 2 with reference to the work of Alexander, Arendt, Buber, Derrida, Mouffe and Przeworski, this suppression of debate not only undermines mechanisms by which violence might be avoided but also results in the inevitable promotion of violence. The vicious cycle that this creates for both the emergence of violence and of 'extremism' is now explored and addresses three distinct questions, starting with whether society needs 'extremism'.

Whether society needs 'extremism'?

The social order created by the emergence of 'extremism' is precipitated by the genre that calls politicians to legislate against 'radicalization' and 'extremism' and that casts teachers (and those in other civic roles such as doctors) as informants. This role is inferred within policy documentation by a duty that they have 'due regard to the need to prevent people from being drawn into terrorism' (HM Government 2015). However, such an inference or connection between 'radicalization' and 'extremism' and terrorism would not exist without the conflation of 'extremism' and violence in the language that we use.

Thus, the question that needs to be asked is if the emergence of 'extremism' and its continued association with violence are required to maintain the legislative and informant genres that are critiqued. An expansion of this question might be, do 'radicalization' and 'extremism' 'need' to be perceived as violent to maintain these genres? It is of note that 'need' is in quotation marks in Bhaskar's original schema for CDA. 'Need' is problematic from a critical realist perspective as we might suppose that any social order or network of practices can be – and will be – maintained by any number of generative mechanisms. Thus, expanding the question further, we are asking if 'extremism' is a significant or contributory factor in the maintenance of the genres.

While not a demonstration of causation, the contemporaneous emergence of the violent connotation of 'extremism', and 'radicalization, and the genres described earlier do support the suggestion that language has contributed to the genre of policymakers to legislate against 'radicalization' and 'extremism' and the genre that casts teachers and doctors as informants. Henceforth, these genres will be referred to as the 'legislative genre' and the 'informant genre'. So, having established that the emergence of 'extremism' might have contributed to the emergence of these genres, the question of whether it was a significant contributory factor remains and leads us to question if these genres could have emerged in the absence of 'extremism'. As was explored in the preceding chapter, before 'radicalization' and 'extremism' were nominalized, they were referred to as emergent from failure of government. Any political or legislative focus was, thus, on the failure of government rather than on 'radicalization' and 'extremism'. Without 'radicalization' and 'extremism' having been nominalized, it is not conceivable that legislation would have been focussed on them rather than on the failure of government, and it is therefore reasonable to suggest that the legislative genre would not have emerged.

While the legislative genre resulted in the inferred duty that those working in civil spaces should have 'due regard to the need to prevent people from being drawn into terrorism' (HM Government 2015), it is not clear that such a duty would have led to the informant genre if 'radicalization' and 'extremism' were not associated with violence. This is quite apart from the fact that the legislative genre would not have emerged in the absence of 'extremism' and thus would not have imposed the informant genre. Heath-Kelly and Strausz refer to CVE being supported by a supposed understanding of '"radicalisation processes" . . . (in the so-called "pre-criminal space")' (Heath-Kelly and Strausz 2018), and the aforementioned description of the progressive association of 'radicalization' and 'extremism' with violence shows how these processes may have been progressively justified in language.

Why, if at all, is 'extremism' needed?

Real IRA to 7/7

In the analysis of the News Corpus, there is a pronounced increase in the usage of 'radicalization' and 'extremism' in articles about acts of terrorism in 2005. All acts of terrorism on the British mainland between 2000 and 2005 had been perpetrated by Irish republicans. The London bombings of 2005 differed in that they were motivated by objection to British foreign policy further afield. Prime Minister David Cameron would later claim that the bombings were caused by an 'extremist ideology' in his speech to the Munich Security Conference (Cameron 2011), but both a well-publicized martyr video left by the suicide bombers (BBC 2005) and the testimony of the former head of MI5 to the Iraq Inquiry claim they were motivated by objection to British foreign policy (Manningham-Buller 2010). By being nominalized, 'radicalization' and 'extremism' are able to be used by David Cameron in this speech to describe 'ideology' that has *caused* violence. Thus, even in the face of the London 7/7 bombers speaking from beyond the grave in well-publicized videos to tell him that the cause of the bombings was foreign policy – a position supported by the head of his internal intelligence service – the nominalization results in the prime minister's failure to address the causes of violence that could not have been more clearly stated.

Having come to describe the causes of terrorism, 'radicalization' and 'extremism' can be seen to be associated with subsequent acts of terrorism throughout the rest of the News Corpus. That the 7/7 bombers were Muslim enabled an Orientalist perspective on them that was also shown in the historical usage of 'radicalization' and 'extremism' to describe political opposition at the fringes of the diminishing British Empire. Originally applied to independence movements across Africa, and then throughout the Middle East, before discussions of 'radicalization' and 'extremism' were applied to the Troubles in Northern Ireland. As the discourse crept closer to home, the next place for it to be applied was the British mainland, and Parliament next discusses the 'radicalization' of British Muslims. Thus, the discursive focus on 'extremist ideology' and 'a process of radicalization' as seen in Cameron's speech and in recent political discourse more generally might also be emergent from a colonialist discourse that is 'needed' for the maintenance of white supremacy and that can be traced back to the early twentieth century.

The new language of New Labour

The nominalization of 'radicalization' and 'extremism' is also emergent from the new language of New Labour (Fairclough 2000), and the analysis of the preceding chapter revealed that this aspect of the discourse corresponded with a shift in parliamentary calculus as New Labour gave up the left's role of perennial opposition. The pre-New Labour positioning of the left in opposition is in line with Laclau and Mouffe's exploration of *Hegemony and Socialist Strategy* from their book of the same name (Laclau and Mouffe 1985). In the more recent preface to the second edition of their book, Laclau and Mouffe suggest that there is 'very little hope' for the left so long as they insist on 'occupying the centre ground' (Laclau and Mouffe 2001), suggesting that the success of the left is dependent on them having 'an adequate grasp of the nature of power relations and the dynamics of politics' (Laclau and Mouffe 2001). It might be argued that the texts from before the nominalization of 'radicalization' and 'extremism' and the emergence of the new language of New Labour showed that the left *did* have 'an adequate grasp of the nature of power relations and the dynamics of politics', as they successfully sought to make material gains for the lives of their constituents – even if that meant renouncing their own power. The nominalization of 'radicalization' and 'extremism', however, hides the nature of power relations and the dynamics of parliamentary politics and indicates that the left under New Labour had relinquished the struggle against hegemony as they sought to be in power to assert their own hegemony. It was noted in Chapter 4 that the leader's speech to the Labour Party Conference in 2017, by Jeremy Corbyn MP, indicated Labour's brief return to an appreciation of the dynamics of parliamentary politics and Laclau and Mouffe's socialist strategy.

Fairclough suggests that New Labour was an attempt to 're-define a political programme that was neither old left nor 1980s right' from the perspective of the 'centre and centre left' (Fairclough 2000). Not only was this emergent from what Fairclough describes as 'an international discourse of the 'Third Way', but he also describes New Labour as seminal in the export of the Third Way to a global audience.

> New labour has been instrumental in setting up a series of international 'seminars' on the 'Third Way', attended not only by Blair and Clinton but also by leaders from other countries, including Brazil, Sweden, Italy, and more recently, Germany. (Fairclough 2000)

As has been briefly explored in earlier chapters, the Third Way was developed by Giddens (Giddens and Pierson 1998, Grice 2002) and provided the philosophical foundations for New Labour and their claiming of the centre ground and abandoning of the perennial opposition that Laclau and Mouffe describe. As was also explored earlier, the structuration model that underpins Gidden's work to support the Third Way fails to account for change over time. This might go some way to explaining why the new language of New Labour from which the nominalization of 'radicalization' and 'extremism' emerged fails to account for the nature of power relations and the dynamics of parliamentary politics over time.

Fairclough describes another aspect of the genre of New Labour as 'discourag[ing] dialogue and debate' (Fairclough 2010). This is seen in the absence of any debate on Prevent being held in Parliament under the New Labour Government, and this ensured that it was not submitted to the scrutiny of Parliament. Though the parliamentary calculus that might have challenged Prevent over the potential repercussions of this oppressive policy was not recognized in the new language of New Labour, it may have been expressed within Parliament more generally. The lack of any parliamentary debate ensured that such scrutiny was not faced by Prevent under the New Labour Government that first created it. The nominalization of 'radicalization' and 'extremism' ensured that such scrutiny was limited, even when Prevent was finally debated in Parliament after the formation of the Coalition Government in 2010.

Thus, 'extremism' may be seen to have become connected to British Muslims as a result of the London bombings of 2005. The connection emerging from a century-old colonialist discourse that had migrated home via Northern Ireland and was applied to the mainland via a focus on British Muslims – enabling an Orientalist focus to progressively turn from the further reaches of the diminishing Empire and on to the home population. This shift was enabled by a focus on the British Muslim population that developed even though it was clearly indicated by both the bombers and the head of the United Kingdom's internal intelligence service that the bombings had more to do with British foreign policy than the perpetrators' religious identity. Combined with the nominalization of 'radicalization' and 'extremism' – a characteristic of the new language of New Labour – this resulted in the causes of 'radicalization' and 'extremism' being obscured, undermining the parliamentary calculus that had previously resulted in politicians of the left and right calling for a moderation of policy. This obfuscation of the causes of 'radicalization' and 'extremism' is related to the hiding of change over time and supported by the philosophy of Giddens whose structuration model underpins the Third Way of New Labour (Giddens and Pierson 1998, Grice 2002).

While this offers a historical understanding of the emergence of 'extremism', Bhaskar advises that we use the semiotic triangle as the minimum theorization required for 'the intelligibility of language use and the possibility of meaning' (Bhaskar 2008, 2016), and this helps to explore the next question to understand how 'extremism' is produced and reproduced.

How is 'extremism' produced and reproduced?

Consideration of the semiotic triangle for when the words 'radicalization' and 'extremism' had not been nominalized results in the diagram shown in Figure 6.1.

In this formation, the previously discussed parliamentary calculus is intact. That is to say that, by being conceptualized as emergent from the failure of government, 'radicalization' and 'extremism' reinforce the need for effective government. In doing so, they restrict government failure as the government are deterred from the creation of oppressive policy by the risk that this might result in 'radicalization' and 'extremism'. In turn, this restricts the emergence of the words and the phenomena that they describe. This was seen in the preceding chapter where parliamentarians were shown to warn against oppressive government policy for the risk that it would foment 'radicalization' and 'extremism'. The effectiveness of this mechanism in restricting 'radicalization' and

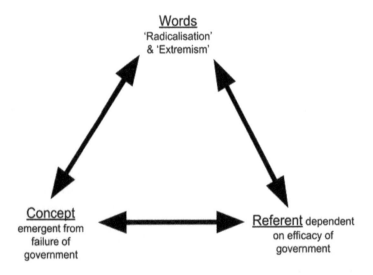

FIGURE 6.1 *The semiotic triangle for parliamentary calculus.*

'extremism' is supported by the corpus analysis that showed the words to be rare before they tended to be nominalized and showed a significant increase in their usage after their nominalization became common practice.

This interrelationship between the words, concept and that which they refer to collapses when the words are nominalized, coming to be seen as entities rather than processes. The concepts cease to be seen as emergent, and this results in the non-dynamic or ossified semiotic triangle shown in Figure 6.2.

By ceasing to be dynamic, the feedback loop that encouraged effective government and discouraged the emergence of 'radicalization' and 'extremism' is ossified. This means that the calculus that restricted the emergence of 'radicalization' and 'extremism' is no longer effective. As the referent has been deagnetified, it ceases to be seen as emergent from failure of government so no longer acts as a threat against oppressive policy formation. It would therefore be expected that nominalization of 'radicalization' and 'extremism' will result in the proliferation of both the words and concepts, as was seen in the preceding chapter.

While nominalization ossifies the semiotic triangle, the association of 'radicalization' and 'extremism' with violence sets up a new dynamic as is indicated in Figure 6.3. It should be noted that

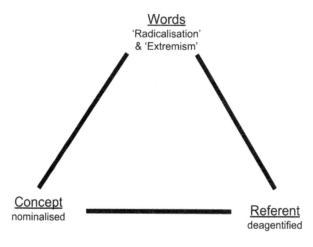

FIGURE 6.2 *Ossified semiotic triangle of parliamentary calculus.*

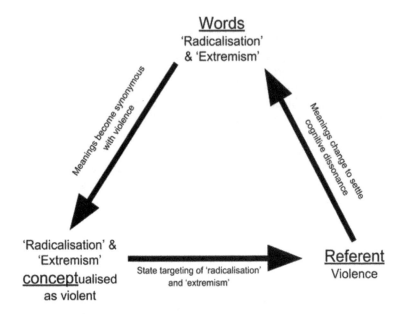

FIGURE 6.3 *The vicious semiotic triangle of 'radicalization' and 'extremism'.*

the arrows – in only pointing in one direction – indicate a constant cycle of reinforcement, as opposed to the feedback loop of the first triangle mentioned earlier.

In this version of the semiotic triangle, conceptualization of 'radicalization' and 'extremism' as violent will have two main effects:

- People will retreat from the expression of views that might associate them with 'radicalization' and 'extremism' for fear of being perceived as violent.

- The perception of the violence of 'radicalization' and 'extremism' will result in the state targeting them, as has been seen in the emergence of Prevent and counter-extremism more generally.

As was discussed in Chapter 1, the targeting of 'radicalization' and 'extremism' by Prevent has resulted in the silencing of debate for fear of being reported to the security services. This presents a mechanism by which the reconceptualization of 'radicalization' and 'extremism' as violent will result in the silencing of debate and – as was discussed in Chapter 2 – the silencing of debate undermines mechanisms by which peace is promoted in a democracy. Thus, as is also theorized in the diagram mentioned earlier, the referent – the political ideology referred to as 'extreme' or 'radical' or the 'extremist' or 'radical' person referred to – may then actually become violent, further catalysing the meanings towards violence. And, by the continuation of this process, 'extremism' can be seen to be emergent from a process that also foments the continued catalysation of violence.

The ossification of the semiotic triangle and the corresponding undermining of the parliamentary calculus that is precipitated by the nominalization of 'radicalization' and 'extremism' may have made the third semiotic triangle and the promotion of violence inevitable. That is to say that the escalation of 'radicalization' and 'extremism' becomes inevitable after their nominalization because the feedback loop by which they were previously restricted has been removed. Having lost this feedback loop, the possibility of failure of government increases as the warning against oppressive policy that 'radicalization' and 'extremism' offered has been removed. Thus, there is an increase in the potential for conflict as more oppressive policy is enacted. Ironically and perhaps inevitably, the nadir of this is policy such as Prevent that is aimed at preventing 'radicalization' and 'extremism'. Thus, it may be that 'radicalization' and 'extremism' have precipitated violence as a result of the vicious cycle that was set up by their nominalization.

The abandonment of parliamentary calculus

While this offers some understanding of what caused the increase in 'radicalization' and 'extremism' seen in the corpus analysis, it does not explain why the apparently well-established parliamentary calculus that was previously demonstrated by the usage of 'radicalization' and 'extremism' was abandoned. An understanding of this might be achieved by exploring and critiquing the philosophical foundations of New Labour and their 'new language' from which recent manifestations of 'extremism' have emerged. As is discussed earlier, Giddens' Structuration Theory underpins the approach of New Labour,[1] and in Chapter 2 we heard how Bhaskar did not initially recognize that there was a distinction between his and Giddens' conception of society and that it took his colleague Margaret Archer years to do so (Bhaskar 2016).

Professor Margaret Archer has explored the distinction between Bhaskar's Transformational Model of Social Activity (TMSA) and Giddens' Structuration Theory (Archer 1995), and the main distinction that she makes between the two theories is around emergence. She proposes that, in a Critical Realist account of society, structure and agency are emergent from one another and are therefore anterior to one another. Stucturationists, Archer tells us, reject emergence (Archer 1995), and she names their mutual constitution of structure and agency 'elisionism', also referring to structurationists 'systemness' of structure and agency, as a singular social practice (Archer 1995). Archer suggests that this singularity of structure and agency is incorrect and that they should be differentiated because of their distinct 'properties and powers which only belong to each of them and whose emergence from one another justifies their differentiation' (Archer 1995).

To summarize Archer's distinctions between Structuration Theory and Critical Realism: Critical Realist theorization takes account of change occurring over *time*; of the *relative autonomy* of structure and agency from one another; and of both structure and agency having the property of exerting independent causal influences in their own right. Though Bhaskar says that he did not initially recognize these distinctions, specifically those related to time (Bhaskar 2016), each can be appreciated in his theorization of the Transformational Model of Social Activity (TMSA), which distinguishes between the agency of individuals and the structure of society, showing how each is distinct from but effects the other (Figure 6.4).

The TMSA might be seen as an approximation of the philosophical underpinnings of the previously explored parliamentary calculus around 'radicalization' and 'extremism'. Parliamentarians who previously warned against oppressive policy for its capacity to foment an 'extreme' response from the electorate recognized the effect that they as individuals might have on the electorate (*society* in the TMSA) and that other *individuals* might have on them as members of society. As Archer explores, implicit in this understanding of the emergence of agency is that these changes happen over time. Failure to appreciate this change over time, the

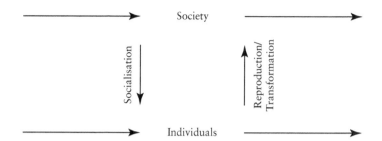

FIGURE 6.4 *Bhaskar's Transformational Model of Social Activity (TMSA) (Bhaskar 2016, Bhaskar 2016).*

elisionism of Structuration Theory that Archer describes (Archer 1995), might have precipitated the nominalization of 'radicalization' and 'extremism' and the subsequent inevitable erosion of the parliamentary calculus around the use of the words.

A recognition of these errors, a failure to recognize the emergence and relative autonomy and independent causal influence of structure and agency from one another over time, may explain the predisposition of the new language of New Labour to use nominalization. Other examples of this might be New Labour's use of 'the market', 'change' and 'globalization', and each – like 'radicalization' and 'extremism' – obfuscates agency and responsibility (Fairclough 2000). Thus, in the same way that nominalization of 'radicalization' and 'extremism' leaves us subject to them, nominalization of other tropes of Blair and New Labour such as 'the market', 'change' and 'globalization' also leaves us subject to them. In each case, had nominalization not occurred, each might be seen as emergent from human agency, and we would, thus, not find ourselves subject to them.

Who benefits from 'extremism'?

The counter-extremism industry

Returning to the exploration of 'extremism', the next question to be addressed is, who benefits from 'extremism'? Elaborating this question, we are asking, 'do those who benefit most from the way social life is organized have an interest in the problem not being resolved?' (Bhaskar 2016, Faure Walker 2019). At its most basic level, this can be answered by Upton Sinclair's famous quote: 'It is difficult to get a man to understand something, when his salary depends on his not understanding it' (Sinclair 1934). Following Sinclair, the importance of funding to the proliferation of orthodox terrorism studies (OTS) that support the government's focus on 'radicalization' and 'extremism' is now explored. As was explored in Chapter 2, orthodox (as opposed to critical) terrorism studies tend to address problems as they are seen in the world, rather than questioning the social structures that might have contributed to the existence of the problem in the first place (Joseph 2009). It is therefore in the nature of OTS that supports the expansion of the policing of 'radicalization' and 'extremism' not to question the extent to which policy has emerged from expanding budgets to tackle 'radicalization' and counter 'extremism'.

Kundnani and Hayes' formidable report on *The globalisation of Countering Violent Extremism policies* (Kundnani and Hayes 2018) explores the expansion of budgets to tackle 'radicalization' and 'extremism', and they focus on the budget of the European Union (EU) which is due to 'significantly increase' from the currently apportioned budget of €400 million between 2007 and 2020 (Kundnani and Hayes 2018). The mutual support for the British government and the EU in their agendas in this area is demonstrated by the

> consistent funding for the EU Syria Strategic Communications Advisory Team (SCAT), which has established 'a network of Member States looking into ways to tackle the national and local communications challenges in discouraging their citizens from travelling to Syria or other conflict zones'. SCAT is modelled on and staffed by former employees and consultants to the Research and Information Communications Unit, which leads the UK's counter-terrorism propaganda operations. 'Counter-narratives', or as they are explicitly referred to in one of the work programmes for the EU's security research programme, 'counter-propaganda techniques'. (Kundnani and Hayes 2018)

This funding to tackle 'extremism' has been applied across EU member states, including €314,000 to Cambridge University for the 'Development, testing and production of de-radicalising educational resources for young Muslims in Great Britain and the European Union' and €291,000 to the United Kingdom's West Yorkshire Police in 2011 for 'Social Media Anti-Radicalisation Training for Credible Voices' (Kundnani and Hayes 2018).

Not only does this indicate that a non-critical or orthodox approach to terrorism studies is being promoted in both academic and government fields, but Thompson (2018) has recently shone a light on the ridiculousness of regional police forces' social media campaigns which, like the Home Office's Counter-Terrorism Media Summary that is produced by RICU and is discussed in Chapter 1, appear to be more focused on the promotion of a threat than on addressing a problem.

> Like other counter-extremism 'initiatives', Prevent is a state-sponsored political construct that depends upon political marketing to promote it as a security proposition that can be justified by politicians and police as dealing with a real and present danger. (Thompson 2018)

Thus, it might be suggested that these well-funded social media campaigns serve more to promote than to address a threat of terrorism. The police receiving a £50 million fund to 'fight against terrorism' (PressAssociation 2017) at the height of austerity's winnowing away of their budget in other areas (Institute for Government 2020) might provide a motivation for their online posturing to promote the threat of terrorism.

The expansion of the UK government's 'strategic communications' – a thinly veiled rebranding of 'propaganda' that a Home Office official is reported as describing as 'sound[ing] horribly cold war' (Hayes and Qureshi 2016) – is described by Hayes and Qureshi in *'WE ARE COMPLETELY INDEPENDENT' The Home Office, Breakthrough Media and the PREVENT Counter Narrative Industry* (Hayes and Qureshi 2016). They document the creation of twenty supposedly independent civil society organizations and their close connection to the Research Information and Communications Unit (RICU) of the Home Office. The civil society organizations include the Armed Forces Muslim Association, family support groups, supposedly independent religious groups such as Imams Online and pseudo-academic supporters of counter-extremism such as the Quilliam Foundation that is described on its website as 'the world's first counter-extremism organisation'. The connection of these supposedly independent civil society organizations to government counter-extremism agendas is made by Hayes and Qureshi's compelling evidence to demonstrate that communications specialists Breakthrough Media have been funded by the Home Office and supported by Breakthrough Media to provide content and online hosting for the organization in question. It is perhaps not surprising that these organizations and their employees who are dependent on budgets to target 'radicalization' and 'extremism' are also the most vocal supporters of this policy area.

One such supporter is Tony McMahon who worked as a 'Consultant on CVE networks' for Breakthrough Media from 2013 to 2019. Describing his work on LinkedIn, he tells us that 'Breakthrough Media serviced the Home Office Prevent contract and my primary responsibility as a consultant was to build a civil society network from scratch starting in 2013' – apparently seeing no irony on being contracted by the state to 'build a civil society'. During this time, McMahon co-authored *The Battle for British Islam: Reclaiming Muslim Identity from Extremism (Khan and McMahon 2016)* with soon-to-be counter-extremism commissioner Sara Khan. Their book opens with the story of a teenage girl called Muneera, who tried to travel to Syria to join the Islamic State after she had been convinced by their online propaganda that it would be like an 'Islamic Disneyland' (one hopes that the name Muneera is a pseudonym to protect the girl's real identity). Curiously, this is a story that has been told to me by numerous senior police officers, members of the Home Office for Security and Counter-Terrorism (OSCT) and Prevent workers up and down the country. The story also made its way into a US Department of State press briefing in 2016 (Speckhard 2016), was repeated in a Ted talk by Yasmine Green, director of research and development for Google Jigsaw,[2] in 2018. And, even made its way into *Vogue* in 2019 (Hattersley 2019).

Each teller of the story claims that it demonstrates the need for counter-extremism strategies like Prevent. The trouble is that is does not show this. It is certainly a dramatic story that will horrify any parent. But, it is hard to see how a strategy like Prevent that makes children scared to discuss their desire to travel to the Islamic State – or any other political positions that might be considered 'extreme' by some – makes it more, and not less, likely that the alarm would be a raised to prevent them from travelling. This highlights one of the common conceits of counter-extremism and Prevent, that they are 'safeguarding' children. Counter-extremism strategies like Prevent make it less likely that children will discuss the concerns that would lead to government agencies like schools, social services and the police from becoming involved in their protection. Thus, what the story of Muneera shows is that our children would be more effectively 'safeguarded' by less and not more counter-extremism.

Neoliberalism and 'murketing'

The process of creating apparently independent organizations to spread a message, McMahon's work for the Home Office, 'to build a civil society network from scratch', mirrors the expansion of neoliberalism via the funding of apparently independent think tanks and has been extensively explored by both Mirowski (Mirowski 2018) and Fairclough (Fairclough 2000). Fairclough brings this analogy closer to home by exploring the emergence of New Labour and their spreading of 'the international discourse of neo-liberalism' via 'the proliferation of political think tanks' (Fairclough 2000). Mirowski brings this style of proliferation together with the state and security services preoccupation with social media when he describes the process of 'murketing':

> The neoliberals have developed a relatively novel way to co-opt protest movements, through a combination of top-down hierarchical takeover plus a bottom-up commercialization and privatization of protest activities and recruitment. This is the extension of the practice of 'murketing' to political action itself. Pop fascination with the role of social media in protest movements only strengthens this development. (Mirowski 2013)

Thus, the foundation of quasi-independent civil society organizations by Breakthrough Media to support counter-extremism might be seen as a continuation of the expansion of the neoliberal project from which they emerge.

Both Fairclough and Mirowski explain that a tenet of neoliberalism is 'a new penal common sense' that supports a 'retreat from public welfare' and 'a punitive stance towards those who are victims of economic change' (Fairclough 2000, Mirowski

2018). Returning to 'extremism', one can see that the 'new penal common sense' is aligned with the post-parliamentary calculus logic of 'extremism'. While parliamentary calculus insisted on social security to avoid unrest, neoliberalism calls for the retreat of public welfare and 'the normalisation of insecurity of employment' and 'criminalisation of deprivation' (Fairclough 2000). Having abandoned the parliamentary calculus that promoted social justice to avoid 'radicalization' and 'extremism', a commitment to the loss of public welfare makes the criminalization of resistance necessary to the maintenance of state power. As Mirowski explains, 'neoliberal policies lead to unchecked expansion of the penal sector' (Mirowski 2018). In this context, recent reports of Prevent being used to target environmental campaigners should be no surprise (Information Rights Tribunal 2018). Nor should it be a surprise that the government's Counter-Terrorism and Border Security Act (HM Government 2018) has faced criticism for the risk that it might criminalize opposition to counter-terrorism law itself (House of Commons 2018, para. 7–18).

The vicious cycle of targeting Muslims

While structurally, as has been explored earlier, 'radicalization' and 'extremism' are inclined towards the oppression of any opposition to the government, they have tended to be focused on the oppression of the British Muslim population. This targeting of Muslims is shown in the Home Office's own data that shows that 65 per cent of referrals to Prevent were for 'Islamist extremism' (Home Office 2017), an alarming number in light of the Office of National Statistics stating that only 4.4 per cent of the UK population are Muslim (Office for National Statistics 2012). The analysis carried out in the previous chapter indicates that this disproportionate targeting of Muslims might be related to earlier colonialist discourses that privileged British interests over resistance to the British Empire and movements for self-government – for example, Viscount Hinchingbrooke's denigration of the 'merits and cause of black Africa' in 1960.

As was explored in Chapter 2, this 'routine privileging of white interests' is described by critical race theory, which Crawford (2017) uses to convincingly explain the emergence of both Prevent and the government's promotion of Fundamental British Values. The decivilizing of Muslim lifestyles and celebration of white British norms as culturally superior that Crawford explores (Crawford 2017) are not limited to Prevent and the government's promotion of fundamental British values but are part of a broader Islamophobic narrative in British Society. This can be seen in the *Times* being criticized by the Independent Press Standards Organisation (IPSO) for presenting a 'misleading' and 'distorted' picture of a Muslim foster family (IPSO 2018) and the editor of the *Daily Express* admitting to a parliamentary committee that his newspaper had created 'Islamophobic sentiment' (House of Commons 2018), a trend that has been diligently documented by Miqdaad Versi for the Muslim Council of Britain (Subramanian 2018).

Alison Scott-Baumann and her team of researchers recently carried out the largest ever study on the experience of Muslims on the campuses of British universities (Guest, Scott-Baumann et al. 2020, Scott-Baumann, Guest et al. 2020). Not having set out to research Prevent, Scott-Baumann and her team found the strategy being referred to repeatedly in the 140 hours of interviews that they carried out with Muslim and non-Muslim students on six campuses (four universities and two Muslim colleges with courses validated by universities). Their book *Islam on Campus: Contested Identities* (Scott-Baumann et al 2020 OUP) focuses mostly upon their ethnographic findings, and their research report (Guest et al 2020) focuses mostly upon their online survey of 2,022 students attending 132 universities – it was this awareness of Prevent that brought me into contact with Scott-Baumann and led to our working together at SOAS University of London. A major finding of Guest and Scott-Baumann's *Islam on Campus* research was that Prevent appeared to promote anti-Muslim sentiment in some of the students who they interviewed and surveyed.

That the media has also continued to promote anti-Muslim sentiment suggests that the public has an appetite for it. This might also suggest that the government's strategy on 'radicalization' and 'extremism' is, like Islamophobic media stories, part of a vicious cycle of the vilification of Muslims that precipitates the public's appetite for their targeting by oppressive policy.

David Toube, policy director for the Quilliam Foundation that was noted earlier for its association with government, recently provided a demonstration of Mirowski's description of 'murketing' and its use of social media. Striking out on Twitter, Toube was quick to denounce Guest's and Scott-Baumann's genuine academic research that challenged the government line on countering 'extremism'. This involved *ad hominem* attacks on the authors and the citing of a blog that Toube had written for the Quilliam website. In his blog post, which he referred to as 'research' in his tweets, he misrepresents the data from the *Islam on Campus* report and then fails to sufficiently analyse the data that he does look at. This enables him to make his fallacious arguments against Scott-Baumann's and Guest's well-reasoned conclusions.

Interestingly, Quilliam's blog site refers to itself as a 'Journal', and, alongside Toube's reference to his blog as 'research', this offers a veneer of academic credibility without him having to submit to academic standards of peer and ethical review that would prevent much of his and Quilliam's work from seeing the light of day. Presciently, Toube further demonstrated the 'fascination with the role of social media' in murketing when he responded to an article that I wrote on 'Pseudoscience, Think Tanks and "Intellectual Landscaping": Exposing the Wilful Ignorance of the Right' (Faure Walker 2020) by making further *ad hominem* attacks against me on Twitter.

Toube's faux intellectualism has echoes of meetings that I have attended with civil servants working on counter-extremism and who also promote a veneer of academic credibility in their use of language to describe their work. Repeatedly referring to the 'peer review' and 'open source' of 'research' from government-commissioned quangos and agenda-driven think tanks without offering any indication that the standards expected of genuine academic work have been met. Toube has shown a continued interest in 'extremist ideology' (Toube 2020) yet fails to interrogate what he means by this or to examine his own ideological assumptions, and, as such, his blind defence of counter-extremism is unsurprising as, like Will Baldét, who was discussed in Chapter 2, his own writing and elegance to common-sense understandings of the world reveal the ideological nature of his position.

In this chapter it has been shown that 'extremism' has emerged from and contributed to the maintenance of neoliberalism. This is supported by the analysis of the preceding chapter that showed it to have emerged from the discourse of New Labour, an early adopter and exporter of neoliberalism. This has been catalysed by increasing budgets to target 'radicalization' and 'extremism', creating quasi-independent bodies – in a process that mirrors the expansion of neoliberalism – that constantly reinforce the need for more resources and policy interventions in this area. The press have faced criticism for their promotion of Islamophobia, and the government might also have a part to play in this cycle, their vilification and disciplining of Muslims fuelling a cycle that demands the further targeting of Muslims.

Prolific intellectual and 1990 Slovenian presidential candidate Slavoj Žižek has warned that democratic mandates might lead to the oppression of minorities:

> The problem is that democratic elections give such a Government a legitimization which makes it much more impervious to criticism by movements: it can dismiss movements as the voice of an 'extremist' minority out of sync with the majority that elected the Government. (Žižek 2011)

In light of this observation, Žižek adds that a strong civil society may be the most effective foil to government power in a democracy. That the British government has created a network of pseudo-civil societies and faux intellectuals to support their nadir of oppressive policy leads one to question what mechanisms might be left that could moderate the state's ever-expanding oppressive power (Bhaskar's power$_2$). The next stage in the approach to CDA described in earlier chapters aims to 'identify possible ways past the obstacles' to challenging this oppression, so lends itself to the exploration of Žižek's observations on government, democracy, 'extremism', and civil society. Thus, in the next chapter we explore ways past the problem of the emergence of 'extremism'.

CHAPTER 7

Challenging the violence of counter-extremism

Returning to Korzybski's dog biscuits

Chapter 3 opened with the apocryphal story of Alfred Korzybski's dog biscuits and how he would trick his students into eating them to demonstrate the power of words. Korzybski was clearly making a point beyond the palatability of pet food. He was showing his students that our world is intimately affected by the language that is used to describe it. What we don't know is if Korzybski went on to propose a resolution to the problem that he described; presumably he did not, as being unable to eat dog biscuits is hardly something to lose sleep over. Conversely, the violence that is precipitated by the emergence of 'extremism' is a problem that demands our attention. So, while we should not lose sleep over the dog biscuits, the emergence of 'extremism' demands that we progress with our analysis, and this moves us to ask the question, how can the emergence of 'extremism' be contested?

The problems associated with the emergence of 'extremism' and that need to be contested are the legislative and informant genres that emerge from the nominalization of 'radicalization' and 'extremism'. Nominalization in this context is emergent from the neoliberal discourse of New Labour that has obfuscated the parliamentary calculus that previously warded off the development of potentially oppressive government policy and the 'radical' and 'extreme' responses that it might solicit. While parliamentary calculus previously guarded against the emergence of civil unrest, the 'new penal logic' of neoliberalism (Fairclough 2000, Mirowski 2018) aims to address the civil unrest that might be inevitable to post-parliamentary calculus and the logic of neoliberalism. This new penal logic has led to a self-fulfilling cycle of the funding of quasi-independent think tanks and civil society organizations to target 'radicalization' and 'extremism' – rather than trusting our politics to deliver a harmonious society, the pre-crime industry has flourished. These organizations feed into the logic that drives the support for this ever-expanding area of policy as well as their own even-increasing budgets. That this new logic has been disproportionately focused on Muslims can be traced back to a colonialist discourse that routinely privileges white interests while decivilizing Muslims (Crawford 2017).

That these obstacles are intimately intertwined and related to one another suggests that their contestation will be a complex task. However, the earlier explored critique of structurationist elision and recognition of emergence indicates that, while still recognizing their emergence from one another, each obstacle can also be addressed individually due to its relative autonomy and for its exertion of independent causal influences (Archer 1995). In the following paragraphs we explore how this might be done.

In Bhaskar's original schema for critical realist CDA, he states, 'this stage . . . looks to hitherto unrealised possibilities for change in the way life is currently organised' (Bhaskar 2016). One unrealized possibility is the transcendence of the vicious semiotic triangle that was described in the preceding chapter. How this might be done is explored below by developing a theory that brings together both the semiotic triangle and Bhaskar's Transformation Model of Social Activity (TMSA). As explored in the preceding chapter, the semiotic triangle for 'extremism' suggests a dystopian cycle for the production of violence but the introduction of the TMSA – by bringing in an appreciation of the possibility of change over time – reveals the ongoing 'depth struggle' that in turn reveals a way towards a more utopian future. The depth struggle here relates to what Bhaskar refers to in his book of the same name as *Dialectic: The Pulse of Freedom* (Bhaskar 2008).

For to exist is to be able to become, which is to possess the capacity for self-development, a capacity that can be fully realized only in a society founded on the principle of universal concretely singularized human autonomy in nature. This process is dialectic; and it is the pulse of freedom. (Bhaskar 2008)

It is clear from the preceding chapter that 'human autonomy' is restricted by the violent discourse of 'radicalization' and 'extremism'. The recognition of the referential detachment that is necessary for the intelligibility of language (Bhaskar 2008, Bhaskar 2016, Bhaskar 2016) and is enabled by the theorization that will be carried out in this chapter will contribute to our understanding that our 'engagement with reality is inexorably linguistic and that reality must be referentially detached from [our] language use (Bhaskar 2008)

Bhaskar refers to this realization as a 'meta-reflexivity totalizing situation' that will allow for 'reflexive monitoring of everyday activities', a necessary step towards agency which he also refers to as 'transformative negation of the given' (Bhaskar 2008). This notional possibility of transcending the oppressive language that is described by this book presents a concrete utopia that might enable us to transcend the violence that is currently precipitated by 'extremism'. While it is often suggested that 'utopian thinking leads to the slaying of millions', Hegel's 'slaughter bench of history', Hartwig has explained that this conception is adopted by and sustains the oppressive aspects of society (Hartwig 2007), the oppression hiding the emancipatory dialectic that sustains it. Thus, the 'concrete' notion of 'utopia' is adopted unapologetically here and from a critical realist perspective more generally (Hartwig 2007, Bhaskar 2016).

The violence and oppression that emerge from 'extremism' create a barrier to the dialectic pulse of freedom. By failing to appreciate the dynamic nature of 'extremism', we are 'imprison[ed] in a non-utopian present without historicity or futurity' (Jameson in Hartwig 2007). This chapter describes a concrete utopia that enables us to have a history and future in the context of 'extremism' and, in doing so, will allow us the possibility of being released from its bonds.

The semiotic triangles described in the preceding chapter all presented a dystopian view of 'extremism' as in each case it inevitably spawned oppression and violence. To describe a more utopian semiotic triangle for 'extremism', we might start with the concepts of 'radicalization' and 'extremism' and consider the scenario in which they are conceptualized as non-violent. This would result in the state no longer targeting the referent, and strategies like Prevent would no longer be promoted so people would not be silenced by fear that they might be reported to the security services. Added to this, debate would not be silenced for people's fear that they might be perceived as violent. As explored in preceding chapters, in the context of the classroom, Parliament and in society more generally, this enabling of debate creates a mechanism by which the non-violence of all involved can be promoted. Through this process, the promoted non-violence of whoever is being referred to results in the meanings of 'radicalization' and 'extremism' becoming less associated with violence as the utopian semiotic triangle repeats itself. This results in the utopian semiotic triangle shown in Figure 7.1.

While the aforementioned theorization of the semiotic triangle and those in the previous chapter explain a number of processes in the development and emergence of 'extremism', they are each separate. Thus, a unified theory that incorporates each of the semiotic triangles is required if we are to fully understand the emergence of 'extremism'. To achieve such a theory, we need to first

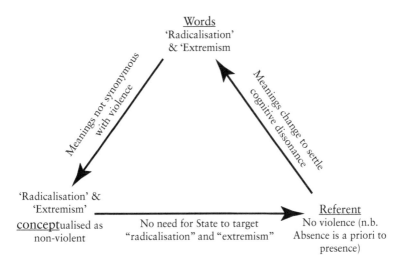

FIGURE 7.1 *Utopian Semiotic Triangle for 'radicalization' and 'extremism'.*

recognize that time is absent from the aforementioned theorizations and return to the earlier exploration of the distinction between Bhaskar's TMSA and Giddens' Structuration Theory. The semiotic triangles that have been described, like Giddens' theory, do not offer an account of change over time; it could be argued that their inexorable cyclical nature sees them stuck in time. To conceptualize the semiotic triangle in the context of time, we need to create a model that not only has a time axis, but also shows the progression from one triangle to the next as time passes. By drawing on the TMSA, which shows the emergence of the structure of society from the agency of individuals and vice versa over time, we can expand and unify the various semiotic triangles into the semiotic helix shown in Figure 7.2.

By bringing time into the theory like this, we can see not only how all of the preceding semiotic triangles might be linked to one another, but it also enables us to imagine how they might be transcended. The earlier versions of the semiotic triangle for 'radicalization' and 'extremism' forced us into an endless cycle of the reinforcement of violence. As ever, and perhaps especially, those who are apparently in power as state actors and who are fulfilling the cycle by the state targeting of 'radicalization' and 'extremism' are as subjected to the effects of 'radicalization' and 'extremism' as anyone else. Thus, we might follow Bhaskar in describing the vicious semiotic triangle as 'projectively duplicating a hyperreal world where slaves become masters' (Bhaskar 2008). The description of 'extremism' in the context of time enables us to transcend the 'projected duplication

FIGURE 7.2 *Semiotic Helix: Bringing time into the semiotic triangle.*

of the hyperreal world' as we can now envisage a notional future outside of the previously theorized cycle of violence.

Over the preceding two chapters, significant barriers to the transcendence of 'extremism' have been described – not least, ever-increasing budgets for the targeting of 'extremism'. The way in which these budgets have been used to promote a neoliberal penal logic through the creation of quasi-independent civil society organizations is a significant barrier to emancipation. It might be argued that the self-reflexive cycle that these quasi-independent civil society organizations and the logic of the violent discourse of 'radicalization' and 'extremism' create restricts the dialectic possibility of being by hiding the nature of being behind the aforementioned hyperreal world. And, as 'being [is] a condition for knowledge' (Bhaskar 2008), this also restricts the possibility of knowledge.

The theorization of the semiotic helix might allow for an understanding of our relation to 'radicalization' and 'extremism' and, thus, the nature of ourselves in a way that was not possible while being restricted by the logic of the vicious semiotic triangle. This knowledge may enable those who have been elided into the suffocating logic of 'extremism' to be released from its grip and to become. It must however be recognized that there are other barriers in the way such as the pseudo-civil societies that have emerged from counter-extremism and which are supported by the ever-increasing budgets that this industry calls for. Added to this, critical race theory suggests that the racist targeting of Muslims as is seen under Prevent is to be expected. As such, the theorization of a concrete utopian discourse for 'extremism' does not guarantee the undermining of the oppressive targeting of 'radicalization' and 'extremism'. However, in the world of real generative mechanisms that critical realism aims to describe, 'radicalization' and 'extremism' do appear to have made some contribution to this oppression. Thus, describing 'extremism' in a way that might transcend the previously described vicious semiotic triangle might make some contribution to the dialectical pulse of freedom and to the free flourishing of all. The theorization of the semiotic helix indicates that the violent discourse of 'radicalization' and 'extremism' can and should be contested and how this might be done forms the focus of the remainder of this chapter and the next and final chapter.

The possibilities for overcoming the promotion of violence by 'extremism' will take on two forms, ways in which this violence can now be surmounted and emergent emancipatory praxis that is yet to be realized. These problems include: the nominalization of 'radicalization' and 'extremism; the loss of parliamentary calculus; neoliberalism; the new penal logic; the legislative genre; the informant genre; the description of the semiotic helix; quasi-independent civil society and supporting budgets; and the vicious cycle of the racialized targeting of Muslims.

Some of the suggestions of how to overcome these problems made throughout this chapter – when taken in isolation – might appear to hold little chance of success. As Fairclough points out about the suggestions that might emerge from critical discourse analysis:

> The Government will not, I imagine, be that eager to take up these recommendations. Nevertheless, we must keep emphasising this: the way things are does not exhaust the possibilities for the way things could be. (Fairclough 2000)

However, taken as a totality of emergent possibilities for the transcendence of 'extremism', these isolated suggestions that the government and their well-funded quasi-independent civil society may not want to hear suggest possibilities for the way things could be. The pulse of freedom demands that we explore the problems associated with achieving these possibilities so that we might act on them. Each problem is explored and reflected on in the following text, so as to propose ways in which each might be transcended.

Nominalization of 'radicalization' and 'extremism'

The nominalization of 'radicalization' and 'extremism' is perhaps the most fundamental aspect of the emergence of 'extremism' that needs to be addressed if the problem is to be surmounted. It is fundamental as it hides the underlying causes of 'radicalization' and 'extremism' and, thus, prevents them from being addressed. This means that both policymakers and those subjected to policy to target 'radicalization' and 'extremism' are limited in their ability to address the problem. It is an uncomfortable thing to examine the language that we use as it dramatically challenges our preconceptions about the world. So, standing back and taking a metaView of language solicits strong feelings and resistance – as more than one civil servant has said of my work, 'you're reading too much into the language'.

Not only is nominalization a difficult subject to discuss, but it is problematic for the way in which it hides the underlying causes of 'radicalization' and 'extremism' and, in doing so, prevents their discussion and eventual resolution. Describing the underlying causes of 'radicalization' and 'extremism' is vital to their transcendence. However, I have experienced barriers to doing so, and this was exemplified in a public debate that had been organized by a community group in the London Borough of Slough with the support of the Home Office and with the stated intention of enabling people to discuss Prevent (Khaldun 2018). Audience members directed questions to a four-person panel that I was on alongside a local Prevent worker, a representative from the Home Office's Office for Security and Counter-Terrorism (OSCT), and the local chief inspector of police. As the event proceeded, the audience became palpably frustrated with the representative from the Home Office's failure to engage with their concerns. The concerns that they raised included frustration with UK foreign policy and the marginalization of Muslims due to austerity and Prevent itself. These concerns might be seen as describing failures of government as was explored in earlier chapters.

Halfway through the debate, I attempted to mediate by describing how nominalization of 'radicalization' and 'extremism' was masking their causes and making it hard for the other panel members to understand the frustrations of the audience. I was careful to situate my description in clear examples, many of which are described in the preceding chapters. The representative from the Home Office persisted in his ignorance of the contribution that 'radicalization', 'extremism' and Prevent made to the marginalization of Muslims, even in the face of the members of the audience joining me in describing this process to him. He did not respond to my suggestion that the nominalization of 'radicalization' and 'extremism' was problematic as he continued to use the words to describe deagentified phenomena. In response to my description of my research, he said that my concern was 'academic', inferring that it ought to be ignored as inconsequential. A number of audience members challenged him on his dismissal of actual research and approached me after the event to discuss their frustration that he had dismissed my research in this manner.

This wilful ignorance of research and expertise is similar to Michael Gove MP's infamous proclamation that 'we've had enough of experts' (Laybats and Tredinnick 2016, Sky News 2016). Both Gove and the aforementioned representative from the Home Office's disparaging of expertise presents a considerable challenge to the dissemination of academic research and expertise as they are not appealing to any rational argument. Rather, they are relying on a fallacious proclamation in the same way that Thatcher did in her catchphrase, 'there is no alternative', and which Bhaskar describes as a TINA compromise formation.

Both of the aforementioned examples of the disparaging of expertise are demonstrations of 'a truth in practice [that] is held in tension with a falsity in theory' (Hartwig 2007, Bhaskar 2008), as in both examples the individuals decrying of expertise demonstrate a contradiction in their practice which relies on those who they decry as 'academic' or 'experts'. Gove demonstrates this by his reference to economic forecasts in the same interview, economic forecasts presumably made by 'experts' who he has not had 'enough of', so he appears to have only 'had enough of experts' who don't support his agenda. Similarly, the Home Office representative in Slough decried 'academic' arguments while repeatedly referring to other academic research – albeit research that he either misrepresented or which was from the aforementioned counter-extremism supporting and Home Office-funded quasi-academic organizations.

While we might thus refer to both arguments as 'TINA compromise formations', there is an additional layer to the argument used in these two examples, 'a wilful blindness to evidence, a mistrust of authority, and an appeal to emotionally based arguments often rooted in fears or anxieties' (Laybats and Tredinnick 2016). Laybats and Tredinnick (2016) go on to explore how this type of 'post-truth political discourse' has been exacerbated by social media. That the government have led social media campaigns and quasi-independent civil societies to create and support their own echochamber (Thompson 2018) results in it being evermore urgent that the fallaciousness of these proclamations be called out. There is unlikely to be a silver bullet for the transcendence of this problem, but highlighting it alongside the other possibilities for transcending 'extremism' that are explored in the following text might lead to enough awareness to support the words being employed in a different way.

Loss of parliamentary calculus

The nominalization that is inherent to the new language of New Labour and that has continued to dominate political discourse since the demise of New Labour obfuscates the causes of and the human agency behind issues besides 'extremism', and Fairclough proposes that we might see a similar process in relation to words such as 'change', 'the market' and other facets of life (Fairclough 2000). Nominalization, thus, masks any alternative vision for the future. This is aligned with Laclau and Mouffe's critique of New Labour and the centrist left lacking 'a vision about what could be a different way of organising social relations' (Laclau and Mouffe 2001).

Laclau and Mouffe propose that the left go 'back to the hegemonic struggle' (Laclau and Mouffe 2001), and this indicates that the parliamentary calculus might not simply be a historical relic in the parliamentary records but could be something that the left ought to aspire to return to. The left should aspire to return to this moderating calculus as not only do Laclau and Mouffe propose it as a solution to the excesses of government but the analysis of previous chapters also supports this assertion. This is, however, easier said than done but Fairclough's suggestion for the promotion of 'real dialogue and debate' (Fairclough 2000) might go some way to supporting this.

As a description of a real generative mechanism for the moderation of oppression, parliamentary calculus describes a concrete utopia, for it is a real mechanism by which oppression is discouraged and, thus, by which the pulse of freedom is supported. However, as the moderation that parliamentary calculus encourages relies on responses to oppression, oppression is a necessary aspect of the calculus described, and it might therefore be described as less than utopian. Thus, while parliamentary calculus is certainly a real contributory factor to the depth struggle, its dependence on oppression indicates that its description does not get to the more fundamental and true order from which it emerges (Bhaskar 2012). So, while recognizing parliamentary calculus as an important mechanism to limit oppression, we should not hold it as sacred. For true emancipation, parliamentary calculus may perhaps itself need to be transcended.

Neoliberalism and the New Penal Logic

The seminal tome on the expansion of neoliberalism in the second half of the twentieth century is Mirowski's *Never Let a Serious Crisis Go to Waste* (Mirowski 2013). Mirowski does not offer any solutions to the neoliberal problem that he describes – one reviewer noting that he 'is careful, perhaps too careful, not to suggest any kind of positive alternative to the economics he derides . . . the book stays firmly at the level of critique' (Pryke 2015). However, Mirowski's exploration of the flaws and fallacies of neoliberalism might indicate what alternatives could look like. In fact, engaging with such a critique of neoliberalism reveals deeper parallels with 'extremism' than have already been explored. In the aforementioned review, while summarizing what critique Mirowski does engage in, Pryke indicates an alternative when he writes in relation to the 2008 financial crisis:

> The parlous state of academic economics meant that it was intellectually ill equipped to engage in any form of critical self-reflection. The absence of a rigorous methodology and the banishment of history and philosophy from the discipline, whilst simultaneously constantly proclaiming its scientific credentials . . . meant that economists quickly lost control of explanation of the crisis. (Pryke 2015)

When compared to Qureshi's withering critique of the study *The 'Science' of Pre-crime: The Secret 'Radicalisation' Study Underpinning PREVENT* (Qureshi 2016), the parallels between neoliberalism and the violent discourse of 'radicalization' and 'extremism' can be seen to run deep. Both lack methodological rigour, are historically and philosophically unfounded and, despite each of their repeated reference to their scientific basis, rely on too precarious a set of beliefs to be able to engage in self-reflection. In the same way that each of these traits meant that economists were ill-equipped to deal with the financial crisis of 2008 (Mirowski 2013), the counter-terrorism industry built around the targeting of 'radicalization' and 'extremism' holds little hope of effectively engaging with the problem of political violence.

While Mirowski is careful not to offer solutions – or to use the language of CDA, 'possible ways past the obstacles' that he describes – we might extrapolate and bring together two of his observations to form a possible solution. The first is the overarching thesis of his book:

> Since economists were caught off-guard during the onset of the crisis, both journalists and the general public had initially to fall back on vernacular understandings of the disaster, as well as cultural conceptions of the economy then prevalent. (Mirowski 2013)

The second is Mirowski's observation that neoliberals 'win by taking advantage of "the exception" to introduce components of their program unencumbered by judicial or democratic accountability' (Mirowski 2013). These 'vernacular understandings' and 'cultural conceptions' might, when applied to 'extremism', be taken to mean the pseudoscience of pre-crime (Qureshi 2016, Goldberg, Jadhav et al. 2017), the 'common sense' that supports counter-extremism and also the routine privileging of white interests that critical race theory anticipates. Each of these having been fallen back on in 'exceptional times' and the notion of terrorism being exceptional and therefore demanding an exceptional response has been debated extensively. The debate perhaps receiving the most attention when Max Hill QC (the government's Independent Reviewer of Terrorism Legislation) faced criticism in the press (Gibb 2017, McCann and Ensor 2017) for warning against the continued expansion of counter-terrorism legislation that he referred to as '"knee-jerk something must be done" lawmaking' (Max Hill QC 2017).

Bringing these problems together, we must be vigilant against falling back on 'vernacular understandings' and 'cultural conceptions' of 'extremism' and the pseudo-science that connects 'radicalization' and 'extremism' to terrorism, especially in exceptional times. These exceptional times may refer to the aftermath of an act of political violence but the ever-expanding problem of the emergence of 'extremism' might also be seen to be placing us in ever-exceptional times; the association of 'radicalization' and 'extremism' with violence suggesting that political divergence from the norm might always be exceptional due to the violence that is presumed to be manifest in the words.

As was discussed in earlier chapters, the new penal logic is consistent with and necessary to the maintenance of neoliberalism. It is necessary as the neoliberal submission to the 'justice' of the market dictates that there are necessarily losers who must by extension be controlled (Fairclough 2000). Mirowski cites the adage of Benjamin Constant, 'The Government, beyond its proper sphere ought not to have any power; within its sphere, it cannot have enough of it', as a favoured quote of neoliberals (Mirowski 2013). This is the logic that underpins the 'unchecked expansion of the penal sector' that is so characteristic of neoliberalism (Mirowski 2013), and New Labour's abandoning of the parliamentary calculus of old Labour opened the door to the unchecked expansion of this new penal logic. Where the former parliamentary calculus restricted government oppression and worked towards the maintenance of social justice, the logic of neoliberalism leaves social justice to the market and requires the new penal logic to control those who the market would inevitably fail.

Neoliberalism and its associated new penal logic has been presented as banal by Thatcher's proclamation that 'there is no alternative', an argument that was repeated by subsequent prime ministers, Blair and Cameron, as they persisted in the expansion of neoliberalism and its associated punitive trends (Bell 2014). As discussed in earlier chapters, this catchphrase has also been used to justify Prevent to me. While recent political leaders have presented it as banal in its presentation as the only option, neoliberalism is anything but banal for those on the margins who are impacted by its punitive logic. In Dan Hancox's *Story of Grime*, he also explores how the neoliberal agendas of New Labour that drove the gentrification of poorer areas of London was accompanied by repressive policing of the original residents who were often forced out of their own homes by the increasing property prices and developments that neoliberalism delivered (Hancox 2018). For the young black men who are the focus of Hancox's book, the neoliberal penal logic that resulted in the loss of their homes (Hancox 2018), surveillance of their families (Hancox 2018) and the suppression of their music (Hancox 2018) was anything but banal. The story that Hancox presents is all too familiar to the experience of my Muslim students who were targeted by the same new penal logic via Prevent. Many of my students who reported their sense of being surveilled by Prevent had, like the subjects of Hancox's book, also lost their homes due to the gentrification of East London.

While leading politicians have fallaciously claimed that there is no alternative to these punitive neoliberal agendas, Bell (2014) argues that there is, in her paper, 'There is an alternative: Challenging the logic of neoliberal penalty' (Bell 2014). She describes this as no small task as 'Delegitimizing neoliberalism and seeking to undermine its key logics will allow a greater focus to be placed on achieving social justice' (Bell 2014), arguing that this might be achieved by 'moving away from populism and becoming truly popular' (Bell 2014). Writing that this could be achieved by not only engaging policymakers 'but also with all those affected by the penal system, be they offenders, victims or onlookers' (Bell 2014). As has already been discussed, the government's creation of a pseudo-civil society has the capacity to drown out genuine community concerns. However, as well as describing the marginalization of young black men in London, Hancox also describes how their engagement in the political process contributed to the resurgence of the left in UK politics. He quotes grime MC JME:

> I'm alright if the NHS gets privatised. I'll just spit two bars, get a bit of money and go fix my ribs. But people that grow up with nothing – like I did – I'm doing it for them. I thought: 'you know what? I'm gonna make them have a voice'. (JME in Hancox 2018)

JME did make 'them have a voice'. When Prime Minister Theresa May called a snap election in April 2017, the Labour Party was 24 per cent behind her Conservative Party in the polls. Hancox describes how such a margin threatened to 'wipe out the British left for decades', perhaps providing a motivation for May having called the election at this time (Hancox 2018). However, JME and his fellow grime MCs and DJs, who had been born into the oppressed fringes of neoliberalism, had other ideas.

Their aptitude for social media had been nurtured by a decade of having to market their music without the support of major record labels, and this enabled them to reach millions who, like them, had been disenfranchized by neoliberalism. Not surprisingly, they were motivated by and threw their support behind the first major party leader to offer an alternative to the ideology that had marginalized them. Their campaign, epitomized by the #grime4corbyn hashtag that virally spread across social media, made a huge difference to the election by engaging those who Bell describes as 'affected by the penal system' (Bell 2014) and who would otherwise not have voted.

> It had been an election in which grime could very plausibly be said to have made a difference. Turnout nationally was at a 25-year high – and this was driven by an unprecedented surge in young and BAME voters. Ipsos Mori polling suggested the 18-24 vote increased 16 percentage points on 2015, while turnout among BAME Britons increased 6 points: the substantial majority of new voters, those who had not voted in the 2015 election, had chosen Labour. (Hancox 2018)

Labour in this election, unlike those under New Labour, presented an alternative to neoliberalism. In response to the injustice that had been meted out to young BAME voters by neoliberalism, they voted for change. The resurgence of the left indicates how parliamentary calculus functions when given a left of genuine opposition.

Legislative genre

While the legislative genre is an aspect of the new penal logic of neoliberalism and 'extremism', the notional possibility of overcoming this problem is better defined and may thus be more easily achieved than responses to neoliberalism and 'extremism' explored earlier. While the strength of the legislative genre lies in legislation, the protocol that accompanies any legislation also opens up the possibility for the problem to be challenged. Such a possibility was recently realized in response to a recent manifestation of the legislative genre and 'extremism', the Counter-Terrorism and Border Security Act (HM Government 2018). Government proposals for the expansion of counter-terror powers were criticized by the aforementioned government's Independent Reviewer of Terrorism Legislation, Max Hill QC, when he appeared before a Parliamentary committee to scrutinize the Bill that would eventually become the act referred to earlier.

As part of the scrutiny that any bill must undergo as it progresses through Parliament, parliamentary select committees make public calls for evidence in relation to the proposed Bill. In response to a call for evidence related to the proposed Counter-Terrorism and Border Security Bill (HM Government 2018) from the Joint Committee for Human Rights (JCHR), I submitted evidence related to the proposal that the Prevent Strategy be expanded (House of Commons 2018). By focusing my evidence on these aspects of the Bill, I was able to submit evidence within the parameters of the call for evidence but also join other individuals and organizations in calling for a full and independent review of Prevent. The JCHR would go on to cite mine and others' evidence in making the following call for a review of Prevent:

> We are concerned that the Prevent programme is being developed without first conducting an independent review of how the programme is currently operating. We are also concerned that any additional responsibility placed on local authorities must be accompanied by adequate training and resources to ensure that the authorities are equipped to identify individuals vulnerable to being drawn into terrorism. We reiterate our recommendation that the Prevent programme must be subject to independent review. (House of Commons 2018)

The JCHR, like other parliamentary select committees, is made up of members of the different political parties. While it is not possible to know if the aforementioned recommendation would still have been made without my evidence to the committee, the citation of my evidence (House of Commons 2018) in the section that leads to this recommendation suggests that it may have made some contribution. That the JCHR report has been written by a number of MPs with the aim of informing parliamentary debate indicates that it may have made some contribution to the scrutiny of Prevent in Parliament.

The legislative genre to legislate against 'extremism' has been theorized earlier to have emerged from New Labour, and Fairclough suggests that the problems of New Labour and the genres that it promotes might be transcended by promoting debate

(Fairclough 2000). Legislation requires that this debate take place in Parliament, and this ensures that, in a political system like the United Kingdom, anyone can contribute. While right-wing think tanks have come to dominate the debate, with organizations like the Policy Exchange and Institute for Economic Affairs sitting at the heart of government (Faure Walker 2020), the passage of legislation through Parliament ensures that independent and expert voices are able to inform legislation. The importance and potential for this was demonstrated when the Counter-Terrorism and Border Security Bill (HM Government 2018) finally received royal assent to become an act of Parliament. As a result of the recommendations of the committee that I had provided evidence to, an amendment to the bill made the Independent Review of Prevent a legal requirement for the government to fulfil.

While there is still much controversy over the Independent Review of Prevent, not least that it had to be delayed by a year after Prevent's greatest supporter, Lord Carlile, was employed as the reviewer before having to step down over his lack of independence, the demonstrable fact that legislation can be changed by reasoned academic arguments shows that the legislative genre that insists on the policing of 'extremism' is surmountable. With think tanks like the Policy Exchange and the Institute of Economic Affairs having close connections to government, Michael Gove MP having been chair of the former and the latter having groomed Dominic Raab MP through his political career, the possibility of informing government policy may seem remote. But, the passage of legislation through Parliament ensures that, while they may dominate government, right-wing think tanks are not able to dominate the writing of Law.

With standards of ethical and peer review holding academic work to a high standard that would prevent much of the 'research' of government supporting think tanks from ever seeing the light of day, I have recently been working with SOAS University of London to support academics to inform policy. It may seem self-evident that academia should be informing policy, rather than right-wing agenda-driven think tanks; however, this is not always the case, and the Policy Exchange's recommendations for gutting the environmental protections and housing standards enshrined the United Kingdom's planning and building regulations that were recently adopted by the government (Airey 2020). Speaking on BBC Radio 4, the writer of the report for the Policy Exchange, Jack

Airey, reveals the neoliberal logic of his proposals, 'if you do not own the land next to your home . . . if you want to object or stop the development then you should buy the land'. Airey's proposals infer that those without millions of pounds to spare do not have the right to protect their homes and, perhaps more importantly, the environment that they live in. His suggestions that have since been adopted by the government remove democratic rights of individual citizens and hand them to the market.

The gutting of the planning system and environmental protections on the advice of a right-wing think tank shows how far we are from independent voices such as academics informing policy. However, it is only by normalizing independent academic research as the trusted evidence to inform policy that there will be hope that the emergence of 'extremism' and the policy-led evidence to support it might be transcended.

Informant genre

Related to the legislative genre, the informant genre casts teachers and other public sector workers as informants. While the legislative genre has resulted in legislation – in the form of the Counter-Terrorism and Security Act (HM Government 2015) and the Counter-Terrorism and Border Security Act 2019 (HM Government 2019)– to enforce the informant genre, the informant genre preceded the legislation when the Trojan Horse hoax forced Prevent into schools a year before the legislation caught up (Chapter 1). That the informant genre preceded legislation to enforce it via the Counter-Terrorism and Security Act (HM Government 2015) and the Prevent Duty (HM Government 2015) indicates that there is at least one generative mechanism for the genre alongside the legislation from which it also emerges. My own experience of thinking that 'something had to be done' to address 'extremism', as was reported in Chapter 1, indicates that the mechanism might be found in language.

The vicious cycle of 'extremism' and the perpetual promotion of violence, by promoting the association of 'radicalization' and 'extremism' with violence, in turn promotes the informant genre by making it commonsensical that 'radicalization' and 'extremism'

– in their violent connotation – should be policed and suppressed by civil society and the security services. For the informant genre to be challenged, it is therefore essential that the association of 'radicalization' and 'extremism' with violence also be challenged.

The exploration of the informant genre is, perhaps, the most pertinent to me due to my former professional role as a teacher being recast to also embody the role of informant. As is discussed in the introduction, it was my being cast in this new role that first prompted me to take an interest in 'radicalization' and 'extremism'. Critical realism helps in efforts to answer the question of whether the informant genre can and should (and can't and shouldn't) be contested. As a professional requirement for teachers that is enforced by both OfSTED and the Counter-Terrorism and Security Act (HM Government 2015), Prevent must be followed by teachers. 'Must' as it is a legal requirement and overt refusal to follow Prevent could result in teachers losing their jobs. However, it is possible for this genre to be contested in less overt ways. This was seen when my lobbying against Prevent led to students – who had previously been silenced by the fear that the genre would lead to their being reported to the security services – being empowered to re-engage in political debate with me.

A broader example of this mechanism to undermine the genre might be seen in the Royal College of Psychiatrists' position statement on Counter-terrorism and Psychiatry (the Royal College of Psychiatry 2016). The statement is written so as not to suggest that Prevent is not followed – presumably to avoid accusation of undermining a legal duty – but a comprehensive critique and call for review of Prevent is proposed. In the same way that my vocal opposition to Prevent went some way to undermining the genre in my classroom, it is possible that this statement from the Royal College of Psychiatrists and others that may follow might do the same in the consulting rooms of psychiatrists, enabling their surveiled patients to speak more freely again

Description of the semiotic helix

It may seem that the problem of describing the semiotic helix is somewhat more abstract than the other problems explored in this chapter. However, from a critical realist perspective, the real generative mechanism that is described by the semiotic helix is no less real. In the previous chapters, it was theorized that failure to appreciate the philosophical foundations and history of 'extremism' that the semiotic helix describes was sustaining the vicious semiotic triangle and led to the promotion of violence. The description of the philosophical foundations and history of 'extremism' – as might be done by describing the semiotic helix – therefore becomes vital to the transcendence of violence. This promotion of the intricacies of language follows the advice of Fairclough, who explains that

> the language element has in certain key respects become more salient, more important than it used to be, and in fact a crucial aspect of the social transformations which are going on – one cannot make sense of them without thinking about language. (Fairclough 2003)

He writes this in reference to his discussion of the work of Bourdieu and Wacquant on neoliberalism (Bourdieu and Wacquant 2001), making it particularly apt to the critique of the emergence of 'extremism' that has been shown to be closely associated with neoliberalism.

As the most abstract problem related to the emergence of 'extremism', the difficulty in describing the semiotic helix may be the most difficult to address. An appreciation of change over time might however be achieved with or without an awareness of the helix, though it is proposed here that the helix might be a helpful way of understanding this. Thus, perhaps the priority should not be so much that we learn from history. Rather, to learn that we are in history. Doing so reminds us that we are engaged in an ongoing depth struggle against master–slave relations, and such recognition is necessary if we are to realize our concrete utopia and transcend the violence of 'extremism'.

Quasi-independent civil society and supporting budgets

The funding, formation and support of quasi-independent civil society by the government presents a significant problem for the surmounting of 'extremism' as the problem lies at the nexus of a mundane and a philosophical problem. The mundane was referred to in the aforementioned quote from Upton Sinclair, 'It is difficult to get a man to understand something, when his salary depends on his not understanding it' (Sinclair 1934). As was explained in the preceding chapters, the growing budgets to target 'radicalization' and 'extremism' provide a strong incentive for those who benefit from the quasi-independent civil society to not understand the philosophical problem on which their funding depends.

The TINA compromise formation that sustains these organizations is emergent from the linguistic connection that has been made between 'radicalization' and 'extremism' and violence – the proposal that policing 'extremism' will reduce the risk of future acts of violence. This categorical error is supported by the quasi-independent civil societies, which are in turn supported by the error as it ensures funding and support from the government. Thus, the perception that there is no alternative to the government's targeting or 'radicalization' and 'extremism', as has been said to me by civil servants, is not only based on a categorical error but has also resulted in 'the multiply mediated compounding of categorical error upon error' (Bhaskar 2008) as the funding for quasi-independent civil society that supports counter-extremism results in cycles of further support for counter-extremism and further funding.

To address TINA formations, Bhaskar proposes dialectic – which he defines as 'argument, change and freedom (and each rationally presupposes its predecessor)' (Hartwig 2007, Bhaskar 2008) – which will 'expand the universe of discourse so as to remove the contradiction between the erstwhile contraries' (Hartwig 2007, Bhaskar 2008). In a world that is dominated by master–slave relations (Bhaskar 2016), it may appear that there is little hope that more discourse will result in the triumph of the pulse of freedom but Bhaskar argues that any false demi-reality must be emergent from a more fundamental and true order (Bhaskar 2012). While resistance to a well-funded quasi-independent civil society whose existence supports the fallacy upon which it is based and which maintains an ever-increasing policy agenda and budget may seem futile, we should remember

That the emergent, false or oppressive level (of social being, i.e. demi-reality, which might also be called Tina-reality), is unilaterally dependent on the more basic, true, and autonomous order, even though it may dominate and even threaten its existence, just as it typically mystifies, occludes and denies it. (Bhaskar 2012)

Thus, it is quite possible that by revealing the demi-reality of common-sense understandings of 'extremism', considered analysis might reveal this 'more basic, true, and autonomous order' upon which they rely (Bhaskar 2012). This possibility might be explored by looking at a recent example of the government's quasi-independent organizations, the Commission for Countering Extremism. While the Commission presents itself as 'a transparent body operating independently of Government' (Commission for Countering Extremism 2018), it has faced much criticism from those who see it as anything but independent and Commissioner Sara Khan has, like the aforementioned quasi-independent civil societies (Hayes and Qureshi 2016), faced particular criticism for being a creation and puppet of the Home Office (BBC 2018, Grierson 2018).

In a recent statement that expressed the views of over 100 academics about the Commission (Islam21c 2018, The Gulf Times 2018), concerns were raised that the Commission had not engaged with recent criticisms of Prevent that had been expressed by the Joint Committee for Human Rights (House of Commons 2018). In this context, it might be suggested that the commissioner's subsequent evidence drive is a political tactic; with the Joint Committee for Human Rights having gathered evidence from genuine civil society organizations and this leading them to repeat calls for an independent review of Prevent (House of Commons 2018), the Commission's formation might be seem as a cynical move to gather 'evidence' that is more aligned with the government's agenda than the findings of the Joint Committee for Human Rights. While this might be a cynical move, the Commission's attempt to emulate the legislative genre has led to ways in which it might be challenged and, perhaps, co-opted to lobby against the expansion of strategy to counter-'extremism'.

The Commission for Countering Extremism's charter was published on the government website, and in a section titled 'How it will work', it is stated that the commission will 'advise and agree with the Home Secretary the Commission's work programme and the remit and terms of reference for the studies it proposes to undertake'

(Commission for Countering Extremism 2018). In a meeting at the Home Office, I was assured that these terms of reference would ensure that any evidence submitted to the Commission would be published in their final report. This assurance was offered to encourage me and other critics of Prevent that this was not a cynical exercise and that we would be heard and, therefore, should engage with the Commission.

According to the Commission's charter that was published in March 2018, the Commissioner should 'agree with the Home Secretary the Commission's work programme and the remit and terms of reference for the studies it proposes to undertake' (Commission for Countering Extremism 2018). Yet, when I met with the representatives from the Home Office four months later in July, the Commission was two months into their 'evidence drive' and had not published their terms of reference. It was only after a series of questions in Parliament, most notably from the Bishop of St Albans on 13 September, that the Commission were forced to publish the terms of reference of their work, on 20 September, seven days after the Bishop's questions were raised. However, when the Commission's terms of reference were eventually published, they offered no such reassurance and framed the Commission's work on how much of a threat 'extremism' posed and how it should be addressed, denying the possibility that they would gather evidence to question the need to counter 'extremism'.

Such detailed focus on the approach of an obscure government commission might be dismissed as pedantry but Qureshi explores the importance of such knowledge. His focus is on his work to expose the pseudoscience of pre-crime (Qureshi 2016) which has been discussed in previous chapters and which he says,

> Highlights how important knowledge is. We should not simply accept generalised assumptions that are made within the security context, especially, without a thorough investigation of what the terms being used are, and what science or knowledge base underpins those assumptions. (Qureshi 2018)

Going on to say,

> Knowledge, as a site of resistance, permits us to re-own our identity, as well through language and narrative. Faux-knowledge,

when applied to communities, serves only as a weapon to harm them (Qureshi 2018).

Thus, while perhaps pedantic, focus on the construction of 'faux-knowledge' via these quasi-independent organizations must be a constant focus for resistance of oppression, and this can be no more important than when associated with the systematic and historical oppression of Muslims.

Vicious cycle of racialized targeting of Muslims

The targeting of Muslims by Prevent is the nexus of numerous historical and sociological factors. Outside of the various vicious cycles for the catalysing of oppression theorized here, critical race theory offers some frame of reference from which to understand this routine privileging of white interests and the corresponding dehumanization of Muslims (Crawford 2017). The privileging of white interests can be seen throughout history; and writer, civil rights advocate and visiting professor at Union Theological Seminary Michelle Alexander's *The New Jim Crow* (Alexander 2010) explores this in the American context to show how the shackles of slavery have morphed into racist drug laws and a racist criminal justice system. Closer to home, Hancox's book, *Inner City Pressure: The Story of Grime* (Hancox 2018), sees the vilification of grime as connected to a long history of racialized policing in the United Kingdom that was – like the vilification of Muslims – stoked by 'the burgeoning New Labour disciplinary regime' (Hancox 2018). The parallels with Hancox's story of the racist policing of grime and more recent strategies such as Prevent run deep: both resulted in the controversial targeting of minority ethnic communities in an effort to reduce violence; both failed to address any underlying causes of violence; both emerged from the new penal logic of neoliberalism and New Labour, forcing an outgroup to conform or face sanction; and, both were manifested in state surveillance that did untold damage to community relations and individuals within the communities targeted.

The harm done by recent targeting of Muslims in the name of the War on Terror is investigated by Asim Qureshi, who makes repeated reference to *The New Jim Crow* (Alexander 2010) in his exploration of the harm done by the trauma associated with the state targeting of generation after generation of the Muslim community in the name of the war on terror (Qureshi 2018). In the face of the extensive literature and testimony to the harm that these racist structures cause, we might ask why they persist? Qureshi offers an answer.

> Without an enemy, without an outsider to feed those flames, those in power will lose their position of control. (Qureshi 2018)

The analysis of previous chapters adds to this picture by drawing a connection between colonialist discourses from throughout the last century and the current targeting of Muslims by Prevent and counter-extremism. The targeting of Muslims having enabled the oppression that Britain had meted out to 'foreign' people under its Empire to turn inwards and onto Britain's home population. The focus on Muslims might have been further catalysed by European identity and Derrida is credited with exploring the need for Europe to have an outsider – Islam – to sustain its own identity. (Isyar 2014)

With such strong historical precedents, the surmounting of this problem might – like the others discussed in this chapter – seem impossible. However, Alexander ends her book with a quote from James Baldwin's advice to his young nephew, who, he says, has been 'born into a society which spelled out with brutal clarity, and in as many ways as possible, that you were a worthless human being' (Baldwin in Alexander 2010). While Baldwin is referring to his nephew being perceived as 'worthless' for the colour of his skin, we might extend his concern to any number of other racist structures and representations. Not lest to the racialized targeting of Muslims that is discussed here and his advice continues to be as valid today as it was half a century ago when Baldwin wrote:

> those innocents who believed that your imprisonment made them safe are losing their grasp on reality. But these men are your brothers – your lost, younger brothers. And if the word integration means anything, this is what it means: that we, with love, shall force our brothers to see themselves as they are, to cease fleeing from reality and begin to change it. . . . We cannot be free until they are free.

In offering this hope, Baldwin is elaborating an argument that is closely aligned with Bhaskar's description of the 'more basic, true, and autonomous order' referred to earlier (Bhaskar 2012). We will not only come closer to approaching this truer order by overcoming the racialized targeting of Muslims, but also by overcoming all the problems that are associated with the emergence of 'extremism'. The next and final chapter will show that surmounting these problems is no easy task as they are part of a concatenated crisis, 'the crisis system' (Bhaskar 2016). But appealing to the metaReality that Bhaskar describes in his later work shows how this might be achieved.

CHAPTER 8

The crisis of 'extremism'

Stuck in an alleyway

On 1 April 2009, I was stuck in an alleyway off Bishopsgate, a street in the financial heart of London. I had come down to Bishopsgate to join the Climate Camp protest and was now trapped along with thousands of other protesters. Climate Camp was one of a series of peaceful protests that were held across London in response to the G20 summit of world leaders who were meeting in London to discuss their response to the recent financial crisis. The financial crisis had revealed the fragility of global financial systems that relied on unsustainable regimes of credit and debt; the collapse of this system would come to be known as the credit crunch. The week of protests saw numerous events and thousands of protesters peacefully marching through London to demand that the decisions that world leaders made at the summit would put people and the planet above the continuation of unsustainable and exploitative financialized economics. The Climate Camp was aimed to raise awareness of carbon trading as a significant aspect of this financializaton, enabling corporations to continue polluting while paying to 'offset' their environmental harm.

In the day leading up to the Climate Camp, I had been keenly following the news between teaching lessons in the school in North London where I was the Head of Geography and, like my fellow protestors, had been undecided as to whether I should join the protest or not throughout the day. Around noon, reports came in that the newspaper seller Ian Tomlinson had died after being assaulted by the infamously violent Tactical Support Group (TSG) of the London Metropolitan Police, and this was accompanied by images of bloodied protestors and details of many people being 'kettled' for hours. Kettling was a now-infamous tactic of the police to contain protesters in ever-tighter and crowded cordons, holding people against their will for many hours. Reportedly to prevent the protestors from causing harm, kettling was much criticized for being a collective punishment that relied on illegal detention of protestors. Added to this, there was very little evidence of violence from the self-proclaimed peaceful protestors, yet news footage at the time showed ongoing violence from the police.

Later in the afternoon of the same day, I was informed that the police had met with the organizers of the Climate Camp and agreed that they would respect our right to protest. This gave me the assurance that I needed to take a bus into Central London after work and join the protest. Arriving at the camp, there was a carnival atmosphere with protestors dancing to mobile solar powered sound systems and chatting with the police. However, the situation soon took a sinister turn as police numbers swelled and members of the TSG with riot shields started to push the crowd in on itself. This was the moment that I found myself trapped in the alleyway off Bishopsgate and witness to a violent incident by a police sergeant who I reported to the Independent Police Complaints Commission (IPPC) and which was also reported in the national press:

> Rob Faure-Walker, 27, a teacher who witnessed the alleged assault and has given evidence to the IPCC, said police and protesters had been talking and joking amicably before the sergeant arrived. 'He just burst through the police cordon, pushing a couple of police out of the way,' Faure-Walker said. 'He picked a woman up off her feet and threw her to the ground. It is my opinion that she was lucky not to have been more seriously injured than she was. She had her back to him at the time, and was talking to someone else, when it happened. I've no idea why he did it. Even other police officers looked shocked at what happened.' Faure-Walker demanded the officer's badge number, which was attached to his shoulder. 'He walked around looking agitated for the next few minutes before I lost sight of him.' Separately, a journalist demanded the officer's number after noting what he saw as the aggressive treatment of demonstrators around the same time. By the following day, when he was filmed striking

Fisher, the sergeant's badge number was concealed. Faure-Walker said he recognised the sergeant as the officer who had thrown Surridge to the floor when he saw footage of the attack on Fisher broadcast on the news. (Lewis 2009)

This incident led to my contribution to legal campaigns against oppressive police tactics (Al Jazeera English 2009). As well as the more physical policing of protests, oppressive police tactics at the time included the undercover monitoring of protest groups and individuals. This was a frequent topic of conversation – and paranoia – at the time, and these concerns were realized by later media reports that revealed that the police had been monitoring members of the same protests that I had been part of (Hattenstone 2011).

Prevent and counter-extremism have clearly emerged from the same logic that seeks to rationalize the policing of peaceful protest by presuming that this will thwart potential future acts of violence. As well as being used to fallaciously cast all Muslims as a potential violent threat, this logic has more recently been turned back against environmentalists as Prevent has been used to target environmental protestors (Pidd 2018); Greenpeace has been included alongside neo-Nazis in advice issued by the Counter-Terrorism Police (Dodd and Grierson 2020); and the oil industry funded free-marker think tank Policy Exchange, which includes senior Conservative politician Michael Gove MP as a founder and chairman, has called for environmental protest group Extinction Rebellion to be designated 'extremist' (Hughes 2019).

The G20 protests that followed the financial crisis were in part focused on the ongoing environmental crisis. And, these crises of the economy and the environment can in turn be connected to a crisis of politics and identity more generally, as democracy and individual conscience are undermined by the policing of peaceful protests. This concatenated system of crises has been described by Bhaskar and other critical realists as the crisis system (Bhaskar 2016, Naess and Price 2016):

The various crises feed into each other: the ecocrisis exacerbates the economic crisis, which produces ethnic and political tensions, which threaten the international political structure or system; so that we have in effect the concatenation of the crises in such a way that they mutually reinforce one another. (Bhaskar 2016)

The analysis of the preceding chapters might lead to the conclusion that we are subject to the various logics of 'extremism'. That we are trapped in the vicious cycle of violence and 'extremism' or under the constant threat of the new penal logic. While this is true, we are to a certain extent trapped, and these powers are not inexorable. The oppressive structures of power$_2$ relations are not inexorable as they hide and are dependent on a deeper and emancipatory truth, as has been explored in the context of the dialectic pulse of freedom (Bhaskar 2008). While inevitable, our emancipation and the pulse of freedom is in a dialectic with the master–slave relations that hide it and is thus not always realized. In exploring the 'concatenated global crisis' of ecological, ethical, economic and existential crises, Bhaskar points towards some of the theory elaborated in this book by describing an aspect of the existential crisis in 'violence and war, terror and the threat of terror' (Bhaskar 2016).

This book has explored some of the generative mechanisms for the concatenated crises and has investigated how they are mutually supportive and emergent from one another. However, it has also been shown that they are not inevitable and that the pulse of freedom demands that they be overcome. Bhaskar describes the crisis system as 'the crisis of the e's', ecological, ethical, economic and existential crises (Bhaskar 2016); so, this book might be seen as a description of a fifth 'e' as 'extremism', which has been shown to be intimately connected to these four other crises. They, therefore, provide a framework by which our positionality (as social beings) might be understood in the context of 'extremism', so each of the other crises is now explored in turn. As these are social concerns, the exploration is necessarily personal as I draw on my experience to describe the impact of each crisis in the first half of the chapter. While the crises tend to be negative, they are not cause to despair, and an appeal to metaReality indicates that the oppressive forces of counter-extremism can and should be transcended. To this end, this chapter and the book closes with the imminent critique of the latest attempts to impose and justify counter-extremism, both in the United Kingdom and around the world, and in an exploration of how the pseudoscience of counter-extremism might help us to better understand the fallacies of supposedly scientific thinking that have led to the British and American government's disastrous response to other policy areas, including climate change and global coronavirus pandemic.

Ecological crisis

The Climate Camp was not the only environmental protest that I was involved in around the time of the financial crisis. My commitment to see change towards a future in which the protection of the planet is a priority saw me take part in countless political actions to raise awareness of the ecological crisis that we face.

> Dozens of cyclists blocked a London bridge in protest at the Government's environmental policies. . . . Protester Rob Faure Walker, 27, a teacher from north London, said the Government was failing 'in any way' to plan to reduce carbon emissions. . . . Mr Faure Walker spoke out against the building of new coal-fired power stations and the expansion of Heathrow airport. . . . 'People have to realise that they can't live their lives the way that they have become accustomed to,' he said . . . 'We can't fly short-haul whenever we want.' (BBC 2009)

Taking part in these mass protests had bought me into contact with oppressive aspects of state power. As well as bearing witness to the physical assault of protesters by the police, I also found myself subject to kettling and occasional violence from the police (Al Jazeera English 2009). 'Extremism' is not only used directly to target and suppress protests against the ecological crisis but has also distracted me from the very same struggle. This has occurred as I find myself working to critique 'extremism' rather than continuing in my former role as a geography teacher, a primary role of which is the promotion of a sustainable ecological future for the planet. This demonstrates the difficulty of responding to the crises as we are inevitably drawn from one and into the next, presenting a visceral ethical crisis over how to proceed in the face of these multiple problems that the pulse of freedom urges us to engage with.

Ethical crisis

The ethical crisis is experienced as a sense that we are not able to do enough to respond in an ethical manner to the crises that we are faced with. During my prior engagement in environmental activism,

I saw it as a mark of some success when commitments in support of environmental protection made their way into mainstream politics as all of the main political parties made pledges to environmental protection in their manifestos for the 2010 general election. My concern for the environment was also a motivation for becoming a schoolteacher, training as a geography teacher so that I might be able to teach others about the importance of protecting world around us. This gave me a sense of ethical fulfilment. In critical realist terms, engaging with the 'inherent value of nature' (Calder in Hartwig 2007) through dialogic engagement in the problem of ecological destruction was my concrete utopia, as I was able to work towards the resolution of the environmental crisis that was my primary concern.

While I have disengaged from environmental activism, my concern for the environment has not diminished. Though, perhaps an empirical manifestation of my own Western upbringing, this leads to a sense of guilt and even hopelessness at times. This is how the ethical crisis is felt as I am unable to respond to all of my concerns as a result of my own limited resources. While I am fortunate to now work in academia and to be able to pursue my critique of the crisis of 'extremism', a lack of alternative options forces many others to continue to work in schools and adopt the Prevent Strategy. This is a concern that I have discussed with many former colleagues, and while I was involved in a panel discussion after a play about the Trojan Horse hoax in Birmingham, an audience member also expressed this concern. Unlike me, they did not have an alternative career to fall back on, and they aired their own frustration and helplessness at feeling trapped in a job that forced them to adopt counter-extremism strategies that they did not agree with. This teacher and my former colleagues were forced into this ethical crisis by a corresponding economic crises.

Economic crisis

Described by Bhaskar as 'the economy becoming disembedded from social structure' (Bhaskar 2016), the economic crisis has been compounded by 'extremism', but this isn't the whole picture. Journalist and academic Warwick Mansell (2007) has explored the recent obsession that governments around the world have with exam data, and an aspect of this has been teachers being forced – in response to the precariousness of their employment – to focus solely on their pupils' exam results, rather than on their holistic education. As Mansell (2007) and the House of Commons Children, Schools and Families Committee report on Testing and Assessment (House of Commons Children Schools and Families Committee 2008) have explored, there is a fundamental difference between what is taught, what is learned, what is tested and the test score. And, the failure of policymakers to make these distinctions has resulted in teachers being compelled to focus on the test score. This compulsion is a financial one as teachers' salaries are judged by the test scores of their pupils in the form of performance-related pay (Mansell 2007), and school budgets are determined by the number of pupils in the school, their parents' decision about which school to send them to largely guided by the test scores (Mansell 2007). Thus, the money that teachers receive has become 'disembedded from the real economy' (Bhaskar 2016) or their ability to teach their students, presenting a very real existential crisis for teachers.

I experienced this existential crisis for the majority of my teaching career, constantly torn between providing my students with what I regarded to be a valuable education and coaching them to pass national tests – these two tasks not always being aligned. This means that the compulsion that I and other teachers coach our students to pass national tests presents a very real existential crisis to being a teacher. That this pre-existing existential crisis is now accompanied by the informant genre that has been imposed on teachers by Prevent only serves to compound this crisis. The crisis deepens as the interpersonal relationships between teacher and student that are described as vital by educational theorists as diverse as Buber (Buber 1923, Buber 1947), Dewey (1916), Freire (1970) and White (2017) are undermined.

Existential crisis

The existential crisis stems from teachers no longer being paid for providing an education to their students. As discussed earlier, teachers are now dissuaded from engaging in their students' education, in favour of a narrow focus on improving their students' ability to perform well in tests, while also acting as informants on their students. The teacher or pedagogue has been replaced by a narrow-focused bureaucrat and informant. Callahan (1962) warned of this trend away from education and towards bureaucracy and testing as far back as 1962 in his book, *Education and the Cult of Efficiency* (Callahan 1962). He describes this regime of teaching to the test as emergent from early management consulting of the 1910s to 1930s and the desire to measure. The teacher and the education that they could provide is being tested and measured out of existence. While the interpersonal relationship of teacher and pupil might have previously been a sanctuary from this harm, it too is now threatened by the surveillance of Prevent and the informant genre.

While these trends in education present an existential crisis for the teacher, the creation of the faux civil societies that were discussed in the previous chapter present an existential crisis for the state. As has been discussed in the preceding chapters, this quasi-independent civil society is drowning out the voice of real civil society. This means that the quasi-independent civil societies, which were presumably set up with the intention of supporting the state, actually destroy a mechanism by which the state would otherwise be kept democratically accountable. They are contributing to the destruction of the democratic state.

Difficulties in overcoming the crisis system

Related to the crises discussed earlier are challenges to overcoming them, and Bhaskar describes four 'impediments to the realisation of the good society', including the domination of personal by social relationships; a deficit in solidarity; the atrophying of the public sphere; and the increasing lag of moral evolution of the species behind its technological evolution (Bhaskar 2016). Examples of each of these have been discussed earlier. The social relations promoted by 'extremism' are forced onto and weaken interpersonal relations between teacher and pupil. A failure in solidarity has enabled the emergence of 'extremism' as Prevent would have been universally opposed and never emerged were there not a deficit in solidarity. This lack of solidarity is akin to the 'democratic deficit' that Scott-Baumann et al. refer to throughout their book, 'whereby citizens are ignorant of aspects of their relationship with the state and the Government sees no need to enlighten them' (Scott-Baumann, Guest et al. 2020). From the existential crisis of teachers, to the undermining of authentic civil society, to the rise in violence in response to the silencing of dissent, the public sphere does appear to be in decline. Bhaskar's final point that relates to technology is also pertinent to Prevent.

One of the most infamous online scandals in recent years has been the unmasking of the data and marketing company Cambridge Analytica, and their possible illegal and immoral influence on elections (HM Government 2018). Accused of illegally using Facebook data to predict and influence the behaviour of voters in elections around the world, they came under scrutiny in the press (Guardian 2018), and this led to the questioning of former Cambridge Analytica employee and whistle-blower Christopher Wylie by Parliament's Digital, Culture, Media and Sport Committee in 2018. In his testimony, Wylie reveals morally questionable practices to influence voters in elections in the United Kingdom and around the world. He also reveals a connection between Cambridge Analytica's parent company (SCL) and Prevent, inferring that the government might have been engaging in morally questionable technological practices in relation to countering 'extremism'.

> There is a quote from somebody who until very recently ran the Prevent programme . . . that doesn't mean that [SCL] work on Prevent but I know that people who have worked on Prevent have also worked with SCL on projects. It is a question to maybe ask the Home Office. (HM Government 2018)

While this passing reference to Prevent might not under normal circumstances merit a second thought, it is made notable by Bhaskar's prediction of the emergence of questionable technological practices from the crisis system. Given the prescience of Bhaskar's observations about the crises, we might take note of his final point, that there is a lag in our moral evolution that may be enabling the emergence of these questionable technological practices (Bhaskar 2016).

Wylie's evidence against the moral crisis of Cambridge Analytica; protests against the economic and ecological crises; and opposition to the emergence of 'extremism' might be seen as aspects of the 'drive to freedom' that are 'clearly identifiable throughout the world today'. Bhaskar cites examples of the Arab Spring in 2010 and the Egyptian revolution of 2011 as other examples of this (Bhaskar 2016). Up to this point, I have focused on these 'pulses of freedom' as dialectic responses to the master–slave relations of the crisis systems that they challenge. The opposition of the pulse freedom to the crises of ecology, extremism, ethics, the economy and existence places us in the dialectic, or a world of duality. While this enables the pulse of freedom to be manifest, it does not transcend the oppressive forces that our freedom opposes.

To transcend this duality and the oppression on which it depends, we must seek the truer world of non-duality. At the end of the last chapter, we saw that James Baldwin had pointed towards this 'more basic, true, and autonomous order' (Bhaskar 2012) in his letter to his nephew. It is this 'metaReality' that we now explore.

metaReality and PREVENT

Bhaskar has proposed the predominance of metaReality in the examples of the trust (metaReality) that underpins commercial transactions (demi-reality) and in war (demi-reality) presupposing peace (metaReality). In both instances and in the similar situation that Baldwin describes to his nephew, the demi-real can only exist in consideration of the metaReal. That this logic does not work in reverse – that is, trust can occur without commerce and peace without war – demonstrates that the demi-real is not required to sustain metaReality and suggests the predominance of metaReality (Bhaskar 2016).

All of the problems described in this book – that is, the nominalization of 'radicalization' and 'extremism', the loss of parliamentary calculus, neoliberalism, the new penal logic, the legislative genre, the informant genre, the description of the semiotic helix, quasi-independent civil society and its supporting budgets, and, the vicious cycle of racialized targeting of Muslims – exist within the dystopian logic of 'extremism', a demi-real world of master–slave relations. They are all contingent on a lack of trust, a lack of solidarity, a lack of understanding and the presumption of violence over peace. Neoliberalism and the new penal logic are sustained by the acceptance of the predominance of the market and the need for winners and losers (Fairclough 2000). Both the legislative and informant genres and the racialized targeting of Muslims rely on a lack of trust and solidarity and a presumption that violence will emerge if not controlled. The creation of quasi-independent civil society is an extension of this demi-real logic.

Challenging these problems is made difficult by the imposition of demi-reality. My time and resources are limited, and the impositions explored earlier compelled me and other teachers to receive training in Prevent when we might otherwise have been engaged in more meaningful activity such as teaching. Being forced to adopt Prevent presents a very real existential crisis to the role of teachers and others compelled to engage in counter-extremism, critical realism's recognition of an ontology of multiple generative mechanisms, and distinction between demi-reality and metaReality enables the proposal of a concrete utopia in response to this crisis. In this context, this means engaging with Prevent as is required professionally (demi-reality) while at the same time arguing for the dissolution of Prevent (metaReality). Thus, while enacting Prevent requires a split between one's embodied personality and ground state, recognition of the distinction between the two might allow us to function within both of these apparently contradictory planes of reality.

As discussed in Chapter 1, one of the fundamental problems that emanates from 'extremism' and which prompted my concern was that my students had been silenced because they feared that Prevent meant that speaking out could result in their referral to the security services – they were being silenced by the demi-real world of Prevent. My subsequent lobbying against counter-extremism and Prevent undermined these oppressive forces and resulted in my students re-engaging in political discussion as they were emboldened by the knowledge that I was also a critic of Prevent. While this example does not show that metaReality will necessarily always triumph over demi-reality, it does show that it is by no means defeatist to engage in contradictory projects within demi-reality and metaReality at the same time. Indeed, given that we tend to occupy a world of demi-reality, the contradiction between both having to adopt Prevent and associated counter-extremism initiatives while also contesting them may be a necessary condition for the expression of the pulse of freedom.

In response to the moralizing nature of supporters of Prevent and the war on terror, prolific academic, activist and critic Asim Qureshi reminds us in the title of his book that, whether it be in the refusal of grassroots organizations to take government funds that are contingent on support for counter-extremism, or resisting the emergence of 'extremism' in Westminster, there is *A Virtue of Disobedience* (Qureshi 2018).

How should 'extremism' be contested?

On 11 July 2018, the Commission for Countering-Extremism launched their 'evidence drive' into the government's approach to countering-'extremism' (Commission for Countering Extremism 2018). As was discussed in the last chapter, numerous academics expressed concern that the Commission had been set up to *sell*, rather than *critique*, the government's approach to this controversial policy area. It was felt that the Commission's findings might have already been decided and that, as such, academics engaging in the Commission's evidence drive might be used to support a cynical exercise to create evidence to support and normalize countering 'extremism' in the face of mounting opposition from professional bodies such as the National Union of Teachers (2016), the Royal College of Psychiatry (2016), NGOs such as Open Society (2016), Rights Watch (UK) (2016) and CAGE (Qureshi 2016), and even criticism of counter-extremism from bodies within Parliament (House of Commons 2018).

The terms of reference were eventually published by the Commission, long after the Commission had already started their 'evidence drive' and only after the intervention of the Bishop of St Albans that was discussed in the previous chapter. The terms laid out the questions that the Commission intended to address and were framed around the presumed harm caused by 'extremism' in questions like 'what are the harms caused by extremist incidents?' (Commission for Countering Extremism 2018). That the questions asked about the harm that 'extremism' might cause and how it might be better tackled added to my concern that the Commission would promote rather than alleviate the emergence of 'extremism'. The questions that the Commission were asking did not address concerns for those who are harmed by counter-extremism, including the concern that the government's agenda to counter 'extremism' might make us all less safe by silencing the vocal dissent that prevents actual violence in a functioning democracy.

In the foreword to the terms of reference from the lead commissioner, we are told that 'the first step is addressing the absence of consensus [about "extremism"]' (Commission for Countering Extremism 2018). This seems a strange intention from the perspective of many of the political theorists who have been explored in earlier chapters. Arendt (1969), Derrida (in Borradori 2004, in Isyar 2014) and Przeworski (1991), among others, suggest that the absence of consent is what our democracy thrives on. The commissioner goes on to say that the Commission will do this by 'building the evidence on extremism' (Commission for Countering Extremism 2018). In saying this, the commissioner is demonstrating a complete disregard for the scientific principles that should underpin this 'evidence drive' and which would demand that the 'evidence on extremism' be tested.

The scope of the Commission, we are told, is to 'learn the lessons from previous and existing counter terrorism policies, including those under Prevent' (Commission for Countering Extremism 2018). However, there is also a clearly stated intention not to review the Prevent Strategy, 'As outlined in our Charter, we will not be reviewing the government's Prevent Strategy or the proposed Integration Strategy' (Commission for Countering Extremism 2018). In the context of the ongoing and extensive criticism of Prevent and the government's approach to counter-extremism (House of Commons 2018, House of Commons 2018), the terms of reference make it hard to see the Commission as anything other than a cynical exercise to gather alternative 'evidence' in the face of mounting criticism of counter-'extremism'. The Commission tells us, 'It will help everyone do more to challenge extremism by building public understanding of its harms and impact' (Commission for Countering Extremism 2018). When combined with their dismissal of the need of scientific rigour in their study, this leaves the impression that the Commission is engaged in the promotion of 'extremism' as a threat, rather than in an audit of government policy.

The final question that the terms of reference tell us that the Commission aimed to address is, 'What could a positive, inclusive vision for our country look like?' This might have been a good starting point for the Commission's work. Such a study would show the importance of promoting dialogue and of helping everyone have access to public services like schools and doctor's surgeries. It would have had the possibility of finding that the government's promotion of counter-extremism, countering violent extremism and associated strategies like Prevent are silencing debate and reducing access to education and healthcare. They would have found that there is a risk that these approaches are marginalizing the very people who they purport to support and, in doing so, may be promoting the violent threat that they say they are preventing.

Given the Commission's failure to engage with these issues, their failure to adopt a stance that is a fundamental requirement of scientific knowledge and their commitment to the promotion of a counter-extremism agenda that undermines our democracy and might promote violence, neither I nor other academics and activists who I was in contact with at the time were offered the assurance that we needed to engage in the Commission's 'evidence drive'.

As has been referred to earlier, the Commission's efforts to promote the supposed threat of 'extremism' may have been in response to Parliament's Joint Committee for Human Rights (JCHR) and others' criticism of Prevent and the government's approach to countering 'extremism'. A central factor in the JCHR's criticism has been evidence to the Committee from Max Hill QC, the government's independent reviewer of Terrorism Legislation. Max Hill QC has been cited earlier as a vocal critic of the government's continued expansion of legislation in this area (Gibb 2017, Max Hill QC 2017), so his contribution as the 'terror watchdog' might have seen him challenge the emergence of 'extremism'. However, his sudden removal from the role of independent reviewer of Counter-Terrorism Legislation led to his critique of this area being cut short.

While it is not possible to know the government's motivation for suddenly promoting Max Hill to the Director of Public Prosecutions (DPP) in October 2018, his tenure as 'terror watchdog' of only one year is considerably shorter than his predecessors who, respectively, served for ten and six years. His promotion removed one of the government's most vocal critics at a time when they were trying to pass the particularly controversial Counter-Terrorism and Border Security Bill 2017–19 through Parliament, a bill that further expands government efforts to counter-'extremism' (HM Government 2018).

The continued expansion of counter-extremism legislation supports the theorization of the legislative genre from earlier chapters, and the overarching premise of this book that 'extremism' will continue to be normalized. The normalization of counter-extremism also suggests that we might expect this policy area to continue to be de-securitized as it is moved from the responsibility of the security services and to civil society. This could be seen when the Counter-Terrorism and Border Security Act was passed into law and shifted Prevent from under the control of the police and onto local authorities, though, while the act dictates that this shift should happen, there is little evidence of the police ceding control.

The desecuritization and normalization of 'extremism' can also be seen in the government's rebranding of counter-extremism under the banner of 'Building a Stronger Britain Together' in 2018. Building a Stronger Britain Together, or BSBT, is described on the Home Office website as supporting 'civil society and community organizations who work to create more resilient communities, stand up to extremism in all its forms and offer vulnerable individuals a positive alternative, regardless of race, faith, sexuality, age and gender'. BSBT does this by allowing organizations 'to bid for in-kind support and grant funding for specific programmes that deliver goals set out in the Counter Extremism Strategy' (Home Office 2018).

The government's BSBT leaflet guide to the 'Partnership Support Programme' is co-authored by the Home Office and advertising agency MC Saatchi (Building a Stronger Britain Together 2017). The guide describes how the Home Office and MC Saatchi can provide this support with 'strategy packages', 'website builds', 'training packages', 'casestudy films', 'printed assets' and 'social media campaigns' (Building a Stronger Britain Together 2017). This programme might be seen as a development from the more clandestine activites of RICU that Ben Hayes and Asim Qureshi describe in their report, *We are Completely Independent: The Home Office, Breakthrough Media and the PREVENT Counter Narrative*

Industry (Hayes and Qureshi 2016), and which is discussed in Chapter 6. While RICU's work opperated in the shadows to create quasi-independent civil societies when the legislative and informant genres were still in their infancy, the continued emergence of 'extremism' has enabled BSBT to openly co-opt pre-existing civil society into countering 'extremism'.

BSBT's Annual Progres Report in 2019 announced that they had co-opted 240 civil society organizations with 'around £8.8 million of Government funding since 2016' (HM Government 2019). As it appears that the Commission for Countering Extremism (CCE) is a cynical move to collect evidence to suit a questionable government agenda, it is perhaps not surprising that their recent 'evidence drive' has been directed towards engagement with many of the aforementioned civil society organizations that have been incentivised by government support to support the government's counter-extremism strategy. The Commission proclaiming in a tweet from a BSBT conference that they intended to 'shine a light' on the stories of the co-opted BSBT organization acts as a neat example of the perverse cycle of policy-led evidence that sustains counter-extremism.

The self-fulfilling cycle that promotes the emergence of 'extremism' that has been described in this book leads to the supposition that counter-extremism will continue to expand into new areas. This can be seen in the CCE's recent focus on 'Challenging Hateful Extremism' in their report of the same name (Commission for Countering Extremism 2019). The Commission has also commenced a 'legal review' to 'examine whether existing legislation adequately deals with hateful extremism' (Commission for Countering Extremism 2020). Freedom of information requests that I have made reveal that the Commission has met with the Crown Prosecution Service to discuss the existing cross-government

Commission for Countering Extremism @CommissionCE · Oct 17   ∨
Powerful session today hearing from those working on the frontline about the victims of #extremism. Thanks to #BSBT conference. The deep impact of #extremism is being felt by individuals, communities and wider society. We will shine a light these stories. extremismcommission.blog.gov.uk/2018/09/20/the...

FIGURE 8.1 *The Commission for Countering Extremism at the Building a Stronger Britain Together Conference.*

Hate Crime Action Plan. As was discussed in Chapter 2, Lord Walney's appointment as the government's 'independent adviser on political violence and disruption' (Home Office 2020) appears to be designed to support the Commission in the expansion of the law in this area. Whether the Commission and Walney manage to further entrench 'extremism' by creating a legal basis for efforts to suppress, it is yet to be seen.

Far from being an example of evidence-led policy formation, as we might hope for in a functioning state, the emergence of 'extremism' should be seen as a case study of policy-led evidence. The policy-led evidence is also sustained by the deeply moralizing 'you're either with us or against us' tones of the global war on terror. The absence of evidence to support the need for the continued expansion of counter-extremism and the corresponding emergence of 'extremism' is of particular concern, not only for policymakers, but for us all. Not least as 'extremism' is a significant factor in the continued emergence of division and of political violence. As twenty-four-hour rolling news recently played live footage of the US Capitol building being overrun by crowds carrying flags denoting their bearers' intentions of creating a white nationalist government, recognition of the violence that emerges from efforts to police 'extremism' could not be more importnant. If we are to create a more harmonious and peaceful world, we must first abandon efforts to police 'extremism'.

NOTES

Preface

1 The Home Office's own data that shows that 65 per cent of referrals to Prevent were for 'Islamist extremism' Home Office (2017), an alarming number in light of the Office of National Statistics stating that only 4.4 per cent of the UK population are Muslim (Office for National Statistics 2012). This is discussed further in Chapter 6.
2 The Space Station is kept in orbit around the earth by going fast enough for the centripetal force to counteract the effect of gravity. While they may feel weightless, the astronauts and the Space Station are prevented from flying away into space by the earth's gravity.

Chapter 1

1 At the time of writing, Quilliam Foundation dissolved after speculation that their founder Majid Nawaz's 'flirtations with Q-Anon conspiracy theories about the US elections and the electoral defeat of Donald Trump may have contributed to internal splits and the decision to close down' (Al Jazeera 2021). As Malia Bouattia writes for Al Jazeera (ibid.), 'The Quilliam Foundation has closed but its toxic legacy remains' in the policies and counter-extremism industry that they promoted for 13 years.
2 It is often proposed that Prevent was imposed on the British public by the Counter-Terrorism and Security Act of 2015. However, the act does not refer directly to Prevent. It states that 'specified authorities' should 'have due regard to the need to prevent people from being drawn into terrorism'. Going on to say that 'The Secretary of State may issue guidance . . . about the exercise' of this 'duty' and that 'A specified authority must have regard to any such guidance in carrying out that duty'. Thus, Prevent is imposed by the Prevent Duty Guidance that is issued by the Home Office, with a statutory duty for schools

and healthcare providers and other 'specified authorities' to follow the guidance. This means that the government could, if it chose to, remove Prevent without the involvement of Parliament or any judicial process.

3　An online 'shoot 'em up' game.

Chapter 2

1　A similar flaw in the approach of the Commission for Countering Extremism is discussed in the final chapter.

2　During the extensive reforms to schools under Michael Gove MP's tenure as secretary of state for education from 2010 to 2014, the National Curriculum for England was rewritten to become a 'knowledge based curriculum'.

Chapter 3

1　'Texts' as used here and throughout the book includes written documents and speeches.

2　It is perhaps not surprising that relying on Giddens work has limited Fairclough's critique of New Labour as Giddens was one of the main architects of the Third Way that formed the foundation of New labour's political project (Grice 2002). As well as contributing to the critique of 'extremism', the introduction of the neglected temporal dimension may also add to the critique of New Labour, potentially revealing more flaws in the Third Way than those that Fairclough has already exposed.

3　A fuller exposition of the schema for critical realist CDA that has been developed to explore the emergence of 'extremism' can be found in the *Journal of Critical Realism* (Faure Walker 2019).

4　This is the same definition that Dr Claire Crawford (Crawford 2017); used to demonstrate the emergence of Fundamental British Values from Prevent and that is discussed in the preceding chapter.

Chapter 4

1　In the same month that Johnson announced the prorogation of Parliament, Professor Greg Philo, Mike Berry, Justin Schlosberg,

Antony Lerman and Professor David Miller Philo, G., M. Berry, J. Schlosberg, A. Lerman and D. Miller (2019) published their extensive research into anti-Semitism in the Labour Party, *Bad News for Labour: Antisemitism, the Party and Public Belief.* Taking the need to address actual anti-Semitism with the utmost seriousness, they ask if it is plausible to consider lifelong anti-racist campaigner and leader of the Labour Party Jeremy Corbyn a greater threat to Jews than the burgeoning, openly racist and anti-Semitic far right that continues to emerge across Europe. In line with the ongoing commentary by Professor David Graeber at the time, they point out that the fallacious claims made against Corbyn undermine necessary and ongoing anti-racism while also emboldening the far right.

Chapter 5

1 The impending invasion of Iraq that would occur less than a month later on 20 March.

Chapter 6

1 It is also of note that Giddens' Structuration Theory appears to inform Fairclough's approach to CDA Fairclough (2013), adding to the importance that any problems with this theory be explored.
2 On their website, Jigsaw describe themselves as 'a unit within Google that forecasts and confronts emerging threats, creating future-defining research and technology to keep our world safer'. They are at the forefront of the online counter-extremism industry, and their most notable partnership is with Moonshot CVE.

BIBLIOGRAPHY

(2016). London Borough of Tower Hamlets -v- B. *EWHC 1707* (Fam). F. Court, https://www.judiciary.gov.uk.

Abbas, T. (2017). 'The "Trojan Horse" plot and the fear of Muslim power in British state schools.' *Journal of Muslim Minority Affairs* **16**: 426–41.

Adams, R. (2016). High court overturns lifetime bans for Trojan horse teachers. *The Guardian*.

Ahmed, N. (2021). Government's independent anti-radicalisation appointment WAS 'RIGGED'. *Byline Times*.

Airey, J. (2020). Rethinking the planning system for the 21st century. Policy Exchange.

Aked, H., M. Jones and D. Miller (2019). Islamophobia in Europe: How governments are enabling the far-right 'counter-jihad' movement. Public interest investigations.

Al Jazeera English (2009). UK 'kettling' tactic sparks anger. https://www.youtube.com/watch?v=GerPAVXYT34.

Alderson, P. (2015). *The Politics of Childhoods Real and Imagined: Practical Application of Critical Realism and Childhood Studies.* London, Routledge.

Alexander, M. (2010). *The New Jim Crow*. New York, The New Press.

Alexander, R. (2008). *Towards Dialogic Teaching: Rethinking Classroom Talk*. York, Dialogos.

Ali, N. (2020). 'Seeing and unseeing prevent's racialized borders.' *Security Dialogue* **51**(6): 579–96.

Ames, J. (2019). Mr Justice Hayden causes outrage with 'man's right to sex with wife' Comments. *The Times*.

Archer, M. (1995). *Realist Social Theory: The Morphogenetic Approach.* Cambridge, Cambridge University Press.

Arendt, H. (1969). *Crises of the Republic*. San Diego, Harcourt.

Baker, J., C. Gabrieltos and T. McEnery (2011). 'The representation of Islam and Muslims in the UK press, 1998–2008 | ESRC | Economic and Social Research Council.' From http://www.researchcatalogue.esrc.ac.uk/grants/RES-000-22-3536/outputs/read/238ea074-7725-4461-b75a-b2a4eb2790ba.

Baldét, W. (2017a). Prevent: A personal reflection. *Huffington Post*. online.

Baldét, W. (2017b). The hate equation. *Huffington Post*.

Baldét, W. (2019). 'As Well as combating terrorism, we must tackle the underlying ideology of Islamisim.' https://www.conservativehome.com /platform/2019/08/will-baldet-as-well-as-combating-terrorism-we-must -tackle-the-underlying-ideology-of-islamisim.html.

Baldét, W. (2020a). Preventing violent extremism: Stepping out of our echo chambers. *Open Democracy*, @openDemocracy.

Baldét, W. (2020b). Preventing violent extremism: We need to talk about Kieron. *Open Democracy*, @openDemocracy.

BBC (2005). London bomber: Text in full. *BBC Online*.

BBC (2009). Green demo cyclists block bridge. BBC.

BBC (2015). 7/7 attacks: What happened that day? @BBCNews.

BBC (2018). New counter-extremism tsar Sara Khan faces calls to quit, @ BBCNews.

BBC (2019a). Birmingham LGBT teaching row: How did it unfold? BBC.

BBC (2019b). Protesters banned from LGBT row school. BBC.

Bell, E. (2014). 'There is an alternative: Challenging the logic of neoliberal penality.' *Theoretical Criminology* 18(4): 489–505.

Bergman, R. (2020). *Humankind: A Hopeful History*. London, Bloomsbury.

Bhaskar, R. (1975). *A Realist Theory of Science*. London, Verso.

Bhaskar, R. (2008). *Dialectic: The Pulse of Freedom*. Abingdon, Routledge.

Bhaskar, R. (2012). *The Philosophy of MetaReality: Creativity, Love and Freedom*. London, Routledge.

Bhaskar, R. (2016a). *Enlightened Common Sense: The Philosophy of Critical Realism (Ontological Explorations)*. Abingdon, Routledge.

Bhaskar, R. (2016b). *The Order of Natural Necessity: A Kind of Introduction to Critical Realism*. CreateSpace Independent Publishing Platform.

Birt, Y. (2019). Astroturfing and the rise of the secular security state in Britain. Medium, @Medium.

Borradori, G. (2004). *Philosophy in a Time of Terror: Dialogues with Jurgen Habermas And Jacques Derrida*. London, University of Chicago Press.

Bouattia, M. (2021). The Quilliam Foundation has closed but its toxic legacy remains. *Al Jazeera*, online.

Bourdieu, P. and L. Wacquant (2001). 'New-Liberal Speak: Notes on the new planetary vulgate.' *Radical Philosophy* 105: 2–5.

Bowcott, O. and R. Adams (2016). Human rights group condemns Prevent anti-radicalisation strategy. *Guardian*, @guardian.

Bridge Initiative (2018). Factsheet: Douglas murray. https://bridge.georg etown.edu/research/factsheet-douglas-murray/, Georgetown University.

Buber, M. (1923). *I and Thou*. London, Bloomsbury.

Buber, M. (1947). *Between Man and Man*. London, Routledge & Kegan Paul Ltd.

Building a Stronger Britain Together (2017). Partnership Support Programme. H. O. M. Saatchi. https://www.gov.uk/guidance/building-a -stronger-britain-together.

Bush, G. (2003). 'President bush discusses freedom in Iraq and Middle East.' From https://georgewbush-whitehouse.archives.gov/news/releases /2003/11/20031106-2.html.

Busher, J., T. Choudhury, P. Thomas and G. Harris (2017). What the Prevent duty means for schools and colleges in England: An analysis of educationalists' experiences. Aziz Foundation.

Callahan, R. (1962). *Education and the Cult of Efficiency*. London, University of Chicago Press Ltd.

Cameron, D. (2011). PM's speech at Munich Security Conference – GOV. UK. https://www.gov.uk/government/speeches/pms-speech-at-munich- security-conference.

Cantle, T. (2001). *Community Cohesion: Report of the Independent Review Team – The 'Cantle Report'*. H. Office, London.

Cavendish, C. (2014). Birmingham schools have hard lessons to teach about local authority failings. *The Sunday Times*.

Centre for Ethnicity and Racism Studies (2012). The Media and Muslims in the UK, University of Leeds.

Centre of Media Monitoring (2019). State of Media Reporting on Islam and Muslims. https://mcb.org.uk/report/state-of-media-reporting-on-i slam-and-muslims/.

Charlton, L. (2019). What Is the Great Replacement? *The New York Times*.

Chomsky, N. (1981). 'The Carter Administration: Myth and Reality.' *Radical Priorities*.

Clarke, P. (2014). Birmingham schools: Education Commissioner's report. https://www.gov.uk/government/publications/birmingham-schools-edu cation-commissioners-report.

Cobain, I. and N. Osman (2020). UK counter-terror programme targeted BAME women using Instagram influencers. *Middle East Eye*.

Cobain, I. and A. Ross (2020). UK counter-extremism propaganda unit extending reach around the globe. *Middle East Eye*.

Comments, R. (2004). Your view: Should the Government negotiate with terrorists? – Telegraph. *The Telegraph*. Online, @Telegraph.

Commission for Countering Extremism (2018a). Charter for the commission for countering extremism. GOV.UK https://www.gov.uk/ government/publications/charter-for-the-commission-for-countering- extremism.

Commission for Countering Extremism (2018b). Commission for countering extremism launches evidence drive. GOV.UK https://www

.gov.uk/government/news/commission-for-countering-extremism-laun
ches-evidence-drive.

Commission for Countering Extremism (2018c). Terms of reference.
GOV.UK https://extremismcommission.blog.gov.uk/2018/09/20/the-
commission-publishes-its-terms-of-reference/.

Commission for Countering Extremism (2019). Challenging hateful
extremism. GOV.UK https://www.gov.uk/government/publications/ch
allenging-hateful-extremism.

Commission for Countering Extremism (2020). Commission for
countering extremism launches a legal review to examine effectiveness
of existing legislation relevant to hateful extremism. GOV.UK https://
www.gov.uk/government/news/commission-for-countering-extremism
-launches-a-legal-review-to-examine-effectiveness-of-existing-legislat
ion-relevant-to-hateful-extremism.

Crawford, C. (2017). 'Promoting "fundamental British values" in schools:
A critical race perspective | SpringerLink.' *Curriculum Perspectives*
37(2): 197–204.

Crozier, M., S. Huntington and J. Watanuki (1975). *Crisis of Democracy:
Report on the Governability of Democracies to the Trilateral
Commission*. New York University Press.

Curtis, A. (2016). HyperNormalisation. BBC.

Dawkins, R. (1989). *The Selfish Gene*. Oxford Paperbacks.

Dean, M. (2007). *Governing Societies: Political Perspectives on Domestic
and International Rule*. Maidenhead, Open University Press.

Dearden, L. (2019). Shamima Begum: Number of people stripped of UK
citizenship soars by 600% in a year. *Independent*.

Department for Communities and Local Government (2012). Creating
the Conditions for Integration. GOV.UK https://assets.publishing.serv
ice.gov.uk/government/uploads/system/uploads/attachment_data/file
/7504/2092103.pdf.

Dewey, J. (1916). *Democracy and Education*. New York, Macmillan.

Diamond, J. (2018). A brand new version of our origin story. *New York
Times*.

Dodd, V. and J. Grierson (2020). Greenpeace included with neo-Nazis on
UK counter-terror list. *The Guardian*, @guardian.

Donaghy, L. (2014). Ofsted's slur on the Muslim community of Park View
School. *The Guardian*, @guardian.

Fairclough, I. and N. Fairclough (2013). *Political Discourse Analysis: A
Method for Advanced Students*. Abingdon, Routledge.

Fairclough, N. (2000a). 'Language and neoliberalism.' *Discourse &
Society* **11**(2): 147–8.

Fairclough, N. (2000b). *New Labour, New Language?* London,
Routledge.

Fairclough, N. (2003). *Analysing Discourse: Textual Analysis for Social Research*. Abingdon, Routledge.

Fairclough, N. (2010). *Critical Discourse Analysis: The Critical Study of Language* (Second Edition). Abingdon, Routledge.

Fairclough, N. (2013). 'Critical discourse analysis and critical policy studies.' *Critical Policy Studies* 7(2): 20.

Fairclough, N. (2015). *Language and Power* (Third Edition). London, Routledge.

Fairclough, N., B. Jessop and A. Sayer (2007). 'Critical realism and semiosis.' *Journal of Critical Realism* 5(1): 9.

Faure Walker, R. (2015). A critical discourse analysis of the prevent counter-terrorism strategies, UCL Institute of Education, 69.

Faure Walker, R. (2017a). By casting teachers as informants, British counter-extremism policy is promoting violence. *The Conversation*. Online.

Faure Walker, R. (2017b). 'How preventing terror is promoting violence.' *Discover Society* (41). Articles, Issue 41. https://archive.discoversociety .org/2017/02/01/how-preventing-terror-is-promoting-violence/.

Faure Walker, R. (2018a). Counter-Terrorism in the Classroom. *Violent Extremism in the 21st Century*. G. Overland. Newcastle, Cambridge Scholars Publishing.

Faure Walker, R. (2018b). 'Prevent | PREVENT digest.' From https://www .preventdigest.co.uk.

Faure Walker, R. (2018c). Use of the word 'radicalisation' is ballooning – and it's hiding the real causes of violence. *The Conversation*, Online.

Faure-Walker, R. (2019a). 'Teachers as informants: Countering extremism and promoting violence.' *Journal of Beliefs & Values* 40(3): 368–80. D OI:10.1080/13617672.2019.1600321.

Faure Walker, R. (2019b). 'The UK's PREVENT Counter-Terrorism Strategy appears to promote rather than prevent violence.' *Journal of Critical Realism* 18(5): 487–512.

Faure Walker, R. (2020). Pseudoscience, think tanks and 'intellectual landscaping': Exposing the wilful ignorance of the right. Novara Media.

Fenton-Smith, R. (2017). Understanding prevent. BBC Radio 4: 38 minutes.

Fernandez, S., R. Faure Walker and T. Younis (2018). 'FOCUS: The "where" of Prevent.' *Discover Society*.

Fitzgerald, J. (2016). 'Counter-radicalisation policy across Europe: An interview with Maarten van de Donk (Radicalisation Awareness Network).' *Critical Studies on Terrorism* 9(1): 7.

Foreign & Commonwealth Office (2018). UK-India working together to counter extremism. GOV.UK https://www.gov.uk/government/speeches /uk-india-working-together-to-counter-extremism.

Fox, C., A. Doyle and I. F. Iman (2020). Racial division is being sown in the name of anti-racism. *Spectator*.

Freire, P. (1970). *Pedagogy of the Oppressed*. London, Penguin.

Frekete, L. (2018). *Europe's Fault Lines: Racism and the Rise of the Right*. London, Verso.

Gibb, F. (2017). We don't need any more laws against terror, says watchdog Max Hill QC. *The Times*.

Giddens, A. and C. Pierson (1998). *Conversations with Anthony Giddens*. Stanford, Stanford University Press.

Gillborn, D. (2005). 'Education policy as an act of white supremacy: Whiteness, critical race theory and education reform.' *Journal of Education Policy* 20(4): 485–505.

Gilligan, A. (2014). Trojan Horse: How we revealed the truth behind the plot. *The Telegraph*, @Telegraph.

Goldberg, D., S. Jadhav and T. Younis (2017). 'Prevent: What is pre-criminal space?' *BJPsych Bulletin* 41(4): 208–11.

Gove, M. (2007). *Celsius 7/7: How the West's Policy of Appeasement Has Provoked Yet More Fundamentalist Terror – And What Has to Be Done Now*. London, Phoenix.

Grice, A. (2002). Architect of 'Third Way' attacks New Labour's policy 'failures'. *The Independent*. online, @independent.

Grierson, J. (2018). Choice of new UK anti-extremism chief criticised as 'alarming'. *Guardian*. London, @guardian.

Griffiths, S. and R. Kerbaj (2014a). The crescent in the classroom. *The Sunday Times*.

Griffiths, S. and R. Kerbaj (2014b). Trojan Horse 2' in London. *The Times*.

Guardian (2016). The Guardian view on Labour in opposition: Come together | Editorial. *Guardian*. online, @guardian.

Guardian (2018). The Cambridge analytica files. *The Guardian*, @guardian.

Guest, M., A. Scott-Baumann, S. Cheruvallil-Contractor, S. Naguib, A. Phoenix, Y. Lee and T. Al-Baghal (2020). Islam on Campus, SOAS, Coventry University, Durham University, Lancaster University.

Gunter, J. (2017). A reckoning in Charlottesville. *BBC Online*, @BBCNews.

Hancox, D. (2018). *Inner City Pressure: The Story of Grime*. London, William Collins.

Hansard (2006). Communities and local government/environment, food and rural affairs, house of commons debate (20th November 2006) Column 263.

Hansard (2011). Quilliam foundation, house of commons debate (Tuesday 15th March 2011) Column 22WH.

Hansard (2014). Extremism & Birmingham schools, house of commons debate (Monday 9th June 2014) Column 245–284.

Hansard (2018). Counter-Terrorism and Border Security Bill, House of Lords debate (17th December 2018) Volume 794.

Harari, Y. (2014). *Sapiens: A Brief History of Humankind Hardcover*. Harvill Secker.

Harley, N. (2020). Teaching youngsters to make anti-extremism videos 'effective' in tackling radicalisation. The National, @TheNationalUAE.

Hartwig, M. (2007). *Dictionary of Critical Realism*. M. Hartwig. Abingdon, Routledge.

Hattenstone, S. (2011). Mark Kennedy: Confessions of an undercover cop. *Guardian*, @guardian.

Hattersley, G. (2019). The women at the forefront of the fight against extremism. *Vogue*.

Hayes, B. and A. Qureshi (2016). We are completely independent: The home office, breakthrough media and the PREVENT Counter Narrative Industry, @UK_CAGE.

Heath-Kelly, C. and E. Strausz (2018). 'The banality of counterterrorism "after, after 9/11"? Perspectives on the Prevent duty from the UK health care sector.' *Critical Studies on Terrorism*.

HM Government (2008). Prevent strategy 2008. UK, The Stationary Office Limited.

HM Government (2011a). PREVENT Review. UK, The Stationary Office Limited.

HM Government (2011b). Prevent strategy 2011. UK, The Stationary Office Limited.

HM Government (2013). Tackling extremism in the UK: Report by the extremism taskforce. UK, The Stationary Office Limited.

HM Government (2015a). Counter-Extremism Strategy. H. Office.

HM Government (2015b). Counter-Terrorism and Security Act. UK, The Stationary Office Limited.

HM Government (2015c). PREVENT duty guidance for England and Wales. UK, The Stationary Office Limited.

HM Government (2018a). Counter-Terrorism and Border Security Bill 2017–19. Home Office.

HM Government (2018b). Evidence from Christopher Wylie, Cambridge Analytica whistle-blower. C. Digital, Media and Sport Committee, @UKParliament.

HM Government (2019a). Building a stronger Britain together (BSBT) progress report 2019. H. Office.

HM Government (2019b). Counter-terrorism and Border Security Act 2019. Parliament.

Hochschild, A. (1998). *King Leopold's Ghost*. London, Pan Macmillan.

Holmwood, J. and T. O'Toole (2018). *Countering Extremism in British Schools?: The Truth about the Birmingham Trojan Horse Affair*. Bristol, Bristol University Press.

Home Office (2001). Community cohesion: A report of the independent review team. H. Office. London, Home Office.

Home Office (2015). Local delivery best practice catalogue: Prevent strategy. https://powerbase.info/index.php/File:OSCT-Prevent_catalogue-March_2015-OCR.pdf.

Home Office (2017). Individuals referred to and supported through the Prevent Programme, April 2015 to March 2016. H. Office, HMSO.

Home Office (2018). Building a Stronger Britain Together. https://www.gov.uk/guidance/building-a-stronger-britain-together.

Home Office (2020). Lord Walney announced as independent adviser on political violence and disruption. *Lord Walney will take on a New Unpaid Role as Independent Adviser on Political Violence and Disruption.* online.

Hooper, S. (2017). What is an extremist? UK government admits it still doesn't know. *Middle East Eye.* online.

Hooper, S. (2020). Senior Prevent official accused of 'doxxing' over deleted tweet. *Middle East Eye.*

House of Commons (2018a). Home Affairs Committee: Hate crime and its violent consequences. https://publications.parliament.uk/pa/cm201617/cmselect/cmhaff/609/609.pdf.

House of Commons (2018b). Joint Committee on Human Rights: Freedom of Speech in Universities. House of Commons, HMSO.

House of Commons (2018c). Legislative scrutiny: Counter-Terrorism and Border Security Bill. Joint Committee on Human Rights.

House of Commons Children Schools and Families Committee (2008). Testing and assessment. House of Commons.

House of Commons Communities and Local Government Committee (2010). Preventing violent extremism: Sixth report of session 2009–10. London, The Stationary Office. https://publications.parliament.uk/pa/cm200910/cmselect/cmcomloc/65/65.pdf.

House of Commons Education Select Committee (2015). Extremism in schools: The Trojan horse affair seventh report of session 2014–15. London, The Stationary Office.

HRC (2017). Report of the special rapporteur on the rights to freedom of peaceful assembly and of association on his follow-up mission to the United Kingdom of Great Britain and Northern Ireland, United Nations.

Hughes, L. (2016). David Cameron: More Muslim women should 'learn English' to help tackle extremism. *Telegraph.*

Hughes, S. (2019). Group that called extinction rebellion 'Extremist' is funded by big energy. *Vice News.*

Humanists UK (2018). Bishops in the House of Lords. https://humanism.org.uk/campaigns/secularism/constitutional-reform/bishops-in-the-lords/.

Huntington, S. P. (1996). *The Clash of Civilizations and the Remaking of World Order.* London, Simon & Schuster.

Hymas, C. (2020). Ex-Charity commission chief emerges as frontrunner
    for Government anti-radicalisation role: William Shawcross is
    understood to be seen within Government as well qualified for the job
    of independent reviewer of Prevent. *The Telegraph*. online.
Information Rights Tribunal (2018). EA/2016/0297-0301.
    KEVIN BLOWE (Appellant) and (1) THE INFORMATION
    COMMISSIONER, (2) HOME OFFICE, (3) CHIEF CONSTABLE OF
    GREATER MANCHESTER (Respondents). https://www.pdpjournals.c
    om/docs/887929.pdf.
Initiative, B. (2018). Factsheet: Douglas Murray. https://bridge.georg
    etown.edu/research/factsheet-douglas-murray/, Georgetown University.
Institute for Government (2020). Performance tracker 2019: Police. https
    ://www.instituteforgovernment.org.uk/publications/performance-tra
    cker-2019.
IPSO (2018). Ruling20480-17 Tower Hamlets Borough Council v The
    Times. I. P. S. O. (IPSO). https://www.ipso.co.uk/rulings-and-resolution
    -statements/ruling/?id=20480-17.
Islam21c (2018). Joint Statement: Commission for Countering
    Extremism. Islam21c, @Islam21c.
Isyar, A. C. a. B. (2014). *Europe after Derrida: Crisis and Potentiality*.
    Edinburgh Scholarship.
Jackson, R. (2005). 'Security, democracy, and the rhetoric of counter-
    terrorism.' *Democracy and Security* 1(2): 147–71.
Jackson, R. (2016). 'To be or not to be policy relevant? Power,
    emancipation and resistance in CTS research.' *Critical Studies on
    Terrorism* 9(1): 6.
Jewish News (2020). Mystery over consortium's 'shameful' bid for Jewish
    Chronicle and Jewish News. *Jewish News*. online.
Jones, M. (2020). Assessing communications-based activities to prevent
    and counter violent extremism, Royal United Services Institute
    (RUSI).
Jones, S. (2005). Biking Bush collides with policeman. *The Guardian*, @
    guardian.
Joseph, J. (2009). 'Critical of what? Terrorism and its study.' *International
    Relations* 23(1): 6.
Judith Butler et al. (2019). The government must stop hijacking LGBT+
    education to bolster its Prevent strategy. *Independent*.
Kennedy, D., G. Hurst and R. Gledhill (2014). Times discovers that
    'Trojan horse' letter is a crude forgery. *The Times*.
Khaldun, I. (2018). Slough community voices frustration against 'Prevent
    lobby.' *Islam 21c*. online, @Islam21c.
Khan, S. and T. McMahon (2016). *The Battle for British Islam:
    Reclaiming Muslim Identity from Extremism*. London, Saqi Books.

Korzybski, A. (1933). *Science and Sanity: An Introduction to Non-Aristotelian Systems and General Semantics*. International Non-Aristotelian Library Publishing Company.

Kundnani, A. (2009). Spooked: How not to prevent violent extremism, Institute of Race Relations.

Kundnani, A. (2014). *The Muslims are Coming: Islamophobia, Extremism, and the Domestic War on Terror*. London: Verso.

Kundnani, A. and B. Hayes (2018). The globalisation of countering violent extremism policies, Transnational Institute.

Laclau, E. and C. Mouffe (1985). *Hegemony and Socialist Strategy: Towards a Radical Democratic Politics*. London, Verso.

Laclau, E. and C. Mouffe (2001). *Hegemony and Socialist Strategy: Towards a Radical Democratic Politics* (second edition). London, Verso.

Lakoff, G. (1990). *Don't Think of an Elephant: Know Your Values and Frame the Debate*. White River Junction, Chelsea Green Publishing Co.

Lakoff, G. (2011). The 'new centrism' and its discontents. *The Huffington Post*. Online, www.huffingtonpost.com.

Lakoff, G. (2016). *Moral Politics: How Liberals and Conservatives Think*. Chicago, The University of Chicago Press.

Laybats, C. and L. Tredinnick (2016). 'Post truth, information, and emotion.' *Business Information Review*.

Lewis, P. (2009). G20 police officer under investigation for alleged second assault. *Guardian*, @guardian.

Loushy, M. (2016). *Censored Voices*. Germany. Independent film. https://www.imdb.com/title/tt3457376/.

Lydon, C. (2017). 'Noam Chomsky: Neoliberalism is destroying our democracy | The nation.' https://www.thenation.com/article/archive/noam-chomsky-neoliberalism-destroying-democracy/.

Mac an Ghaill, M. and C. Haywood, eds. (2017). *Muslim Students, Education and Neoliberalism – Schooling a 'Suspect Community'*. Palgrave Macmillan UK.

MacDonald, M., D. Hunter and J. P. O'Regan (2013). 'Citizenship, community, and counter-terrorism: UK security discourse, 2001–2011.' *Journal of Language and Politics* 12(3): 29.

Mackinlay, J. (2009). *The Insurgent Archipelago*. London, C Hurst & Co Publishers Ltd.

Manningham-Buller, E. (2010). Iraq Inquiry – Baroness Manningham-Buller. https://webarchive.nationalarchives.gov.uk/20140204101934/http://www.iraqinquiry.org.uk/transcripts/oralevidence-bydate/100720.aspx.

Mansell, W. (2007). *Education by Numbers*. Michigan, Politico.

Marc Alexander, Jean Anderson, Dawn Archer, Alistair Baron, Mark Davies, Jonathan Hope, Lesley Jeffries, Christian Kay, Paul Rayson and B. Walker (2017). 'Hansard Corpus: British parliament, 1803–2005.' From https://www.hansard-corpus.org/texts.asp.

Marsh, S. (2018). Record number of anti-Muslim attacks reported in UK last year. *The Guardian.*

Mautner, G. (2016). Checks and balances: How corpus linguistics can contribute to CDA. *Methods of Critical Discourse Studies.* R. Wodak and M. Meyer. London, Sage: 154–79.

Mavelli, L. (2012). *Europe's Encounter with Islam: The Secular and the Postsecular.* London, Routledge.

Max Hill QC (2017). 'Rights vs Security: The challenge engaged.' *Tom Sargant Memorial Lecture to Justice.* London. https://justice.org.uk/wp-content/uploads/2017/10/JUSTICE-lecture-MHQC.pdf.

McCann, K. and J. Ensor (2017). UK terror tsar accused of 'naivety' over claims that disciples of hate preachers should not be prosecuted. *The Telegraph,* @TelegraphNews.

Miah, S. (2015). *Muslims, Schooling and the Question of Self-Segregation.* Basingstoke, Palgrave Macmillan.

Mirowski, P. (2013). *Never Let a Serious Crisis Go to Waste: How Neoliberalism Survived the Financial Meltdown.* London, Verso.

Mirowski, P. (2018). *Never Let a Serious Crisis Go to Waste: How Neoliberalism Survived the Financial Meltdown.* London, Verso.

Mouffe, C. (2005). *On the Political (Thinking in Action).* Abingdon, Routledge.

Murray, D. (2010). Blackballed by Cameron. *Spectator.*

Naess, P. and L. Price (2016). *Crisis System A Critical Realist and Environmental Critique of Economics and the Economy.* London, Routledge.

National Union of Teachers (2016). *PREVENT Strategy.* NUT Conference 2016.

Nelson, F. (2020). Kemi Badenoch: The problem with critical race theory. *Spectator.*

NETPOL (2018). Home Office forced by Netpol to release 'counter-radicalisation' training materials, @policemonitor.

Neumann, P. (2008). Introduction. Perspectives on radicalisation and political violence. Papers from the First International Conference on Radicalisation and Political Violence, London.

News, S. (2016). *In or out: Michael Gove in 360.*

O'Connor, S. (2020). It is time to make amends to the low-paid essential worker. *Financial Times.*

Oborne, P. (2018). Trojan Horse affair: When government and media colluded to vilify the Muslim community. *Middle East Eye.*

OCHCHR (2018). End of Mission Statement of the Special Rapporteur on Contemporary Forms of Racism, Racial Discrimination,

Xenophobia and Related Intolerance at the Conclusion of Her Mission to the United Kingdom of Great Britain and Northern Ireland. ONLINE, United Nations.

Office for National Statistics (2012). 2011 Census: Population estimates for the United Kingdom, 27 March 2011. O. f. N. Statistics.

OfSTED (2005). Inspection report: Sir John Cass Foundation and Redcoat Church of England Secondary School. https://reports.ofsted .gov.uk/.

OfSTED (2012). Inspection Report: Park View Business and Enterprise College. https://reports.ofsted.gov.uk/.

OfSTED (2014a). Inspection Report: Oldknow School. https://reports .ofsted.gov.uk/.

OfSTED (2014b). Inspection Report: Park View Academy of Mathematics and Science. https://reports.ofsted.gov.uk/.

OfSTED (2014c). Inspection Report: Sir John Cass Foundation and Redcoat Church of England Secondary School. https://reports.ofsted .gov.uk/.

Omand, S. D. (2004). Contest: A 5 year UK strategy for countering international terrorism. C. Office.

Open Society (2016). Eroding trust: The UK's prevent counter-extremism strategy in health and education, open society justice initiative. https ://www.justiceinitiative.org/publications/eroding-trust-uk-s-prevent-c ounter-extremism-strategy-health-and-education.

O'Regan, J. and A. Betzel (2016). Critical Discourse Analysis: A Sample Study of Extremism. *Research Methods in Intercultural Communication: A Practical Guide*. Z. Hua. Online, Wiley-Blackwell, 281–96.

O'Regan, J. and J. Gray (2018). 'The bureaucratic distortion of academic work: A transdisciplinary analysis of the UK Research Excellence Framework in the age of neoliberalism.' *Language and Intercultural Communication*.

Paglen, T. (2009). *Blank Spots on the Map: The Dark Geography of the Pentagon's Secret World*. New York, Dutton.

Paul, M. (2018). 'Sapiens – a critical review.' *Be Thinking*.

Pearson, A. (2014). Trojan Horse debate: We were wrong, all cultures are not equal. *The Daily Telegraph*, @Telegraph.

Perry, B. (2014). 'Towards an ontogenesis of queerness and divinity: Queer political theology and terrorist assemblages.' *Culture and Religion: An Interdisciplinary Journal* **15**(2): 59.

Peterson, J. (2018). *12 Rules for Life: An Antidote to Chaos*, Allen Lane.

Pettinger, T. (2020). 'British terrorism preemption: Subjectivity and disjuncture in Channel "de-radicalization" interventions.' *The British Journal of Sociology*.

Philo, G., M. Berry, J. Schlosberg, A. Lerman and D. Miller (2019). *Bad News for Labour: Antisemitism, the Party and Public Belief*. London, Pluto press.

Pidd, H. (2018). Anti-fracking activists falsely accused of 'grooming' boy, 14. *Guardian*, @guardian.

Pinker, S. (2012). *The Better Angels of Our Nature: A History of Violence and Humanity*. Penguin.

PressAssociation (2017). UK police given extra £50m to fund fight against terrorism. *Guardian*, @guardian.

Pryke, S. (2015). 'Book Review: Never Let a Serious Crisis Go to Waste, How Neoliberalism Survived the Financial Crisis.' *Review of Radical Political Economics*.

Przeworski, A. (1991). *Democracy and the Market: Political and Economic Reforms in Eastern Europe and Latin America (Studies in Rationality and Social Change)*. Cambridge University Press.

Puar, J. K. (2014). 'Reading religion back into Terrorist Assemblages: Author's response.' *Culture and Religion: An Interdisciplinary Journal* **15**(2): 12.

Qureshi, A. (2016). 'The "science" of pre-crime: The secret "radicalisation" study underpinning PREVENT.' https://www.cage.ngo /product/the-science-of-pre-crime-report.

Qureshi, A. (2018). *A Virtue of Disobedience*. London, Byline Books.

Ragazzi, F. P. S. M. (2018). Students as Suspects? The challenges of counter-radicalisation policies in education in the Council of Europe member states Council of Europe. Strasbourg: Council of Europe.

Ramesh, R. (2014). Quarter of Charity Commission inquiries target Muslim groups: Islamic groups say they are being unfairly singled out, with five British charities operating in Syria under full investigation. *Guardian*.

Rights Watch (UK) (2016). Preventing Education. https://www.rightsan dsecurity.org/assets/downloads/preventing-education-final-to-print-3.c ompressed-1_.pdf.

Rights Watch (UK) (2019). Government removes Lord Carlile as Prevent Reviewer. https://www.rightsandsecurity.org/impact/entry/government -removes-lord-carlile-as-prevent-reviewer-conceding-rwuks-legal-chal lenge-to-his-independence.

Rudd, A. (2017). BBC Question Time. *Question Time*. BBC1, BBC.

Said, E. W. (1978). *Orientalism*. London, Penguin.

Said, E. W. (2003). New Preface to *Orientalism*. London, Penguin.

Sandbrook, D. (2013). *Seasons in the Sun, The Battle for Britain, 1974–1979*. London, Penguin.

Scott-Baumann, A., M. Guest, S. Naguib, S. Cheruvallil-Contractor and A. Phoenix (2020). *Islam on Campus: Contested Identities and the Cultures of Higher Education in Britain*. Oxford University Press.

Sedgwick, M. (2010). 'The concept of radicalization as a source of confusion.' *Terrorism and Political Violence* **22**(4): 479–94.

Shawcross, W. (2021). I want to hear the case for and against Prevent. *The Guardian*.

Sian, K. (2017). 'Born radicals? Prevent, positivism, and "race-thinking".' *Palgrave Communications* **3**(1): 6.

Sinclair, U. (1934). *I, Candidate for Governor*. Los Angeles, University of California Press.

Sky News (2016). In or Out: Michael Gove in 360. https://www.youtube.com/watch?v=t8D8AoC-5i8.

Smith, B. (2020). Home Office launches 'full and open competition' for Prevent strategy reviewer after court challenge. *Civil Service World*.

Speckhard, A. (2016). *The ISIS Defectors Interview Project*. New York, US Department of State.

Stampnitzky, L. (2013). *Disciplining Terror: How Experts Invented 'Terrorism'*. Cambridge University Press.

Stone, J. (2020). 'Bonkers' Liz Truss speech pulled from government website: Rant about Foucault replaced with note saying content has been redacted. *The Independent*.

Subramanian, S. (2018). One man's (very polite) fight against media Islamophobia. *The Guardian*.

Telegraph (2004). Your view: Should the Government negotiate with terrorists? – Telegraph. *The Telegraph*. Online, @Telegraph.

Tereshchenko, A., M. Mills and A. Bradbury (2020). Making progress? Employment and retention of BAME teachers in England. London, UK, UCL Institute of Education.

The Gulf Times (2018). Nearly a hundred academics issue statement raising concerns with commission for counter extremism. *The Gulf Times*.

The Royal College of Psychiatry (2016). *Counter-terrorism and Psychiatry*. London.

Thomas, P. (2014). 'Divorced but still co-habiting? Britain's Prevent/community cohesion policy tension.' *British Politics* **9**(4): 21.

Thompson, G. (2018). 'How and where is Prevent promoted? Digital, visual and spatial representations of UK counter-terrorism.' *Discover Society*.

Tierney, D. (2019). The Moral Maze: Radicalisation and De-radicalisation: 43 minutes. https://www.bbc.co.uk/programmes/m000bxk7.

Toube, D. (2020). Why UK's extremism strategy is shifting. *The Jewish Chronicle*.

Tower Hamlets (2013). Transforming Education for All: The Tower Hamlets Story. Tower Hamlets Local Authority.

Tower Hamlets (2014a). 'Sunday Times article on Trojan horse allegations.' From http://www.towerhamlets.gov.uk/Home.aspx.

Tower Hamlets (2014b). Tower hamlets guidance: Supporting vulnerable children: Preventing violent behaviour and violent extremism in tower hamlets. L. B. o. T. Hamlets.

UAE, N. M. C. (2019). Foreign Correspondents' Club hosts UK counter-extremism expert William Baldet to discuss challenges of fighting Islamist and Far-Right extremism.

Ullah, A. (2020). London university to investigate professor over 'bullying' of Muslim academic. *Middle East Eye*. online.

UNESCO (2018). UNESCO global networking for education to prevent violent extremism. https://en.unesco.org/news/unesco-global-networking-education-prevent-violent-extremism.

United Nations (2020). UN experts decry US rhetoric on designation of terrorist groups. ohchr.org.

Vernalls, R. (2019). Labour MP backs parents protesting against LGBT+ lessons at Birmingham school. *Independent*.

Vickerie, L. (2014). Letter to all Tower Hamlets Secondary School headteachers [by email, 20th June 2014].

Watts, C. (2015). Should the United States negotiate with terrorists? *Brookings*. Online, @BrookingsInst.

White, J. (2017). *Love and Its Place in Education*. London, UCL Institute of Education.

Wilshaw, M. (2014). Letter to Rt Hon Michael Gove MP, Secretary of State for Education. https://assets.publishing.service.gov.uk/government/uploads/system/uploads/attachment_data/file/415115/Advice_note_on_academies_and_maintained_schools_Birmingham_toSoS_Education.pdf.

Wolfson, D. (2020). New JC owner as JC Trust approves sale to consortium: Paper sold to consortium led by Sir Robbie Gibb. Jewish Chronicle. online.

Yeo, C. (2020). Tribunal: Nullified nullification no barrier to deprivation of British citizenship. www.freemovement.org.uk.

Younis, T. and S. Jadhav (2019). 'Islamophobia in the National Health Service: An ethnography of institutional racism in PREVENT's counter-radicalisation policy.' *Sociology of Health & Illness*.

Žižek, S. (2011). *Living in the End Times*. London, Verso.

INDEX